MAK

WORL

Jill Bavin-Mizzi

Bible John: A New Suspect

europe books

ISBN 9791220149785
First edition: April 2024

Edited by Veronica Parise

Bible John: A New Suspect

For Patricia Docker, Jemima MacDonald,

Helen Puttock and their families.

Acknowledgements

I would like to thank my family for their incredible support – from their participation in our search of Scottish cemeteries to their sharing of computer expertise. In particular, thank you Hannah for proof-reading my final draft.

I would also like to thank my friends Alan and Arlette Warnock for sharing their reminiscences of and knowledge about their young lives in Scotland. And, of course, thank you to my close friend, Tracie Wright, for listening to the many twists and turns as this manuscript took shape.

I am indebted to Dr Stuart Boyer for trying to teach me about DNA transmission and for lending his scientific expertise to my genealogy. You're a wonder, Stuart! Thank you also Dr Jeremy Keating for your very valuable assistance with my understanding of the suspect's much discussed dental features.

Thankyou Gordon and Margaret White for helping me with various cemetery and crematorium records and for going to great lengths to examine the Scotstoun and Bankhead Primary School Registers in the Glasgow City Archives. Thankyou also to Michael Gallagher from the Glasgow City Archives for his generous assistance when I needed it most.

I have repeatedly relied on a private investigator, Keith Coventry, for information which I desperately needed. He never once failed me. Thank you so much, Keith.

But, most of all, I would like to thank June for allowing me into her home and trusting me with her recollections. I have, at all times, tried to stay true to your telling of your own story, June.

Chapter 1.

Finding Patricia Docker - Friday 23rd February, 1968

Patricia Docker's body lay in a quiet service lane at the rear of Carmichael Place, only yards from her home. The young woman was lying on her back with one of her legs twisted outwards from the knee - naked except for a wedding ring on the ring finger of her right hand. A neighbour called police after finding Patricia early on Friday morning. When Detective Sergeant Johnstone and Detective Constable MacDonald arrived on the scene, at about 8.10am, they found no sign of Patricia's clothing, but noticed that her right shoe was only partially on and the other was nearby. They saw a used sanitary towel next to her body.[1]

Police Surgeon, Dr James Imrie, examined Patricia while she still lay in the service lane. He noted her facial and head injuries but concluded that none of these wounds were "serious enough to have killed her." Dr Imrie also found ligature marks on Patricia's neck, which indicated to him that she had been strangled. He believed the marks had been made by something strong, like a belt.[2]

Photograph published in the *Scottish Daily Express*, 26th February 1968.

Later that day, Glasgow University Professor, Gilbert Forbes, conducted a post-mortem. He confirmed Dr Imrie's initial findings, establishing the cause of death as strangulation. Professor Forbes believed that Patricia had been beaten and kicked about the head, face and body just before her death. Her right eye had been blackened and there was a laceration on her upper lip. There was also bruising on the right side of her head above her ear. During the post-mortem, Professor Forbes found that, at the time of her death, Patricia was menstruating. While he saw "no clear evidence of sexual assault," a number of former detectives have stated unequivocally in their memoirs that Patricia had been raped.[3]

Detective Superintendent Elphinstone Dalglish led the investigation into Patricia Docker's murder. At the time, he was deputy to Detective Chief Superintendent Tom Goodall. D.S. Dalglish instructed detectives to conduct house-to-house inquiries, fanning out from the service lane. Few people had noticed anything unusual during the night but one neighbour, a schoolteacher, said she heard shouting at "round about midnight".[4] She told police:

> I heard a woman shout out, twice in quick succession 'Let me go.' It was brief and I never heard it again. I thought nothing of it at the time. It was not followed by any kind of screams or any sort of commotion really.[5]

When former detective Joe Jackson was interviewed for the 2021 documentary "The Hunt for Bible John", he explained that he was one of the officers tasked with going from door to door, asking people "if they had heard anything, seen anything, etc." He recalled the schoolteacher's evidence and said that nothing else came from the door-to-door inquiries. Nevertheless, for detectives, this one statement established that Patricia Docker had been murdered in the service lane where her body was found. She had not been killed elsewhere and dumped in the laneway.

***

When Patricia Docker had not returned home by midnight her parents assumed that she was staying overnight at a friend's place but, when she failed to return the following day, they became worried. After reading an article in the evening newspaper about the discovery of a woman's body in his neighbourhood, Patricia's father, John Wilson, went to the mobile police caravan headquarters which had been set up in Ledard Road.[6] He identified the body of his twenty-five-year-old daughter, Patricia Jane Charlotte Docker. She and her four-year-old son had been living with him and his wife Pauline at their Battlefield home for almost a year.[7]

John Wilson told police that his daughter had gone out on Thursday night with some friends from Mearnskirk Hospital, where she worked as a nursing-auxiliary. Apparently, the friends intended to go dancing at the Majestic Ballroom. Wilson said that Patricia had separated from her husband of five years after the couple returned from Cyprus the previous April. Alexander Docker, a in the R.A.F., was stationed at Digby in Lincolnshire.[8] The *Daily Record* reported that detectives contacted the base in Digby and the orderly officer told them: "Corporal Docker is on leave, but not, I understand, in Glasgow." According to police notes, Alex Docker:

> went on leave on 19th February 1968 till 3rd March 1968. On forenoon and afternoon of 22nd February he and his girlfriend travelled by train to Haddington,

13

arriving at his parents' home about 5.30pm. Had tea with parents, then husband and father went for a drink in a local public house, returning at or about 9pm. Remained with parents and girlfriend talking and watching TV. 11.30pm prepared for bed and slept there overnight. ... has no car.[9]

As Professor Judith Rowbotham, says in an interview for the documentary "The Hunt for Bible John", police were able to eliminate Alex Docker as a suspect in Patricia's murder because he couldn't have been in Glasgow at the time, "the logistics were simply not there."

In the days that followed, police held a number of press conferences, appealing for public assistance. D.S. Dalglish described Patricia Docker "as being about 5ft. 3in. in height, of slim build, and with dark brown wavy hair, cut in a medium short style". He told the press that she had "hazel eyes, a snub nose and protruding upper teeth." [10] To this description, D.C.S. Tom Goodall added that, when Patricia left home on Thursday night, she was wearing a grey duffle coat with a blue fur collar, a mustard or yellow knitted-type dress, natural-coloured stockings and brown strap shoes. She was also carrying a brown handbag.[11] For their part, the press reported these descriptions of Patricia at length and, as early as the 24th February, they began circulating photographs of her.

On the 26th February, the *Daily Record* claimed that for "almost five hours", on the preceding day, four officers from the Police Underwater Unit (known as frogmen) searched a mile of the River Cart, near the end of Carmichael Place. The *Scottish Daily Express* was more precise about the search area: "The four frogmen searched the shallow water between Weir's sports ground at Battlefield to the Kilmarnock Road bridge." Apparently,

14

the frogmen discovered something in the River Cart but D.S. Dalglish refused to release any details. The *Evening Times* quoted Dalglish as saying only that the frogmen found "something which had a definite bearing on the case." Years later, writers have suggested that the frogmen found Patricia's handbag, part of her watchcase and a bracelet.[12] Despite a police search of the River Cart embankment on the 4th March, Patricia's clothes were never found.

Witnesses reported seeing three cars in the vicinity of Patricia Docker's murder. On the 26th February, for the first time, police appealed to anyone who had seen a light-coloured Morris 1000 Traveller in or around Battlefield on the Thursday night. They believed the car had pulled over at a bus stop on Langside Avenue near the entrance to Queens Park at approximately 11.10pm. There, the driver picked up a young woman waiting for the No. 34 Corporation Bus. Police also appealed for information regarding a man and woman who were seen driving a white Ford Consul, 375 model, which turned from Braemar Street into Overdale Street at approximately 11.20 pm. Witnesses said that the car was tooted at from behind when it started rolling backwards near the junction of Carmichael Place.[13] The couple in the white Ford Consul immediately contacted police and were cleared of any involvement in Patricia's death but, despite numerous appeals, the driver of the Morris 1000 Traveller never came forward.[14]

For several days, detectives interviewed anyone who attended the Majestic Ballroom on the night Patricia Docker was murdered. It was estimated that there had been one hundred and fifty dancers at that particular session and police appealed to all of them to come forward. The *Glasgow Herald* carried their appeal: "We are still making progress, but we would like to interview all the dancers who were at the Majestic on Thursday night. We can assure them that if they come forward their personal backgrounds will be treated in confidence."[15] Meanwhile, the Scottish newspapers continued to print photographs of Patricia Docker.

Despite all of the publicity, it wasn't until some ten days after Patricia's body was found that a member of the public told police they had seen her at the Barrowland Ballroom in Gallowgate that Thursday night.[16] Detective Chief Inspector George Brownie announced on Saturday the 2nd March that Patricia had attended the Barrowland as well as the Majestic on February the 22nd; that she had "visited TWO city dance halls on the night she died."[17] The press told readers that, after visiting the Majestic Ballroom in Hope Street, Patricia went to a special over-25s carnival dance at the Barrowland. In his memoir *Chasing Killers*, former detective Joe Jackson argues that Patricia had not attended the Majestic at all that night. The early information they received placing Patricia at the Majestic was incorrect. In Jackson's own words: "It was some days before we learned that Patricia had, in fact, gone to the Barrowland instead. This led to the first bum steer: a nutcase who had been at the Majestic insisted that he had danced with the murdered woman. His claim was quickly disproved but centring our investigation on the Majestic lost us valuable time."[18]

When investigators realised that Patricia Docker had been at the Barrowland Ballroom, they began interviewing staff and dancers there. A number of later writers have suggested that, while none of the interviewees remembered seeing Patricia leave the Barrowland with anyone, some recalled her dancing with "two or three different men" that night. At least one of these witnesses indicated that there was nothing noteworthy about any of Patricia's dance partners except that one of them "had light red hair" and "was rather good looking."[19]

In *Chasing Killers*, Joe Jackson says that, after Patricia Docker's murder, "detectives worked fourteen-hour days from 8 a.m. until 10 p.m."[20] But the information they gathered led nowhere. As retired Detective Superintendent Robert Johnstone says, there were "no clues, no fingerprints, no witnesses." [21] Detective Superintendent James Binnie, who was also part of the investigating team at the time, later explained that the trail simply went cold and so the investigation was wound down after only two weeks. [22]

***

For years, cold-case writers and criminologists have used the available information to construct a narrative of Patricia Docker's murder, much as I have just done. But, for all of us, the sources are limited. Given that no-one was ever arrested or tried for this crime, there are no court transcripts in existence. What is more, the police files and Patricia's autopsy report remain closed to the public. Unlike most historical documents, criminal case records are not necessarily opened after a specified period of time. Whenever murder investigations are classified as "ongoing" the relevant documents can remain off-limits indefinitely.

Despite these restrictions on access to information, cold-case writers, criminologists and historians like me are able to reconstruct much of what happened by using details which were deliberately fed to the press by those in charge of the investigation. We also rely on the additional material disclosed, and sometimes even generated, at a later date. For instance, some of the details of Patricia Docker's murder have been revealed in the memoirs of former detectives and in the work of crime writers or documentary filmmakers who have interviewed various participants in the case. Perhaps even more importantly, a good deal of information was released in 2022 when a journalist named Audrey Gillan used actors to read lengthy passages from the original police reports in her podcast, "Bible John: Creation of a Serial Killer".

Some writers are interested in going beyond the reconstruction of Patricia Docker's murder. They search the available evidence for clues in order to continue the hunt for her killer. For example, in their 2010 publication *The Lost British Serial Killer*, David Wilson and Paul Harrison examine one of the significant clues reported by the Scottish press – the fact that Patricia's "unclothed" body was found lying in a service lane while most of her effects were missing. Wilson and Harrison argue that Patricia's killer likely stripped her and removed her clothing from the scene because "he had an understanding of how the police would conduct their investigation … – largely through fingerprints, hair and blood samples, in an age before DNA profiling." [23] The implication, according to Wilson and Harrison, is that the killer had probably offended before or "had some insight into policing." [24] Of course, either of these scenarios is possible, but neither was assumed by investigators at the time. Detectives may have reasoned that, if the killer removed most of Patricia's effects from the crime scene because of some understanding of police procedures, he probably would also have taken her shoes and sanitary towel, both of which he had likely touched.

David Wilson and Paul Harrison go on to suggest an alternative, more plausible, explanation for Patricia Docker's nakedness – that her killer removed her clothing as a dramatification. In other words, he posed her body to send a message to those who found her. Patricia's killer stripped her naked and left her in the open for all to see, posed perhaps as the "whore" he believed her to be. If this were the case, then the removal of Patricia's effects amplified the killer's message. By taking almost everything away, the killer drew attention to, and hence attributed meaning to, the items he chose to leave.

For instance, the killer left a wedding ring on the ring finger of Patricia Docker's *right* hand (despite having taken her bracelet). [25] Positioned as it was, this ring signifies that, although she had married, Patricia was either separated, divorced or simply pretending to be available. The killer may have considered any or all of these options to be a serious moral transgression. It is more difficult to determine the possible significance of Patricia's brown, strap shoes. It might be that, for the killer, they were evidence of her attendance at a dancehall and were left at the scene, also as a moral statement. [26] Maybe, even the sanitary towel, discarded as it was near Patricia's body, held some significance for her killer. According to the former Sheriff of North Strathclyde and of Lothian and Borders, Charles Stoddart, detectives "merely noted" the fact that Patricia Docker had been menstruating and recorded it along with the rest of the pathologist's findings. [27] At this stage, they made nothing more of the sanitary towel.

From a purely practical point of view, the removal of so many of Patricia Docker's effects indicates that her killer was not travelling on foot. It is inconceivable that he ran from the service lane laden with Patricia's belongings. This would have meant carrying her dress, coat, stockings, underwear and handbag through the streets of Glasgow. It might even have meant holding them while hailing a taxi or catching a ride on public transport. The implication is that Patricia's killer used a car. Many years later, the *Guardian* suggested that: "Though they said little about it at the time, the police assumed that the person who had killed Patricia Docker had taken her to Carmichael Lane in a car."[28] In other words, he had either driven her home from the Barrowland Ballroom or picked her up as she made her way home.

The more likely of these scenarios is that the killer met Patricia Docker at the Barrowland Ballroom. Afterall, the Barrowland was approximately four miles from her home. No-one saw Patricia attempting to walk any part of that distance and there were no sightings of her on any of the local buses.[29] In fact, as writer Andrew Hagan suggests in "The Hunt for Bible John," "the journey between [the] dancehall and the site of her murder is almost completely empty of detail" – so much so that "investigating officers at the time were taken aback by how few people were able to identify her movements that night."

There were, however, witnesses who remembered seeing a number of cars of interest that night. As mentioned earlier, one of these was the Morris 1000 Traveller. The driver was seen picking up a woman who was waiting at a bus stop on Langside Avenue near the entrance to Queen's Park. But from that location, Patricia would have been less than half a mile from home. She would not have needed to wait for a bus nor to accept a lift. Years later, Detective Superintendent Joe Beattie asked himself, why Patricia would "be stood at a bus stop so close to her home?" He concluded that it was "unlikely that the woman picked up in Langside Avenue was Patricia Docker."[30]

A second car, observed near Carmichael Place, was the white Ford Consul 375. At least one witness remembered the Ford Consul driving along Overdale Street and being tooted at as it rolled backwards near the intersection with Carmichael Place. But the man and woman who had been in the Ford Consul came forward and were discounted by

20

police. It appears that the more important car was the one which tooted at the Ford Consul. Unfortunately, no description of this third car was ever reported in the press. Nor was there any mention of whether the driver continued along Overdale Street or turned left, either into Carmichael Place or the narrow service lane just before it, where Patricia's body was found the following morning. Investigators must have recognised the possibility that Patricia was a passenger in this third car.

Patricia found here

Map from streetmap.co.uk

As already noted, after murdering Patricia Docker, the killer tossed some of her belongings into the nearby River Cart. The killer could not have reached the River Cart by driving down Carmichael Place because it turns into a narrow walkway. It seems probable that, instead, he drove along Ledard Street and turned left into Millbrae Road. The killer may have tossed Patricia's handbag, watch case and bracelet through an open car window as he crossed Millbrae Bridge. Indeed, press photographs taken soon after the murder, show police frogmen examining a stretch of the River Cart just beside Millbrae Bridge.[31]

Much has been made of the killer's possible exit route. David Wilson suggests, in an article for the *Herald Scotland*, that this exit route is significant because Patricia's killer was very likely "returning home, where he would be safe."[32] But identifying this exit route is problematic. If the killer did cross Millbrae Bridge, then he was initially heading south. He may have continued driving in this direction to Glasgow's outer southern suburbs or even beyond but we cannot be certain of this. Satisfied with having thrown some of Patricia's effects into the River Cart, he might have turned off Millbrae Road at the next intersection, turning west into Riverside Road or east into Earlspark Avenue. He might even have doubled back towards the city.

The only other information that eventually came to light was that Patricia Docker was seen dancing with two or three different men at the Barrowland Ballroom – one of whom "had light red hair" and "was rather good looking."[33] But there was no mention of this man in any of the newspaper reports of the time. The accounts came from later writers who may well have been influenced by hindsight. It seems more likely that, as Charles Stoddart wrote in *Bible John: Search for a Sadist*, there were "No witnesses. No descriptions. Not even much circumstantial evidence. And no breaks."[34]

There is only one thing that we can ascertain about the killer's appearance at this point in time and that depends on whether he met Patricia Docker at the Barrowland Ballroom or on her way home from the dancehall. If he met her at the Barrowland then we know that he was, or appeared to be, at least twenty-five years of age. As already mentioned, the Barrowland had hosted an over-25s carnival dance on that Thursday night.

Chapter 2.
Finding Jemima MacDonald - Monday 18th August, 1969

Margaret O'Brien agreed to look after her sister's three children on Saturday evening, the 16th August 1969, so that Jemima MacDonald could attend one of the Barrowland Ballroom's over-25s nights. Jemima was a single mother and Margaret often took care of her children. Margaret became concerned when Jemima didn't return to collect her children the following day. She overheard some of the neighbourhood children talking about "a body in a building".[35]

They had found a partially-clothed woman sprawled on the floor in a bed recess in a derelict tenement. The woman's body was only twenty to thirty yards from Jemima's flat in Bridgeton's Mackeith Street.[36] At about 10 o'clock on Monday morning, Margaret went to the tenement and found her sister.

Photograph published in the *Scottish Daily Express*, 19th August 1969.

In her recent podcast, Audrey Gillan reveals police descriptions of Jemima's body as it lay in the tenement building:

She was lying face down with her coat half pulled down her back and wrapped up round her waist, as was her kimono skirt. Her shoes were off and her stocking tights removed and torn. Her black patent handbag was missing and has not yet been recovered. The back of her pants and legs were dirty. She obviously had been punched in the face and death was due to strangulation, probably caused by the stocking tights. In addition, tufts of hair had been pulled from her head and were lying on her clothing.

The press mentioned only that Jemima's large, black imitation patent-leather handbag was missing and mistakenly suggested that so too was her dark brown woollen coat.[37] It wasn't until many years later that anyone revealed that a used sanitary towel had been found near Jemima's body.[38]

A post-mortem was conducted later that day but D.C.S. Goodall refused to release any details. In 2019, fifty years after her murder, Jemima's death certificate was opened to the public. This document records the cause of her death as strangulation. According to later writers, Jemima had been strangled with her own stockings. She had also been severely beaten about the head and raped, despite the fact that she was menstruating.[39]

Although her death certificate states that Jemima MacDonald was thirty-one years of age when she was murdered, the press repeatedly referred to her as a thirty-two-year-old "mother-of-three".[40] They published Jemima's photograph and printed D.C.S. Goodall's description of her: "she was 5ft. 7in. tall, slim, had dark hair which had been dyed and was showing traces of fair hair at the roots and front". On the night she was killed, Jemima "was wearing a black pinafore dress, a white frilly blouse, and off-white, sling-back, high-heeled shoes."[41]

Police placed a guard on the three-storey tenement in Mackeith Street while detectives sifted through the rubbish in the flat. If they ever found anything of any significance, it was not reported in the press. Detectives also made door-to-door inquiries in the area, but no-one appears to have heard anything unusual on the night Jemima was murdered.[42] D.C.S. Goodall repeatedly appealed to the public to come forward with any information which might prove relevant. He also asked all dancers who attended the Barrowland Ballroom on Saturday night to contact police.

Witnesses did come forward, enabling detectives to piece together Jemima's movements on the night she was murdered. Jemima had left the Barrowland on foot, walking along Gallowgate and Bain Street. From there, she made her way to London Road, taking a short cut through Landressy Street to James Street. She then continued on towards her home in Mackeith Street. This walk, of less than a mile, would have taken her just over twenty minutes.[43]

During that time, Jemima MacDonald was not alone. She had been seen talking with a man at the Barrowland Ballroom shortly before midnight and this same man accompanied her on her way home. Indeed, one of Jemima's neighbours saw them together at about 12.40pm outside 23 MacKeith Street, where Jemima's body was later found. In the words of the police report, Jemima had appeared unconcerned and waved nonchalantly to her neighbour.[44] D.C.S. Goodall told the press that, according to witnesses, the man was between twenty-five and thirty-five years of age, 6' to 6' 2" tall and slim in build. Newspapers reported alternately that he had "fair, reddish hair" or "reddish, fair hair", "cut short and brushed back." He had a pale, "long, thinnish face" and was well-dressed in a good-quality blue suit with hand-stitched lapels and a white shirt.[45]

In an attempt to identify the man seen with Jemima MacDonald, Detective Superintendent James Binnie contacted the Glasgow School of Art. He was hoping that someone there would be able to produce a colour sketch of the suspect. The task was accepted by George Lennox Paterson, the school's registrar. Lennox Paterson knew that a number of witnesses had already described the suspect to detectives but some of them had not been particularly helpful so he asked to interview only two of the witnesses - a young woman and a young man.[46] Lennox Paterson believed that, if he questioned them himself, he might learn more about the suspect's appearance and demeanour and he wanted to capture the witnesses' general impression of the man in his sketch.

George Lennox Paterson spoke with the young woman first and she was able to describe the suspect's features "in the most general sense". She indicated that the man she saw with Jemima MacDonald was very good-looking "in the conventional sense" and implied that he was quite the "ladies' man." The male witness confirmed some of the details mentioned by the young woman and said that he too considered the suspect to be good-looking.[47]

In *Bible John: Search for a Sadist*, Charles Stoddart argues that George Lennox Paterson recognised the difficulty of constructing an accurate representation of a man who he had never seen. Essentially, Lennox Paterson suggested that he had been tasked with composing his idea of the witnesses' idea of the suspect's face. And, after speaking at length with the two witnesses, Lennox Paterson felt that he did not have sufficient information. In particular, he didn't know enough about the suspect's eyes or lips so he deliberately left the eyes in shadow and the lips vague. "The whole effect", Charles Stoddart claims, "resembled an out-of-focus photograph, but with just sufficient clarity to enable someone to recognise the person depicted."[48]

George Lennox Paterson's sketch of the suspect appeared in thousands of newspapers and on countless

 posters throughout Scotland. To ensure the widest possible circulation, it was also shown on television. Police then sorted through the scores of responses they received, but none of them led to an arrest. On the 28th August, the *Daily Record* suggested that the investigation had "developed into a long, hard slog."

Sketch published in black and white in Tilly Pearce, 'The Hunt for Bible John', *DigitalSpy*, 4th January 2022, Photo Credit BBC.

***

On the 12th October, two weeks after Jemima MacDonald's body was found, D.C.S. Tom Goodall died from a heart attack. He was replaced as head of Glasgow City Police by his deputy, Elphinstone Dalglish and Jemima MacDonald's case was handed over to D.S. James Binnie. By this time, the investigation was winding down. Plain-clothes detectives had been attending dance sessions at the Barrowland for nearly two months to see if Jemima's killer would return but, towards the end of October, they ceased their inquiries there.[49]

In an effort to rekindle public interest in the case, Jemima MacDonald's siblings offered a £100 reward for information leading to the capture of her killer. On the 22nd

October, the *Scottish Daily Express* carried the words of Jemima's eldest sister, Jean Thomas: "This £100 may just be enough for someone to come forward and give the police the vital clue they need. The money comes from myself, three sisters and three brothers. We know it will not bring Mima back but if the man responsible is caught it may save the life of some other poor woman."[50] The family's £100 reward has never been claimed.

***

From the outset, the press drew links between the murders of Patricia Docker and Jemima MacDonald. On the 18th August, the day Jemima was found, the *Evening Times* reminded readers: "Another Glasgow murder victim, Patricia Docker (25), a nurse, was never seen alive again after attending a dance."[51] And the press was quick to point out that both women had attended the Barrowland Ballroom.[52] Nevertheless, a number of detectives have suggested, over the years, that Patricia Docker and Jemima MacDonald may have been killed by different men.[53] In "Unsolved", the 2005 documentary for Grampian and Scottish Television, Detective Inspector Billy Little says that, at the time, the two cases were treated separately and this remains the official position.

But the similarities between the two cases are undeniable. To start with, both Patricia Docker and Jemima MacDonald attended an over-25s night at the Barrowland Ballroom. Patricia and Jemima were both mothers without husbands. They were both slim in build and, given that Jemima had dyed her blonde hair brown, they appeared to have dark hair, "cut in a medium short style". Both women were menstruating at the time they were murdered. In both cases, the killer appears to have escorted his victim almost to her front door, before attacking her. Both women were battered about the head and body and killed in the same way, strangled with an item of clothing. They were then left where they died; their killer having made no attempt to conceal their bodies.[54] And these are only the similarities that we know of. As the *Evening Times* suggested in their 1989 review of the murders, "There may have been other links, but to this day the police have kept them to themselves."[55]

However, there is one notable difference between the two crime scenes. Jemima MacDonald's killer didn't completely strip her, as Patricia Docker's killer had done. But rather than indicating that the killer was a different man, perhaps this change in behaviour was simply a matter of practicality. While Patricia's killer appears to have travelled by car, we know that Jemima's killer was travelling on foot. Taking all of Jemima's effects would have posed an enormous difficulty. So, instead the killer took only what he believed he could get away with – Jemima's handbag. In other words, even the difference in the crime scenes is not problematic. In essence, Jemima's killer took something from the scene, just as Patricia's killer had done.

***

While the murders of Patricia Docker and Jemima MacDonald are officially still being investigated as separate cases, the fact that some senior detectives were prepared to "probe the similarities", means that they gave themselves the opportunity to pool the information from both cases. This tentative pooling of evidence not only makes more information available, it gives investigators the opportunity to search for patterns in the killer's behaviour, should he indeed be the same man. This no doubt helps investigators to recognise the importance of certain clues and to interpret them. They can use understandings from one murder to inform their interpretation of clues from the other.

For instance, police initially reasoned that Patricia Docker had either met her killer at the Barrowland Ballroom or been picked up as she walked home. The fact that Jemima MacDonald was seen leaving the Barrowland Ballroom with her killer, strengthened the belief in a Barrowland connection. Detectives realised that the killer may have been stalking that particular venue. The Barrowland's clientele came mainly from the east side of Glasgow and the dancehall was situated in what was considered to be a very rough area.[56] In an interview for "The Hunt for Bible John", writer Andrew O'Hagan describes this particular district in Glasgow: "That area, that little triangle of the east end of Glasgow, the area around the Barrowland dancehall, was notorious as a place of theft, criminality, drunkenness. There's a sense of violence just simmering there." So, it seems that, for whatever reason, the killer was drawn to this notoriously violent corner of Glasgow in his search for victims.

It is also significant that in both murders, the killer selected his victim from the Barrowland's age-specific over-25s night, rather than from one of the ballroom's general dances which would have included younger women. The killer was deliberately choosing women who belonged to an age bracket generally associated with marriage and motherhood. In *Dancing with the Devil*, Paul Harrison interviews a Barrowland "regular" who explains that: "it was well known that if you wanted a bit more than a dance, then Thursday night was the evening to visit the Barrowland. Many older women were there, the wedding rings came off and identities were disguised."[57] The same might have been said of Saturday's over-25s night, known locally as "grab a granny" night. Perhaps, given the Barrowland's reputation, the killer was looking for women who he believed were available for sex, despite the fact that they were, or had once been, married. It is even possible that he was particularly interested in young mothers. And if, in the killer's mind, many of the women who attended the Barrowland Ballroom's over-25s nights were married, separated or divorced mothers who were out looking for sex, then his selection appears to have been based on a perceived moral transgression.

So, among the women who attended the Barrowland Ballroom on the nights that the killer was searching for a victim, were there any other criteria of choice? As noted earlier, both Patricia Docker and Jemima MacDonald were slim in build and appeared to have dark, shoulder-length hair. And both, quite remarkably, were menstruating. In *One Was Not Enough*, Georgina Lloyd, suggests that, when Jemima's autopsy revealed that, like Patricia Docker, she was menstruating at the time she was attacked, "a chilling thought" entered investigators' minds: "Were they seeking some kind of sex deviate? One with a hang-up about menstruation?"[58] But, of course, the physical similarities between the victims and the fact that they were both menstruating could be coincidental. It is risky, at this stage, to make too much of these commonalities.

If Patricia Docker and Jemima MacDonald were indeed killed by the same man, the fact that he returned to the Barrowland Ballroom to select his second victim suggests that he was not too concerned about being recognised or identified. The same insouciance is reflected in the brazen act of walking Jemima MacDonald home, giving witnesses the opportunity to see the two together. And these actions came at a cost. A number of witnesses did see the killer with Jemima, both in the Barrowland and while he was escorting her home. What is more, these witnesses were able to provide a good deal of information about his appearance. As mentioned earlier, they noted his fair reddish hair, or reddish fair hair, which was, as the sketch shows, cut short, parted to the left and swept to the right. They also described him as being 6' to 6' 2" tall and slim in build, as having a pale, "long, thinnish face" and being very good looking in the conventional sense. And they estimated that he was between twenty-five and thirty-five years of age, which is consistent with the fact that, on both occasions, he attended the Barrowland's over-25s dance nights.

Of interest too, are descriptions of the killer's clothes. A number of witnesses recalled the man being "well-dressed" in a "good-quality" blue suit with hand-stitched lapels. The impression conveyed by the killer's clothing, as indeed by his appearance, is one of a man who was both meticulous and conservative. He was noticeably neat and formal for the late 1960s. This killer was no hippy. What is more, the immediately recognisable "quality" of his suit suggests that he was relatively well-off, or at least wanted to be viewed that way.

It is also significant that in both Patricia Docker and Jemima MacDonald's murders, the killer made no attempt to conceal his victim's body. This means there was no delay in their discovery and the subsequent investigations into their murder. This lack of any attempt to conceal a murder victim is often taken as an indication that the killer is proud of his work or that, at the very least, he is not ashamed of what he has done. While in Patricia Docker's case the killer appears to have posed her body to send a moral message, there is not as much evidence of this in Jemima MacDonald's case – though clearly her coat and skirt had been pulled up around her waist and her shoes and used sanitary towel were again left near her body. But, without the removal of the rest of her effects, any intended message seems to have been lost for those who found her. Certainly, if detectives made any meaning from Jemima's crime scene, their thoughts were not revealed in the press. Nor have any former detectives revealed their analyses in their memoirs.

Chapter 3.

Finding Helen Puttock - Friday 31st October, 1969

Helen Puttock's body was found soon after 7am on Friday 31st October 1969, lying face down in the backcourt of 95 Earl Street, Scotstoun, about a hundred yards from her home. A neighbour named Archie MacIntyre noticed what he thought was a "bundle of rags" in the enclosed, grassed courtyard at the rear of his flat. Macintyre later told the press: "I got a terrible shock

to find it was a woman. I didn't know at the time if she was dead or not." MacIntyre said that Helen's clothes were in disarray: "She was still wearing her coat but it was pulled roughly up over her head".[59] According to the *Evening Times*, Archie MacIntyre ran upstairs to his neighbour, "to phone for the police and [an] ambulance." After failing to rouse anyone, he hurried across the road to a phone booth.[60]

Photograph published in Charles Stoddart's *Bible John: Search for a Sadist.*

When D.C.S. Dalglish and Detective Superintendents Binnie and Beattie arrived in the Scotstoun backcourt, they noticed that Helen's dress had been ripped and her underslip pushed up above her breasts. Her brassiere was torn in two.[61] The cause of Helen's death was indicated by the piece of underwear still tied in a reef knot around her neck.[62] In the 1990s, journalist Audrey Gillan was given access to D.S. Joe Beattie's notes and again she has included them verbatim in her podcast:

> There were abrasions above the ligature which appear to have been made by the deceased attempting to loosen it. There were also abrasions to the jaw and the side of the head which are consistent with a punch or having her head struck off some object. There was bleeding from her mouth and nose.

Later writers have noted that there was a deep bite mark on Helen's right wrist and a used sanitary towel was found tucked neatly under her left armpit.[63]

Years later, the *Herald Scotland* told readers: "There were signs that [Helen] had tried to escape from her killer by scrambling up the railway embankment ... she had been caught, struck with some heavy instrument" and dragged back across the yard. Her heels had dug tracks in the long grass, and there were blades of grass wedged between the soles of her feet and her shoes. Helen's killer had then pulled her to the rear wall of the tenement building where he raped and strangled her.[64]

A police murder caravan was set up outside the close on Earl Street and more than a hundred officers searched the surrounding back courts and the railway line which ran along the rear of the properties. Police found a broken gold chain and Helen's lipstick and eyeshadow near her body. They retrieved her hairbrush from the embankment at the rear of the lot and they found a single, inexpensive cufflink in the close, which Joe Beattie described as "a cheap Woolworth's-type cufflink". Helen hadn't taken a handbag with her to the Barrowland the night before but the small red leather purse she used, which should have contained around ten shillings, was missing.[65]

***

At the time of her murder, Helen was twenty-nine years old. She was staying at her mother's home in Scotstoun with her husband George Puttock and their two young sons – David aged five and Michael aged one. George was a Corporal in the Royal Signals and he was on leave, preparing to take up a new posting in Harrowgate.[66] On Thursday night, the 30th October, Helen and her sister Jeannie decided to go dancing at the Barrowland Ballroom. When interviewed many years later, George Puttock said: "I had tried to stop my wife going dancing; indeed, there had been a two-hour argument." But, he explained, "while I was apprehensive it wasn't really right to stand in the way", so, when Helen insisted, George handed Jeannie enough money to ensure they got a taxi home.[67] Jeannie later recalled that their mother also tried to stop them from going dancing that night. She had reminded them of the recent murders and asked them to stay home. But Helen was determined to go out. She showed her mother her long fingernails and said, "Can you imagine anyone trying anything on me?" Jeannie told detectives that Helen "had a temper," and that, when they fought as children, she "always used her nails." George painted a similar picture: "She was so strong physically. She always said that no-one could get the better of her."[68]

Just after 8.30pm that night, Helen and Jeannie caught a bus into Glasgow, reaching Glasgow Cross at about 9pm. As arranged, they met two friends, Marion Cadder and Jean O'Donnell, in the Traders Tavern in Kent Street. They had a few drinks and left before the tavern closed. Helen and

Jeannie arrived at the Barrowland at around 10pm. They paid the four-shilling fee and entered the small downstairs dancehall known as Geordie's Byre. After about half an hour, they climbed the stairs to the main hall where a live band was playing. Jeannie soon paired-up with a strong dancer and agreed to partner him for the rest of the evening. While they were dancing, she noticed a man leaning against a pillar to the side of the dancefloor quite near Helen. Jeannie watched as he approached her sister and asked her to dance. Jeannie later recalled that, unlike her own partner, this man "didn't show much skill on the dance-floor". He was "more of a shuffler than a proper mover."[69] Jeannie also formed the impression that he was different to the other men in the Barrowland, suave and a little sophisticated. In her words, this man was "a cut above the others," a "wee bit better class."[70]

The two couples met up when the musicians took a break. Jeannie's dance partner introduced himself as "John". Helen's partner said his name was also John. Jeannie responded, "It seems everyone around here is called John!"[71] When Paul Harrison interviewed Jeannie in 2003, she described the scene: "It was a ridiculous coincidence that both men should be called John, but it does happen that John was a popular name at the time. I think we all laughed because none of us believed the names to be real and neither John was insistent that it was their actual name." She recalled: "When it came to Helen's dance partner, he seemed to pause for a second or two before giving his name as John, he seemed [to be] a bit apprehensive and it was the only time I saw him look less than confident because he seemed so certain of himself in every other way".[72]

The couples shared a table and Jeannie noticed what good-manners Helen's John had. He didn't swear like the other men did. He pulled out a chair for Helen to sit on whenever she returned to the table and stood up when the women went to the toilet. Jeannie later said: "Helen and I excitedly laughed about it because it wasn't the sort of thing that happened to us or we were used to." Then, at some point in the evening, Helen's partner returned to the issue of his name. Jeannie told Paul Harrison, that "he seemed reflective and was clearly thinking about something, then he suddenly announced his surname." Jeannie said that the noise in the dancehall made it difficult for her to hear but she thought he said, "Templeton, Sempleson or Emerson." [73]

When the dancing finished at 11.30pm, the sisters went to the cloakroom. Jeannie mentioned the cost of catching a taxi home and Helen said, "It's all right, we'll not need to pay for it. He's paying for it", referring to her dance partner. Jeannie replied "good" and the sisters decided to spend their taxi money on some cigarettes.[74] They joined the two Johns in the foyer and Jeannie paid for a packet of cigarettes from the cigarette machine there. She heard the packet drop but the drawer wouldn't open. Helen's John couldn't open the drawer either and he became angry. According to Jeannie, he demanded to see the manager and said: "I'll get this sorted out." What was unnerving, Jeannie later told Paul Harrison, "was the intensity with which he said it".[75] She explained: "He wasn't outraged or shouting, he was collected and calm but very assertive. It was like a schoolteacher speaks to a young child, he was giving the manager a real dressing down without losing his temper." In Jeannie's mind, his manner was cold, imperious, authoritative, the kind adopted by a man who expects to get his own way.[76] He went on to ask who the local Member of Parliament was, implying that he would lodge a formal complaint. Charles Stoddart suggests, in *Bible John: Search for a Sadist*, that Helen apologised for her dance partner's behaviour. The manager then suggested they take their complaint to the assistant manager downstairs.[77] Helen's John abruptly turned around and headed to the stairwell. As he went, he said something to the group that Jeannie remembered: "My father says these places are dens of iniquity. They once set fire to this place to get the insurance money and then they done it up with the money they got."[78]

By this time, there was a queue exiting the dance hall and so the group was forced to pause on the stairs. Jeannie turned momentarily to her own dance partner. When she turned back, she found Helen deep in conversation with her John.[79] She thought she heard Helen ask where "such bravery" came from. In reply, he said something that Helen clearly did not accept because she shook her head and was "smirking in disbelief". Helen's John then took something from his jacket pocket and showed it to her. Jeannie couldn't see exactly what it was, but it was pink and looked official, like some form of identification card or paper. Nor could Jeannie hear the conversation clearly, but she thought that Helen's John might be "trying to prove that he was really employed as such-and-such, or had been to some place or other." [80] When Helen saw the card or paper, her attitude immediately changed "from playful disbelief to an almost surprised acceptance and air of satisfaction".[81] Jeannie leaned forward and asked if she could see the card or paper too. Helen's John returned the document to his pocket, "looked at her with an air of superiority and, tapping the side of his nose with his index finger, said, "You know what happens to nosey folk."" This remark was not made in jest. John's face was serious, devoid of any humour.[82]

Once outside, the two couples walked towards Glasgow Cross with Jeannie and her dance partner in the lead. Helen's John asked Jeannie's partner, "What are you doing, are you going home now?" Jeannie felt that he was trying to get rid of him. Jeannie's John also seems to have assumed this. He replied, "It's OK. I'm going up to George Square to get a bus." The others set off for a nearby taxi rank. Jeannie turned to Helen and asked "Is he seeing us home? Where does he come from?" Helen replied, "Over there", waving her hand. As far as Jeannie could tell, she didn't wave it in any particular direction. Within minutes, the three boarded a taxi. [83]

Inside the taxi the atmosphere was stilted so Helen and Jeannie tried to make light conversation. They asked John all about himself. What was his job? To which he replied, he worked in a laboratory. Where did he go on holiday? He said, his family "had a caravan at Irvine".[84] At some point in the conversation, he said that he played golf but, no matter how hard he tried, he couldn't get a hole in one. Apparently, his cousin had recently done so. When asked what he did for New Year, or Hogmanay, John said that "he didn't drink, but he prayed." Jeannie got the distinct impression that he had "experienced a strict religious upbringing" and yet, from their conversation, she noticed that John knew most of the pubs in Yoker.[85]

At some point in time, someone mentioned the cost of public transport. John knew the fares, and possibly even the times, for both the buses and the Blue Train services north of the River Clyde.[86] And when Helen expressed concern at the cost of the taxi fare, he said not to worry, he had "plenty of money".[87]

The conversation turned to dancing and John told the sisters that he disapproved of married women going to the Barrowland Ballroom. He asked Helen and Jeannie if they were married. They told him they were. John then said, "You know what happens to the adulterous wife.

41

Did you read it in the Bible?" The sisters indicated that they had not. "She gets stoned to death", he told them.[88]

John described himself as an only child but contradicted this soon afterwards by mentioning his sister. He said that alcohol was not allowed in his home and, when his sister came back drunk once, his father refused her entry to the house.[89] Jeannie believed that John immediately regretted having mentioned his sister and tried to redirect the conversation by saying something about a foster home or foster children.[90] But, by this time, she had formed the impression that the killer was "one of a family of two, his sister and himself".[91]

In Jeannie's words, the group had a "derisory conversation about different classes of people", in relation to football. Then, when Jeannie asked John whether he supported Rangers or Celtic, he replied, "I'm agnostic". Jeannie didn't know what he meant by that term, so she asked, "Does that mean you're an atheist?" John started talking about Moses.[92] He wasn't making direct quotations from the Bible, but Jeannie recognised his words as "having Old Testament connotations." Police later concluded from Jeannie's evidence, that he probably had been referring to the story of the baby Moses hidden in the bulrushes from Exodus 2:3 -2:4.[93]

At about the same time that John was mentioning these biblical passages, the taxi was travelling along Kingsway. He immediately recognised the high-rise flats and quietly muttered something about his father or another relative having worked there.[94] He also said that a children's home had once stood on the site.[95] John took a packet of Embassy tipped cigarettes from his pocket and offered one to Helen. He made no such offer to Jeannie, so she leaned forward and asked if she could have one too. John simply turned his head away. While he was still holding the packet of cigarettes in Jeannie's direction, she helped herself. John then put the cigarettes back into his pocket.[96] Jeannie noticed that he never took one for himself. In fact, she hadn't seen him smoking at all that night and she thought she remembered him saying that he didn't smoke when they were near the cigarette machine in the Barrowland.[97]

John insisted that the taxi driver take Jeannie home before Helen, even though she lived further away, so Jeannie was dropped off near her house in Kelso Street.[98] That was the last she saw of Helen and John. Days later, police managed to trace the taxi driver, a man named Alexander Hannah. Unfortunately, he had not heard the conversation in the taxi and remembered little about his passengers.[99] He did, however, offer some information about what happened between Helen and John after Jeannie left. According to Joe Beattie's notes, "one of the occupants" asked him what the fare was and he said £1 and 6p. The man didn't seem to have any money, Hannah said, but the woman took the exact amount from her purse and gave it to the man. He then leaned through the window and paid the fare.

Interviewed in 2005 for the programme "Unsolved", George Puttock, said that he too tracked down Alexander Hannah who told him that, "he had only been on the taxis a couple of nights so he wasn't familiar with the route." Hannah said that he had made a number of wrong turns and George assumed from this that Helen got so fed up that she told him to stop when he was close enough to her home. Hannah told George that Helen got out of the taxi and crossed the road and that John quickly paid him and ran after her. He said that the man then "got hold of her but she was resisting him". Hannah assumed it was "two lovers having a tiff" and drove off.

43

It was likely only moments later that a witness heard Helen scream. This witness "recalled hearing a woman cry out but put it down to drunken revelry." As Paul Harrison suggests in *Dancing with the Devil*, the sudden cry, followed as it was by silence, indicates that "the attack must have been instantly violent and opportunistic."[100]

At around 2am, a man was seen "walking quickly … in a determined manner" along Dumbarton Road. An almost empty number 6 night-service bus picked him up near Gardner Street as it travelled along Dumbarton Road towards the city. The man paid his fare with money from a red purse and took a seat on the bus. Passengers later described him as "dishevelled with a red mark under one eye".[101] One witness said he thought the red mark was a scratch.[102] The driver, conductor and one of the passengers noticed that the man's jacket was covered in dirt or mud, so much so that he looked as though he had been in a scuffle. What is more, he seemed agitated and kept trying to tuck his loose shirt cuff into the sleeve of his jacket.[103] The man alighted from the bus on Argyle Street just past Gray Street.[104] No witnesses claim to have seen him after that time.

***

Detectives asked Jeannie what she could recall about the man's appearance. She told them that he was between twenty-five and thirty years of age, 5'10" to 6' tall and of medium build. Jeannie said that he had light auburn or reddish hair, fine features and blue-grey eyes.[105] In *Bible John: Search for a Sadist*, Charles Stoddart says that Jeannie later described the killer to him as having "nice eyes, neither soft nor staring, but friendly." She told him that he was about 5'10" and had a "milk and roses

44

complexion" with "sandy hair, not really red but not too far off it...".[106] Bible John's hair, Jeannie explained in a 1996 interview with Audrey Gillan, was not "carrot red". She said, "he didnae have that colouring, kinda red. To me in the dark you would take him for fair-headed but when you seen him in the light it was kinda sandy-fair, you know with the kind of light eyebrows."[107]

Jeannie told detectives that her sister's killer had good straight teeth, with the exception of one tooth, "in the right upper side overlapping the next tooth".[108] She then explained in her interview with Charles Stoddart that, when she was standing next to Helen's John in the Barrowland, "her height brought her only to the point where her eyes were level with his mouth, and she saw that he had two front teeth which overlapped very slightly." What is more, she noticed that one of his upper teeth was missing, "a tooth which a dentist would describe as number four or five at the back of the right-hand side of his mouth." [109]

Jeannie described the killer as being "of smart and modern appearance" - wearing a brownish flecked single-breasted suit, with high lapels and three or four buttons. His trousers had no turn-ups. The man also wore a light-blue shirt, dark tie with red diagonal stripes and a knee-length, brownish coat, made from either tweed or gabardine. His wristwatch had a military-style broad leather strap. The press circulated the details of this description and was quick to point out that it was consistent with descriptions of the man who had been seen with Jemima MacDonald.[110]

In the days that followed, Jeannie worked closely with the Identification Branch of the Police, helping to put together a pencil-line drawing identikit (a tool then commonly used in criminal identification). But on one of her early visits to the Partick Police Office Jeannie saw

George Lennox Paterson's sketch of the man suspected of murdering Jemima MacDonald. She immediately pointed out the striking similarity between that image and her sister's killer.[111] In her interview with Audrey Gillan, Jeannie said that, "it wasnae him but the resemblance was there. It was good enough to make me feel sick."

Some four weeks after Helen Puttock's murder, police again asked George Lennox Paterson to work with their witness to produce a likeness of the suspect - this time it was to be a portrait. Jeannie spent two or three days with Lennox Paterson, responding to his questions about the killer's appearance and demeanour. When Lennox Paterson

had finished, the portrait resembled his earlier sketch of Jemima MacDonald's suspected killer, but with greater definition in the eyes and mouth. Jeannie was very impressed with the result. She told Joe Beattie that Lennox Paterson "should get a medal".[112] In fact, she was so confident, she said: "'That'll get him, nae bother. That's him!'" [113]

A copy of the George Lennox Paterson portrait was included in a special issue notice released by Glasgow City Police – "City of Glasgow Police: Special Notice – Murder of Helen Gowans or Puttock (29)"

Copies of the portrait were widely distributed about seven weeks after Helen's murder.[114] D.S. Beattie told the press: "We think it is a very good painting of the man…"

And the *Glasgow Herald* quoted D.S. Binnie, as saying: "We would like everyone in Scotland to see this painting. Coupled with the description already given, this man must be known. He could be the man living next door: he could be the man you danced with some night: he could be the man sitting next to you in church. He could be anyone, and we would ask anyone who knows or thinks he knows him to come forward. All our inquiries will be treated in the strictest confidence."[115] D.S. Binnie's request was successful in terms of eliciting a large public response. More than six hundred respondents came forward in the first few days and, by early November, Detective Chief Superintendent Dalglish said that police were "facing the task of combing through each report."[116]

***

Investigators also asked Jeannie what she could recall about the killer's conversation and behaviour. Some of these details were immediately fed to the media. In a television news broadcast, D.C.S. Dalglish told viewers: "It is thought that his Christian name may be John". He "is quite well spoken, and probably has a Glasgow accent". The man may speak of being from "a family of two and of having a sister". He may also speak of having had "a strict religious upbringing" and "severe parental attitude towards drink."[117] He might mention passages from the Bible.[118]

When the religious nature of some of the taxi conversation was revealed, John Quinn, who was then writing for the *Evening Times*, immediately dubbed the killer, "Bible John".[119] As former detective Joe Jackson said in an interview for the documentary "Calling Bible John", Helen Puttock's murder was the third "in a series we came to consider the Bible John murders".

In their efforts to identify the killer, police checked their files for men previously convicted of sexual assault and they visited all of Glasgow's psychiatric hospitals but they drew a blank.[120] Detectives in plain clothes mingled with dancers at the many dance halls in Glasgow without any success.[121] They interviewed the 453 hairdressers and barbers who worked in the city, showing them copies of the portrait.[122] No-one remembered having cut the suspect's hair.[123] D.S. Joe Beattie thought that the man's short, neat hair and military-style wrist watch were perhaps indicative of armed forces personnel so he sought help from the forces' investigative branches. They then contacted British bases all around the world, sharing police information and checking the leave dates and destinations of forces' personnel. According to Charles Stoddart, "a small number of very good suspects emerged, but all were eventually eliminated."[124] Detectives questioned all 240 tailors in Glasgow and placed an artist's impression of the suspect's suit jacket in *Men's Wear*, *Tailor and Cutter* and *Style Weekly*".[125] They visited more than 400 golf clubs and dozens of churches.[126] And they interviewed all of the dentists in Glasgow asking whether any of their patients had a slightly overlapping front tooth and a missing tooth in the position that Jeannie had identified.[127] Joe Beattie even asked the Glasgow Dental School to make a plastic replica of the suspect's teeth but all of the men who were identified by dentists as having teeth similar to Bible John's were cleared.[128] And, despite having attended more than 300 identification parades, Jeannie never recognised any of the suspects she saw as her sister's killer.[129]

Armed with the wealth of detail that Jeannie had provided, Joe Beattie was certain they would catch the killer. When he was interviewed years later by Charles

Stoddart, he said: "I was rubbing my hands together during the first week. We knew so much, that to me it was just a matter of time till we pulled him in ... I've never known a case where so much information was available." But, in the end, Beattie was left lamenting: "I was awful unlucky ... we never even got a sniff at him. ...We must have missed him right at the start, and yet we knew almost everything about him."[130] According to journalist Magnus Linklater, Joe Beattie had regrets "to the end of his days" – often referring to Helen Puttock's killer as "the one that got away".[131]

As with the cases of Patricia Docker and Jemima MacDonald, the murder of Helen Puttock turned cold.

Chapter 4.
Jeannie's Evidence

Over the years, there have been many challenges to the efficacy of Jeannie's evidence. The *Sunday Herald* reported in 1996 that: "some police sources go so far as to suggest she had drunk too much that night to be able to remember details about the man who went off with her sister."[132] In response to such claims, Jeannie felt the need to defend herself. When she was interviewed by Audrey Gillan in 1996, she said that she had two whiskeys during the hour she spent in the Traders Tavern, she bought one round for her sister and herself and Helen bought the other. Jeannie explained: 'We didnae drink in the house. My mother would never have allowed it. We only had money for two whiskeys, the ticket in and the taxi fare home." She said, "it wasn't as if we went to the dancing steaming." And Jeannie felt that any effect the whiskeys may have had, wore off in her two hours of dancing. She also pointed out that the Barrowland Ballroom was not a licensed premise. Her memory of "what took place that night", Jeannie told Paul Harrison, was "crystal clear".[133]

But challenges to Jeannie's description of the prime suspect continue. In his 2001 publication, *Power in the Blood*, Donald Simpson suggests that Jeannie's evidence with regard to Bible John's "height and the overlapping front teeth" might have been "confused" because she had had a "few drinks". [134] In their 2010 publication *The Lost British Serial Killer*, David Wilson and Paul Harrison reiterate that Jeannie, "had been drinking that night" and suggest this "might well have affected her memory".[135] And, in 2012, former Detective Inspector Bryan

McLaughlin writes: "I'm certainly not suggesting that she deliberately misled the detectives and I'm sure she would have been convinced of her recollections. But it's no secret that Jeannie, who passed away in 2010, had enjoyed a wee drink on that fateful night although she always insisted she hadn't been more than tipsy."[136]

The motivation for those who have sought to discredit Jeannie's evidence is, in part, an attempt to explain why no arrest was ever made in the Bible John murders. Despite all of the witnesses and all of the clues, the investigation came to a dead end. Jeannie's critics argue that too much emphasis was placed on her recollections and this, ultimately, led the investigation astray. Of course, these critics have their own ideas about the way the case should have been handled.[137] As Les Brown writes in his memoir, *Glasgow Crimefighter*, everyone who worked on the case "has a theory".[138] And, more often than not, there is a secondary motive for discrediting Jeannie's evidence – in particular, her description of Bible John. Some cold case writers and criminologists have challenged Jeannie's description of the killer's height, teeth and hair colour because these features do not fit with the suspect they have in mind.[139]

But Jeannie's evidence has never had to stand alone. There is ample corroboration. Not only does her description of a tall, smartly dressed, twenty-five to thirty-year-old man with light-auburn or sandy-coloured hair resemble witness descriptions of Jemima MacDonald's killer, it is corroborated by witnesses who were inside the Barrowland Ballroom on the night Helen Puttock was murdered. Some of the dancers remembered "seeing Helen with a slim red-haired man". Others described a man "wearing a flecked brown single-breasted three-button suit with high lapels" or remembered a man collecting a "brown tweed or gabardine overcoat from the cloakroom at the end of the night". Still others remembered his wristwatch having a wide leather strap with a narrower strap threaded through it. [140] And there were witnesses who saw the killer later in the night. They too corroborated Jeannie's description of Bible John. As noted earlier, the bus driver, conductor and one of the passengers claimed that a man, who fit the killer's description, boarded the number 6 night-service bus on Dumbarton Road soon after 2am. [141] And we know that this was Helen Puttock's killer because he took his fare from a red purse and, while he was on the bus, he repeatedly tugged at his sleeve and tried to fold the cuff back in. What is more, he appeared dishevelled, with mud on his jacket and a fresh scratch on his cheek. Clearly, Helen Puttock had used her fingernails in her desperate bid to break free, just as she promised her family she would.

Indeed, even the seemingly minor details of Jeannie's evidence have been corroborated. From the outset, Jeannie was very specific in her description of Bible John's teeth. She told detectives that the killer had "one tooth in the right upper side overlapping the next tooth". Helen Puttock's post-mortem revealed a deep bite mark on her right wrist, which testified to the slight overlap in the killer's front teeth. [142] At the time, investigators recognised the value of this material corroboration. It indicated that Jeannie was, as Joe Beattie believed, an excellent witness – "a typical 'Mrs Glesca', sharp as a tack and blessed with a prodigious memory for detail." [143] Joe Beattie told Paul Harrison in an interview years later that, as a witness, Jeannie "was the best [he] could have had because she did not embellish detail, she stuck to the facts she knew were accurate and nothing more." [144]

53

Many years after his wife's murder, George Puttock told the press: "Jeannie always swore that she would never forget the face of Helen's killer and I believed her." He recalled Jeannie saying: "I would have been so sure if I'd seen him … but I never did."[145] And, in her interview with Paul Harrison, Jeannie explained: "I had hundreds of men lined up before me and never once did I recognise him … and that's because I remember everything about him. The cops never had him in a line up."[146]

***

Although there were not many clues with regards to the murder of Patricia Docker, there were considerably more from Jemima MacDonald's murder and, as Joe Beattie suggested, there was a wealth of information about Helen Puttock's killer. We expect serial killers to go to great lengths to avoid detection; to leave scant trace about who they are or where they might be found. But Bible John seems to have taken few precautions. As noted earlier, he left all three bodies in the open, making no attempt to delay their discovery. He risked being seen with Jemima MacDonald when he escorted her on her way home. And, despite witnesses having provided his approximate age, height, build, style of dress and hair colour, he returned for a third time to the Barrowland Ballroom. By then, a sketch of Jemima MacDonald's killer had been pasted on the wall.

Even more remarkably, Bible John spent hours with Jeannie and the man who became known as Castlemilk John. This complication had clearly not been part of the killer's original plan. When Bible John first noticed Helen, she was standing alone to the side of the dancefloor. Jeannie was already up dancing. Nevertheless, despite all

54

of the difficulties posed by the presence of the two potential witnesses, the killer pressed on. Bible John was determined to murder Helen Puttock, irrespective of the evidence that could be amassed against him.

Some writers have assumed that Bible John chose to cover his tracks by leaving a trail of misinformation. They argue that he deliberately salted his conversation in the taxi with false clues. In *The Lost British Serial Killer*, for example, David Wilson and Paul Harrison suggest that: "It is eminently feasible – maybe even likely – that the stories about golf, Moses, pubs in Yoker and so on were all deliberate red herrings, brought up because he knew Jeannie would soon be interviewed by the police."[147] But this contradicts the evidence of the killer's insouciance; the over-confidence, even arrogance, which characterised all three murders. Moreover, there are none of the inconsistencies which you would expect to find in a series of impromptu attempts to mislead. Put simply, there are no obvious contradictions in anything the killer did or said. Indeed, the clues that Bible John so liberally left behind with regards to Helen Puttock's murder are both internally consistent and in keeping with what we know about him from the murders of Patricia Docker and Jemima MacDonald.

***

It is important that we now pool the evidence from all three murders attributed to Bible John in an attempt to examine patterns in his behaviour and conversation. We might be able to learn more about where the killer lived, the implications of his style and manners, his occupation and the way in which his obsession with adultery and menstruation affected his choice of victim.

Where the killer may have lived

As noted earlier, there is some indication that Bible John initially travelled south after murdering Patricia Docker in Battlefield. He had tossed some of Patricia's effects into the water cart, likely as he crossed Millbrae Bridge. But from there, he might have driven almost anywhere. So, it is the killer's escape route after murdering Helen Puttock that has attracted most attention. Afterall, a number of witnesses saw the killer board the number 6 night-service bus as it travelled along Dumbarton Road towards the city, alighting just past the Gray Street intersection. At the time, detectives believed that the killer's choice to alight at the Gray Street bus-stop was significant because of its proximity to the north terminal of the Govan Ferry. As Charles Stoddart suggests, it would have been only a short walk down Kelvinhaugh Street, on to Pointhouse Road, to the terminal at the bottom of Ferry Road.[148] With this in mind, detectives assumed that Bible John was trying to cross from the northside of the River Clyde to the southside, indicating that he may have lived in Glasgow's southern suburbs or beyond.[149]

In *The Lost British Serial Killer*, David Wilson and Paul Harrison challenge this assumption. They argue that the killer did not alight at the Gray Street bus-stop in order to catch the Govan Ferry because the ferrymen, "could not remember anyone resembling Bible John getting on the ferry in the early hours of Friday morning."[150] Some months after Helen Puttock's murder, Joe Beattie interviewed the two ferrymen who had been on duty that night. In *Search for a Sadist*, Stoddart quotes Beattie recalling his interview with the ferrymen:

We discovered they were both verra verra careful Highland chentlemen ... They couldn't be sure; there 'might chust have been someone there as you describe sir,' but 'wouldn't it be an aawful [sic] thing if I said he was there and he wasn't?'[151]

While Beattie attributes the ferrymen's non-committal recollection to their "verra verra careful" attitude, it is undoubtedly concerning. The Govan Ferry would have been virtually empty at 2am on a Friday morning and the killer, with his fancy clothes, dishevelled state and freshly scratched face, must have been conspicuous. Afterall, the ferries which crossed the River Clyde were not large vessels. Surely the ferrymen would have remembered seeing the killer if he had boarded their ferry.

There is of course the chance that Bible John intended to catch the ferry but missed it. He had spent a long time in the taxi, firstly taking Jeannie home and then doubling back with Helen. What is more, throughout this journey, the taxi driver had taken one wrong turn after another. When Bible John was first seen after murdering Helen Puttock, he was described by a witness as "walking quickly ... in a determined manner along the Dumbarton Road."[152] And, when he boarded the night-service bus, one of the passengers noticed that he was "breathless".[153] He was clearly in a hurry. Of course, he may have been hurrying because he was fleeing a murder scene. Then again, he may have been rushing to catch the bus, knowing that the ferry would soon be leaving. Arguably, after alighting the bus, Bible John could have gone in any direction. But, as Charles Stoddart points out, "Beattie had a hunch that this was not so."[154] He was convinced that the killer intended to travel southwards to Govan and perhaps beyond.

What we do know, is that Bible John seems to have had considerable knowledge of the northern area of Glasgow. Jeannie said that Bible John seemed familiar with the fares and possibly even the times of the buses and the Blue Train service operating along the north bank of the River Clyde. He also knew many of the pubs in Yoker and immediately recognised the high-rise flats on Kingsway, as both the site of a former children's home and somewhere that his father or one of his relatives had once worked. There are also indications from the murders of both Patricia Docker and Jemima MacDonald that Bible John was familiar with the streets of Glasgow. He had known an exit route from Battlefield which enabled him to throw Patricia Docker's effects into the water cart. And, after murdering Jemima MacDonald, he managed to leave Bridgeton on foot undetected. All of this knowledge, all of this familiarity, could only come from having lived, for some time, in Glasgow.

Having said this, police were not convinced that the killer was necessarily still living in Glasgow. The *Scottish Daily Express* quoted a "police spokesman" as saying, "This man need not necessarily live in Glasgow. He may well live in a town, miles away."[155] What bothered investigators was that, within days of Helen Puttock's murder, the city of Glasgow was saturated with images of Bible John. Police had contacted hairdressers who may have cut his hair, tailors who might have made his clothes, churches who perhaps counted him among their congregation, even dentists who may have recognised his teeth, but none of the leads paid off. It seemed that no-one in Glasgow knew this man.[156]

<u>The killer's style and manners</u>:

Witnesses in the murders of Jemima MacDonald and Helen Puttock described the killer's hairstyle as short and very neat. And there is some original news footage inserted in the 2020 production, "Calling Bible John", in which a detective describes Bible John's hair as short and "very, very neat". This detective said that it was so neat it appeared to have been lacquered. Although the killer's hairstyle could indicate a military connection, as Joe Beattie considered, it might simply have reflected an underlying, old-fashioned social conservatism. The same could be said of Bible John's style of clothing. In another short section of original footage, a detective shows one tailor a sketch of the brown-flecked jacket, saying, "It's a most unusual suit" and pointing out the "three buttons and high lapels." In response, the tailor explains, "Yes, it's like the old Italian style suit." So, although stylish, Bible John's suit was anything but modern. It was, in fact, cut in an old-fashioned style – an Italian style in a period when Italian craftmanship was already valued.

There can be little doubt that Bible John also relied on old-fashioned manners to demonstrate that he was a cut above the typical Barrowland Ballroom punter. In fact, Jeannie felt that he "stuck out like a sore thumb, not only in his demeanour, but in his behaviour." He was "polite and well-mannered" and Jeannie noticed that he didn't swear.[157] And, he was so chivalrous that both Helen and Jeannie got the giggles. Jeannie later explained that they were not used to such chivalry. As one example of the killer's good manners, Jeannie described how he pulled out Helen's chair to tuck her back in every time she returned to the table. But the act of directing Helen's chair was more than a statement about social refinement.

It served as a subtle show of control over her movement. This control became more overt when Bible John escorted her, as he did his other victims, on her way home. By accompanying all three women "almost to their front doors", he prolonged his show of chivalry, while keeping his intended victim close at hand. He only dispensed with the façade when he was ready to kill.[158]

So, was there any truth to Bible John's implied social superiority? We know that he owned at least two suits. On the night he murdered Jemima MacDonald he wore a blue suit and, when he murdered Helen Puttock, his suit was described as brown-flecked. But many Scottish men would have owned at least two suits in the 1960s. Indeed, evidence suggests that even working-class men owned at least two suits. On the Facebook page, "Glasgow Memories", one contributor posted a photograph of a bricklayer working in a suit in the 1950s. Another contributor responded that her father was an upholsterer who had a new suit made every two years and wore the old suits to work.[159] But what makes Bible John's suits significant, is the quality of both the workmanship and the fabric. The old Italian-style cut, the hand-stitched lapels and the absence of turn-ups on the trouser legs indicate that the suits were tailor-made, not off the rack. They had been crafted and fitted in a way which witnesses immediately identified as "stylish". Moreover, witnesses recognised their "good quality cloth".[160] Jeannie suggested that the brown-flecked suit might even have been made from "Reid and Taylor cloth".[161] It is also worth noting that Bible John wore a tweed or gabardine coat and expensive suede-like half-boots. Clearly, he was not poor or down on his luck.

At the same time, Jeannie did not believe Bible John when he said in the taxi that he had "plenty of money".

She assumed he was lying because, "he didn't seem the generous sort, if the incident of the cigarettes was anything to go by."[162] But, perhaps the issue here is one of perception. Jeannie appears to have been referring to "old money", to intergenerational wealth. Afterall, she described Bible John as "well-spoken, without being lah-de-dah or Kelvinside."[163] And, to this extent, we know that Jeannie was probably right because the cufflink that Bible John lost, when he was struggling with Helen Puttock in the backcourt in Scotstoun, was a cheap, "Woolworth-type" cufflink. It seems very unlikely that someone who had grown up in a wealthy family would have owned a cheap, mass-produced cufflink.

But if Bible John had experienced poverty in his childhood or grown up as a member of Glasgow's working-class, he may well have considered that he had made good, that he had climbed a rung or two up the social ladder. Perhaps his short, lacquered hair, his stylish suits and his chivalry were not just a reflection of his social conservatism, but a conscious attempt to signify his upward social mobility – to put a good deal of distance between himself and his social origins. He certainly made his disdain for Glasgow's working-class culture obvious when he was in the taxi. Jeannie recalled the group having a "derisory conversation about different classes of people", in relation to football.[164] And when she asked Bible John whether he supported Rangers or Celtic, he indicated that he supported neither. As David Wilson and Paul Harrison suggest in *The Lost British Serial Killer*, "in a city where football dominated working class culture, he couldn't be bothered with either Rangers or Celtic".[165] It was clear that he preferred the more middle-class pastime of golf.

The killer's occupation

The only information that detectives shared with the public in relation to Bible John's occupation was that "he does not appear to be engaged in heavy, manual work."[166] When Paul Harrison interviewed Jeannie in 2003, she offered a little more background to this statement. She told Harrison that Bible John's "fingernails were well cared for, almost as if they had been manicured, and his hands weren't grubby or cut, they looked clean and well presented." She said it was obvious he wasn't a manual worker or labourer. Jeannie then compared Helen's dance partner with her own. She said that Castlemilk John had "coarse, strong hands that were obviously used to manual labour" and that he "was much rougher round the edges than Helen's partner".[167]

And this is supported by a claim that Joe Beattie made. Beattie told Charles Stoddart that, early on in the investigation, D.C.S. Tom Goodall shared his thoughts with him. According to Beattie, Goodall believed that the killer was someone who was "beyond the average person's suspicion". He was someone people trusted unreservedly, and this trust emanated from the position he held in the community. Goodall felt that they were looking for a man who belonged to one of a few respected professions – "solicitors, the police, the legal profession, physicians, doctors, the medical profession, firemen, priests, the church and the press."[168] Jeannie believed that, when Bible John showed Helen the piece of paper or card in the Barrowland, she became convinced that he "was somehow genuine and authentic".[169] Perhaps this belief was rooted, as Tom Goodall suggested, in his association with an especially well-trusted occupation. Still, detectives never got a lead suggestive of any particular profession.

Admittedly, Joe Beattie thought that the killer may have been a serviceman or an ex-serviceman. But although many of the men who fit Bible John's age profile would have completed their National Service, Jeannie was adamant that her sister's killer was not still in the forces. She never accepted Beattie's suggestion that the piece of paper or card could have been a military pass. Jeannie felt certain that, if Helen had been shown some form of military identification, she would have distrusted the killer immediately. Helen had been a military wife for a long time and, as Jeannie explained in her interview with Paul Harrison, she had witnessed some pretty bad behaviours and so she would never have trusted a military man.[170]

When he was in the taxi with Helen and Jeannie, Bible John said that he worked in a laboratory. It seems unlikely that this statement was an impromptu attempt to mislead. Bible John could have chosen any number of respectable, but still predictable, responses to a question about his occupation. He could have said that he was a teacher, a lawyer, an accountant. But to claim that he worked in a laboratory is not only unusual, it seems to run counter to his attempts to persuade the women that he was socially superior and had "plenty of money".[171]

Perhaps we need to consider the possibility that Bible John was actually telling the truth. Maybe, at that time in his life at least, he did work in a laboratory. This would certainly be consistent with his well-kept hands and milk-and-roses complexion. What is more, the admission would have been so vague as to be safe. Bible John was not specific about what type of laboratory he worked in, nor where the laboratory was located.

What is more certain, is that when Bible John said that he worked in a laboratory, Helen made no attempt to challenge him, even though she had seen the piece of paper or card. This means that the paper or card was either consistent with some form of laboratory work or it was unlikely to have been evidence of any kind of occupation. If there had been a contradiction between the two, Helen would probably have noticed and said something. But she didn't. For the time that they were in the taxi at least, she and Jeannie appear to have taken Bible John at his word - that he worked in a laboratory.

The issue of adultery and the killer's religion

In *Bible John: Search for a Sadist*, Charles Stoddart argues that the killer was no "religious eccentric" or "Bible thumper". Stoddart is convinced that the coining of the nickname "Bible John" led to a press frenzy. He argues that, in reality, "the only hard facts behind the religious façade are that Jeannie ... remembers a couple of short references in conversation which had biblical connotations".[172] And, more recently, detectives working on the Bible John murders have also suggested that too much emphasis was placed on the killer's religion. Interviewed for the 2005 documentary "Unsolved", Detective Inspector Billy Little said the killer's biblical references "would appear to have been blown out of proportion."

But we need to guard against being too dismissive here. There are undoubtedly more clues with regards to the killer's morality than these positions acknowledge; especially in terms of Bible John's impromptu language and behaviour. For example, his repeated use of the term "adulterous" shows that, for him, such terminology was part of every-day or commonplace expression. And there were, of course, the behaviours which Jeannie noticed. Bible John hadn't been drinking before he attended the

Barrowland that night and he commented in the taxi that at Hogmanay he didn't drink, he prayed. What is more, Jeannie noticed that he didn't swear and, even though he owned a packet of Embassy-tipped cigarettes, she didn't see him smoke at all that night. Indeed, she thought he said that he didn't smoke. And even though Bible John attended the Barrowland Ballroom in search of his victims, there is evidence that he didn't often dance. He was certainly not the regular dancer that so many people have written about – the smooth mover who spent his evenings prowling Glasgow's dancehalls. When Bible John asked Helen to dance, Jeannie noticed almost immediately that he wasn't a proficient dancer. She told Joe Beattie that Helen's dance partner, "wasn't up to much." He could make his way around the floor, but he was "a contact dancer", "more a shuffler than a proper mover".

These patterns in Bible John's language and behaviour were taken seriously by detectives at the time. In his interview with Paul Harrison, Joe Beattie said that: "Every church and kirk in Glasgow of all denominations was visited with priests, ministers and members of the clergy being interviewed about their congregation and their own people."[173] What is more, as Norman Adams points out in *Goodbye, Beloved Brethren*, detectives "questioned families belonging to the sect in Central Scotland" in relation to the Bible John murders.[174] Perhaps the police suspected that there may have been a brethren connection. Afterall, the killer shared their distinctive use of language and his preoccupation with abstinence had much in common with brethren bans on swearing, smoking, drinking and dancing.[175]

But, whatever Bible John's religious affiliations, we know that he shared some of Christianity's moral preoccupation with sin, especially the sin of adultery. His conversations in the taxi, about the badness of "adulterous" women, reveal an intense interest in this particular sin. Indeed, David Wilson and Paul Harrison go so far as to suggest that the "main motivation" behind the Bible John murders was connected to a perceived lack of marital fidelity. They ask, "did he believe that married women who left their husbands at home to go out dancing and look for some 'fierce winchin'" deserved such treatment?"[176] The answer would have to be, yes. Afterall, in the taxi, Bible John first established that Helen and Jeannie were both married and then suggested that, in the Bible, the adulterous wife had been stoned to death.

We also know that the Bible John murders were premeditated. As Joe Beattie said, "He knew he was going to kill".[177] Indeed, Bible John went to the Barrowland Ballroom for that specific purpose. It appears to have been, in his mind, the "den of iniquity" most likely to be attended by the kind of woman he wanted to kill. As mentioned earlier, the Barrowland was widely thought to attract "men and women on the hunt for a bit of romance", despite their being married.[178] So, in the killer's mind, there would have been an abundance of "adulterous women" in this particular den of iniquity.

Bible John then used his belief in the women's adultery to justify his own behaviour. As Wilson and Harrison suggest, he "was not concerned about hiding his handiwork. In fact, he wanted it to be seen." Perhaps, when he posed Patricia Docker, he was not indicating that she was a "whore" as much as that she was an "adulteress". And the excessive violence that Bible John inflicted on Patricia Docker, Jemima MacDonald and Helen Puttock, reflected more than his "his deep-seated hatred of these women". It demonstrated the extent of the punishment he had metered out. It was, perhaps in his mind, commensurate with Mosaic Law which prescribed stoning to death for adultery.[179] He wanted the world to know that he had punished these women appropriately for their adultery. And it must have been important to him that people knew that he, and he alone, had administered these punishments. To that end, he left his calling cards – the Barrowland connection, the repeated strangulations with an item of clothing and, importantly, the used menstruation towels.

Menstruation

There can be no doubt, after the third murder, that menstruation was an important issue for the killer. We know this because Bible John left the women's used sanitary towels at all three crime scenes and, just in case detectives had missed his message in the first two murders, he left Helen Puttock's sanitary towel tucked under her left arm. But the police never passed any of this information on to the press. There was no mention in any newspaper report about the presence of a used sanitary towel. This information was only raised years later by cold-case writers and in the memoirs of some former detectives.[180]

The fact that Patricia Docker, Jemima MacDonald and Helen Puttock were all menstruating when they were murdered is perhaps the most contentious of all the clues connecting the three cases. Cold-case writers and criminologists have acknowledged that the killer's decision to leave the menstruation towel, at least in Helen Puttock's case, "was not an oversight, but a carefully considered piece of behaviour."[181] In *The Lost British Serial Killer*, David Wilson and Paul Harrison go so far as to say that leaving the sanitary towel in each case, "was clearly a message that Bible John wanted to send to whoever found the body, the police and ultimately the public at large."[182]

In *Dancing with the Devil*, Paul Harrison claims that police initially believed that "some sort of sexual flirting had got out of hand" and that each of Bible John's victims refused to have sexual intercourse with him because they had their period. Their rejection then triggered the killer's violence.[183] The police notes on Jemima MacDonald's murder, reproduced as they are in Audrey Gillan's podcast, confirm this. Investigators at the time wrote:

> It would appear that her assailant perhaps had attempted to have sexual relations with her and when he found that she was in her menstrual period became incensed and strangled her.

This theory is more fully expressed by forensic psychologist Professor Ian Stephen in his 1996 interview for "Calling Bible John". Stephen says, and it is worth quoting at length: "one of the other factors I don't think that was thoroughly looked at was the fact that Bible John may have been quite a lad round the dance halls in Glasgow at that time and because of his shy, quiet nature he might have picked up quite a few women and taken them home. Fortunately for them they may not have been menstruating at the time he took them home and it might have been an entirely successful relationship for him and it may have been misfortunate for the individuals who he did kill to be menstruating which seems to be the trigger for the offending."

The problem with this theory is that, given the odds of selecting a menstruating woman (which would be roughly one in four), Bible John must have "picked up" approximately nine other women who were not menstruating. And, while some of these women may have agreed to have sex with him, there would surely have been some women who refused for reasons other than menstruation. Yet, despite all the publicity about the killer, not one of these women came forward to acknowledge having met such a man - a man who was clearly very distinctive.[184] What is more, if Bible John had returned to the Barrowland Ballroom a dozen or more times, he would likely have been considered a regular. But he was not a regular. Indeed, no-one from the Barrowland, no staff members or dancers, recalled seeing him at the venue before.

This means that we are left with a killer who appears to have selected three menstruating women from possibly only three Barrowland attendances. And this is a serious problem for most writers. They simply cannot accept that the killer knew these women were menstruating when he selected them. For example, Molly Whittington-Egan claims in *Scottish Murder Stories* that it is, "ridiculous to suggest that Bible John with his feral instincts could sense [when a woman had her period]".[185] And David Wilson and Paul Harrison write: "It is far-fetched to suggest that he chose his victims who were menstruating. How would he have known, unless they had mentioned it much earlier in the evening, which seems unlikely?"[186] Alan Crow and Peter Samson also wrestle with this issue in *Bible John: Hunt for a Killer*. They ask: "Was there perhaps a feminine streak to his nature, which instinctively drew him and allowed him to "sense" women he was certain were having their periods?"[187]

But is it really so ridiculous to surmise that Bible John knew that these women were menstruating? For menstruating women, there are the obvious signs of checking your dress when you stand up or going to the toilets regularly to ensure that you are not bleeding onto your clothes. And then there are other signs, signs which are very much a product of their time. In the late 1960s, many women did not use tampons when they were menstruating. While they had been sold commercially since the inter-war years they were disposable and, as such, they were relatively expensive. Many women continued to use what Alejandra Borunda refers to as the old "makeshift" strategies. They used commonplace items like small towels or scraps of material which could be washed and reused. Perhaps the most common of these traditional practices, was the adoption of a menstruation towel which hung from an elasticated belt around the waist. The towel was attached at the front and back with safety pins. The whole set up was anything but discreet. The menstruation towels were, as Borunda suggests, "bulky and unwieldy" and they had, not only to be washed, but dried.[188] This meant they were displayed publicly on washing lines or, in winter, on a clothes horse in front of the stove. Most men, especially those who had sisters or who had been married, would have known the system.

It is important to note here that, in each of the three murders, it was a menstruation "towel," not a tampon, that was found at the crime scene. Interestingly, the police notes on Patricia Docker's murder, describe the towel found near her body as a "tampax sanitary towel".[189] It was not a home-made or makeshift menstruation towel. But even the commercially produced sanitary towels had to be attached to a menstrual belt in the late 1960s. It wasn't until 1969 that sanitary pads, as they are now known, were fitted with an adhesive strip.[190]

So, when Patricia Docker, Jemima MacDonald and Helen Puttock went to the Barrowland Ballroom, a keen observer might have seen the tell-tail line of an elastic belt beneath their dress. Perhaps the shape of the safety pins showed through. But, even if these were difficult to see, they could undoubtedly have been felt by a dance partner with his hand on a woman's waist.

There is, in other words, every chance that Bible John knew that Patricia Docker, Jemima MacDonald and Helen Puttock were all menstruating at the time he selected them. In other words, menstruation may well have been one of the killer's signatures as criminologists and psychologists have suggested, but not because he was enraged by his victim's refusal to have sex with him. Bible John selected these women, not only because he considered them to be adulterous, but precisely because they were menstruating.

A number of cold-case writers have suggested that the killer's focus on menstruating women might reflect his acceptance of "the Mosaic law (Leviticus 15.19) that a menstruating woman is 'unclean'".[191] In which case, Bible John may have felt the need to select a woman who was, in his mind, "the lowest of the low". But this awful phrase has historically been reserved for prostitutes and Bible John was clearly not targeting prostitutes. So perhaps, there is another way of understanding Bible John's selection of Patricia Docker, Jemima MacDonald and Helen Puttock. He likely believed, as did most people in the 1960s, and certainly most Christians, that life begins at the moment of conception. And, if he raped a woman, there was a chance that she would conceive a child during the rape – his child. If that happened, if she did conceive, then in the act of murdering her he would also be killing his own unborn child. As extreme as this reasoning might appear to be, it was likely open to someone who was deeply religious or especially moralistic.

Had this been Bible John's reasoning, then he was faced with a serious dilemma. He needed to ensure that his chosen victim would not fall pregnant. Aside from wearing a condom during the rape (and this, given the level of violence, would not have been practical or reliable), the only option open to him, was to rape a woman who was at least temporarily unable to conceive. In the 1960s, it was widely held that a woman could not get pregnant while she was menstruating. Given that Bible John was determined to murder a woman, but perhaps unwilling to kill his own unborn child, he needed to find a menstruating victim

So why would Bible John have been so preoccupied with, or even concerned about, his own hypothetical child? Because of some deep-seated religious fundamentalism? Perhaps. Or maybe he had a more personal reason – one connected to his own upbringing.

Chapter 5.
Suspects and Bible John's DNA

In 1976, when Joe Beattie retired from the police force, all the initial suspects in the Bible John murders had been eliminated and the murders of Patricia Docker, Jemima MacDonald and Helen Puttock had turned cold.[192] For years, the evidence from the crime scenes was stored in the 'Bible John room' of the Marine Police Station, in Partick. Charles Stoddart writes, in *Bible John: Search for a Sadist*, that the room was "crammed with documentation" and "adorned with pictures of the victims" and posters of Bible John.[193] According to Paul Harrison, detectives had retained some "20 boxes packed with files and statements" for the day when they could make an arrest.[194] Stored among this collection were the stockings that had been found tied around Helen Puttock's neck.

When the Marine Police Station closed in 1993 the evidence from the Bible John room was transferred to the new police building in Dumbarton Road. At this time, detectives discussed whether the small semen stain found on Helen Puttock's stockings during the original investigation, might now "yield a clear enough DNA pattern" to assist in their investigation.[195] In 1995 they sent the stockings, for the first time, for forensic testing.[196] Advances in DNA extraction and profiling in the early 1990s offered what the *Sunday Herald* called "a new weapon in the forensic armoury, one that had simply not been around in Joe Beattie's time."[197]

Despite concerns about inadequate storage, scientists managed to extract Bible John's DNA profile from the semen stain.[198] Interest in the Bible John murders was rekindled. A team of four detectives began collecting and testing DNA samples from the original suspects, including George Puttock. He told the *Daily Record* that he was asked to provide a DNA sample and it was only after returning a negative result that he was finally ruled out as a suspect in his wife's murder.[199]

In 1995, Britain established one of the world's earliest national DNA databases - the UK National DNA Database (NDNAD). That year, the *1994 Criminal Justice and Public Order Act* came into effect, allowing detectives to request DNA samples from "anybody arrested for a recordable offence". Previously, samples were only taken from people who had been charged with a "serious arrestable offence", an offence, punishable by imprisonment.[200] Investigators submitted Bible John's DNA profile to this database in search of a match, but no match was found. No-one who had previously been arrested for a "serious arrestable offence", nor indeed anyone who has subsequently been arrested for a "recordable offence", matched Bible John's DNA profile.

***

This failure to find a match in the UK NDNAD has meant that cold-case writers, criminologists and former detectives have continued to speculate about Bible John's identity.

John Edgar (aka "John White"): In his memoir *Glasgow Crimefighter*, retired detective Les Brown claims that, some two years after the murder of Helen Puttock, he and a colleague saw a man and woman arguing. The woman told them that she met the man at the Barrowland Ballroom. The man gave his name as "John White" and said he lived at 28 St Andrew's Street in the centre of Glasgow. Brown and his colleague took John White to the police station where they learned he had given a false name and address.[201] Brown says that they held the suspect at the police station until Joe Beattie could assess him. When Beattie arrived, he told them that, although the suspect "was the nearest yet", he wasn't Bible John.[202] His front teeth didn't overlap and so, on that ground alone, Brown claims, Beattie let the man go.[203]

Many years later, Les Brown was talking with Detective Inspector Bryan McLaughlin who claimed that he also arrested a man he now suspected of being Bible John. In late 1969, soon after the murder of Helen Puttock, McLaughlin saw a man who bore "a striking resemblance" to the portrait painted by George Lennox Paterson. In his memoir, *Crimestopper*, McLaughlin says that the suspect was standing near the Barrowland Ballroom, "eyeing up passing women." McLaughlin and his colleague took the man to the police station, where he gave his name as "John", and, according to Les Brown's version of McLaughlin's story, he too gave his address as 28 St Andrew's Street. The implication is that McLaughlin had picked up the same suspect as Brown. But, once again, Joe Beattie ruled him out because he didn't have an overlapping front tooth.[204]

When he published his memoir in 2005 Les Brown revealed John White's real name, which was John Edgar. This revelation prompted an immediate rebuttal from the man himself.[205] John Edgar denied any involvement in the Barrowland Ballroom murders and offered to take a DNA test to prove his innocence.[206] In 2017, the programme "Trace Evidence – The Bible John Murders" made mention of the fact that Edgar had indeed provided a DNA sample and, on the strength of the results, he was categorically cleared by investigators still working on the Bible John inquiry.[207]

David Henderson: In 1983, a central heating contractor from Glasgow named Harry Wyllie told police that he had "new evidence" about "an old mate from [his] childhood schooldays". Wyllie said he first suspected David Henderson when he returned from Australia to Scotland in the late 1970s and read an article in the *Evening Times* about the Bible John murders. He believed that Henderson closely resembled the portrait painted by George Lennox Paterson.[208] Wyllie told reporters from the *Evening Times*: "I know it is him ... he was a smart dresser for the time. His hair was short and neat. He dressed sharply with a bit of style." According to Wyllie, Henderson grew up in Glasgow's East End and frequented the Barrowland Ballroom.[209]

Harry Wyllie said that, when he gave this information to detectives, they "treated [him] as a joke" so he hired private investigators, Bill Blyth and Richard McCue. They traced Henderson to Holland. He had married a Dutch woman and was living abroad.[210] Although Wyllie insisted that the dossier compiled by these private eyes "confirmed [his] suspicions", detectives remained unconvinced. In *Bible John – Hunt for a Killer*, journalists Alan Crow and Peter Samson claim that "Henderson was quizzed and later ruled out by police."[211] Jeannie told Audrey Gillan, that she was shown a photograph of "the guy from Holland" and, although he looked like Bible John in many respects, he had brown eyes and so she told detectives it wasn't him.

Anonymous suspect suggested to Professor Ian Stephen: In 2000, forensic psychologist Professor Ian Stephen said he was approached by a man claiming to know the identity of Bible John. The new source was a Scotsman who was living in the United States and believed that

76

Bible John was one of his relatives. He claimed that his relative "bore a likeness" to the killer and that he was the son of a Glasgow police officer "who was raised by a church-going aunt". The Scotsman said his relative was living in Lanarkshire with his wife and two children at the time of the Bible John murders and that he was "a keen dancer who frequented ballrooms." By 1970, he had sold his house and moved with his family to England, without ever having been questioned by police.[212]

Professor Stephen, believed that the relative's profile fit that of Bible John so he passed his information on to detectives.[213] In response, he was told: "We will examine carefully the information delivered to us."[214] More than a decade later, Paul Harrison noted that, "Strathclyde Police appeared to be less than enthusiastic about the so-called new lead … [and] nothing further was heard of the matter."[215]

Donald Simpson's "John X": In his 2001 publication, *Power in the Blood*, Donald Simpson claims that he was working in his garden in 1991 when he first met John X, a man in his late fifties who lived near him in western Glasgow.[216] Simpson says he questioned John X, over several years and became convinced by the man's responses that he was Bible John. Simpson cites a litany of circumstantial evidence. For example, John X had red, fairish hair in his youth and dressed nicely. He lived with his parents in Earl Street for some time before the murders and frequented the Barrowland. He had joined the Brethren in 1963, changed to the Pentecostal Church in the mid-1960s and worked as a lay Pentecostal preacher for about four months sometime in the late-1960s.

But, at the end of the day, Donald Simpson admits that John X (whose name was not actually John) had false teeth and so he did not know whether he ever had front teeth which overlapped. What is more, John X had been investigated by detectives some three months after Helen Puttock's murder.[217] By Simpson's own admission, John X was, at that time, eliminated from the Bible John enquiry on the grounds of both height and appearance. He also had what Simpson refers to as a "slim alibi" – he had been at the Park Church, in Woodlands, on the night Helen Puttock was murdered.[218] But, given Simpson's repeated requests, police agreed to meet with John X in the 1990s and they again eliminated him from their investigation on the grounds of his height. Even Simpson concedes that John X was an inch and a half under the minimum height estimation of 5'10".[219]

<u>Paul Harrison's police officer</u>: In *Dancing with the Devil*, Paul Harrison suggests that Bible John was a police officer at the time of the murders. Harrison reasons that "the killer seemed to be one step ahead and … [left] very little in the way of clues or evidence" so he must have been "either involved in the criminal investigation or had someone senior on the inside of that investigation covering his tracks".[220] But, even a cursory glance suggests that the killer left an abundance of clues. As Joe Beattie had said, he'd never known a case where so much information was available. At the very least, there were independent witness descriptions from two of the murders, the bite mark on Helen Puttock's right wrist and the semen stain on her stockings. What is more, these clues were not covered-up. They were recorded and stored.

Paul Harrison argues that key participants themselves believed Bible John was a police officer. He claims that Joe Beattie told him that the only profession that "wasn't properly scrutinised" was the police force and that Joe Beattie was "shattered" to think that the killer could be one of his own officers.[221] Harrison also says that Jeannie shared his suspicions. Apparently she had noticed a man who resembled the killer during one of her many visits to the Marine Police Station.[222] Harrison quotes Jeannie as saying: "When I pointed out the similarities of the individual to Joe he dismissed it as a mistake because the person I showed him was in the police and therefore had to be above suspicion."[223] During their interview, Harrison says, Jeannie suggested that if detectives had "looked a little closer to home", they might have found Bible John.[224]

But Paul Harrison was not the only person to interview Joe Beattie and Jeannie before they passed away. Charles Stoddart interviewed them both prior to 1980 and published much of their conversation in his book, *Bible John: Search for a Sadist*. According to Stoddart, the police officer who Jeannie pointed out at the Marine Police Station was investigated and cleared of any suspicion. Stoddart quotes Beattie as saying: "in fact he was one of the best likenesses we had. In that situation I had to interview him and put my cards on the table. The officer was called in and told 'I'm very sorry, but I'm obliged to interview you in connection with the Bible John inquiry, because you look like him'". This officer was able to account for his whereabouts at the time of all three murders and Joe Beattie was satisfied that he was not involved.[225] And other writers have suggested that the police force did indeed "turn inward", interviewing and clearing a number of suspects on the force.[226]

Peter Tobin (1946-2022): In 2010, Professor David Wilson named Peter Tobin as a suspect in the Bible John murders. Wilson told the *Daily Record* that he became convinced of Tobin's guilt when he considered the evidence presented in his 1991 trial for the murder of Dinah McNicol. Wilson referred to a conversation between Tobin and Dinah,

 saying: "I couldn't believe what I was hearing. He was trying to imply he was socially superior and that he could be trusted. This was exactly the same type of conversation that witness Jeannie … heard in the back of a Glasgow taxi …" Professor Wilson told the *Daily Record* that he would stake his reputation on Tobin being the notorious killer and that, as far as he was concerned, "the case is closed."[227]

Photograph published in the *Daily Record*, 27th February 2010.

In *The Lost British Serial Killer*, David Wilson and Paul Harrison (a different Paul Harrison to the author of *Dancing with the Devil*) argue that Peter Tobin:

> was living in Glasgow at the same time as the first of the Bible John murders. He visited the same dancehalls as Bible John. Like Bible John, he sexually abused women whom he met at dancehalls. And, as of December 2009, had been convicted of murdering

three women and so could be described as a serial killer. Just like Bible John.[228]

As supporting evidence, Wilson and Harrison cite the fact that Jeannie heard Bible John's surname as "something like Templeton, Sempleson or Emerson".[229] It is no accident, they believe, that Peter Tobin sometimes used the surname Semple. Wilson told the *Daily Record*, that this was "a striking piece of evidence that cannot be coincidental."[230]

However, there are problems with this suspect. Peter Tobin married his first wife, Margaret Mountney, on the 6th August 1969, and she claims that they were on their honeymoon in Brighton when Jemima MacDonald was murdered. According to Margaret, Tobin "remained on the south coast and did not return to Glasgow for fully two weeks after that murder."[231] Margaret Mountney also said that, when she first met Tobin in August 1968, he had a noticeable "scar down the side of his left eye".[232] It was a scar, she says, that "would have been one of the first things anyone noticed about his face" and yet none of the witnesses who saw Bible John mentioned him having a prominent scar. But even without this scar, Peter Tobin bears little resemblance to witness descriptions of Bible John. In the late 1960s he had dark brown hair and brown eyes and he was only 5' 6" tall.[233]

Before she passed away, Jeannie was asked whether she thought Peter Tobin could be Bible John and she said no.[234] Jeannie told Paul Harrison: "I looked at photographs of that man, he's creepy right enough, but I saw nothing that resembled the man who I shared a taxi with and went on to murder my sister".[235] What is more, after Peter Tobin's arrest for the murder of Angelika Kluk, a sample of his DNA was compared with the DNA extracted from the semen stain found on Helen Puttock's stockings. It did not match.[236] And yet, even now, there are people who believe that Bible John and Peter Tobin are one and the same man. In a recent interview for the documentary "Hunt for Bible John", retired Detective Superintendent David Swindle felt the need to address this, saying: "There was DNA found on Helen Puttock's tights. One thing's for sure, that DNA is not Peter Tobin's because Peter Tobin's profile has been compared against it. There is nothing to indicate that Peter Tobin was involved in these cases."

John Irvine McInnes (1938-1980): John McInnes attended the Barrowland Ballroom on the night that Helen Puttock was murdered and, as the *Guardian* later stated, "he also matched the description of the tall, slim, smartly-dressed figure remembered by Jeannie and those who recalled the dance partner of Jemima MacDonald".[237] In fact, police questioned McInnes only seventy-two hours after Helen Puttock's body was found.[238]

But it seems that when John McInnes was placed in a line-up, Jeannie passed him by. Indeed, McInnes told some of his friends that "he had been picked up by the police and taken in for FOUR identity parades" without ever being singled-out.[239] And this was no oversight on the part of the witnesses. Like Jeannie, neither the conductor nor a passenger from the number 6 night-service bus, believed that McInnes was the man they saw on the night of Helen Puttock's murder.[240] In 1996, the *Herald Scotland* told readers that Jeannie, "remains convinced to this day" that John McInnes was not Bible John. She acknowledged that there was a strong resemblance between the two men, but it was nothing more than that.[241] According to Jeannie, McInnes's "jug ears" were "absolutely wrong". [242]

Photograph published in *Daily Record*, **2nd February 1996.**

John McInnes was ruled out as a suspect during the original investigation. Nevertheless, his name remained on file and, in the mid-1990s, it resurfaced.[243] A number of investigators felt that McInnes was still a very good suspect. He had been born in 1938, making him thirty-one years old at the time of Helen Puttock's murder.[244] He grew up in Stonehouse and so he had a Western Scottish accent and his family were "well respected members of the Plymouth Brethren."[245] When he was young, McInnes worked for a time at Rowans, a men's clothiers in Glasgow's Buchanan Street. In 1957 he enlisted in the Scots Guard but, after being back-squadded twice, he was discharged in July 1959.[246]

In 1964, John McInnes married Helen Russell in a small brethren ceremony in Muirkirk. The couple had two children before they divorced in 1972. McInnes then moved into the family home in Stonehouse with his widowed mother.[247] At some point in his adult years, he left the brethren. A member of his former Gospel Hall said in an interview with Alan Crow and Peter Samson: "It was a real shame for his mum. It was a real disappointment for her. He just seemed to become depressed with the life he was living and tried to take his own three times before he succeeded. I don't know why he turned against the Church. It was a very sad affair when he did."[248]

In 1980, after committing suicide by severing the main artery under his arm, John McInnes was buried in the family grave – with his father, Robert McInnes, below him. Seven years later his mother, Elizabeth Irvine, was buried above him.[249]

***

In 1995, when detectives sent Helen Puttock's stockings for forensic testing, they knew that a DNA profile might lead them directly to Bible John. As mentioned earlier, having found no match on the national DNA database, detectives began collecting DNA samples from the original suspects in the Bible John murders.[250] By this time, John McInnes had long been buried so Strathclyde Police asked some of his relatives whether they would be prepared to provide a DNA sample.[251] They swabbed John McInnes's son, Kenneth, and his siblings, Janet and Hector.[252] Almost immediately, the press reported that "A match was found" - that investigators "had received a direct hit, a match."[253] Detectives considered that the DNA comparison between the McInnes relatives and the semen sample taken from Helen Puttock's stockings was so strong, that John McInnes must indeed be Bible John. They applied for a special licence to exhume his body.[254]

The *Herald Scotland* reported that, "on the basis of encouragingly close DNA matches, the Crown authorised the exhumation of Mr McInnes's remains."[255] In other words, the local procurator-fiscal found the connection between the McInnes relatives' DNA and that of Bible John, to be "a close enough match to justify exhuming McInnes's body".[256] The McInnes family grave was reopened on the 1st February, 1996.[257] Two

84

leading pathologists were on site to ensure the efficacy of the disinterment - Edinburgh University Professor Anthony Busuttil, who was observing the exhumation on behalf of the McInnes family, and Dr Marie Cassidy, Glasgow University consultant and forensic pathologist for the Crown.[258] As camera crews waited for the exhumation to begin, Superintendent Louis Munn assured them that that, "this is not something that anybody enters into lightly".[259]

John McInnes's remains were taken to a mortuary where bone samples were removed for DNA analysis.[260] These samples were sent to the Strathclyde Police Forensic Laboratory. After months of testing, the Strathclyde scientists were unable to reach any meaningful conclusion. They cited the fact that McInnes's bone samples had been "severely damaged by 16 years' exposure underground." The samples were then sent to the Department of Biological Anthropology at Cambridge University. Cambridge University, in turn, sought assistance from the Institute of Medicine in Berlin.[261]

Meanwhile, Donald McDonald, Professor of Oral Pathology at Glasgow University, was asked to compare John McInnes's teeth with the bite mark found on Helen Puttock's wrist (preserved as it was in a plaster mould). Professor McDonald concluded that, "while Mr McInnes's teeth might have made the marks, because of the limited detail it was not possible to make a valid judgement about probability."[262] This "limited detail" stemmed from the fact that John McInnes had been fitted with dentures some three years after Helen Puttock's murder and so there were simply no teeth to compare.[263] His dental records have not as yet been found.

Eventually, the results of the DNA testing identified significant differences in the DNA profiles of Bible John and John McInnes. In July 1996, the *Glasgow Herald* reported that the McInnes family had been told that John McInnes "was not the murderer of Helen Puttock". He had been comprehensively cleared.[264] Many years later, in an attempt to dispel any residual doubt, Professor Anthony Busuttil, the pathologist working for the McInnes family, explained in an interview for "Serial Killer – Bible John", that: "the person we exhumed was not the person that was being looked for in terms of the Bible John crimes." Detective Inspector Billy Little from Strathclyde Police was equally direct: "I can tell you that the DNA stain recovered on the clothing of Helen Puttock is not John McInnes's."[265]

When it was finally revealed that John McInnes's DNA did not match Bible John's profile, there was a public outcry. John McInnes's brother, Hector, told the press that the whole experience had been distressing and that the three-month delay between the disinterment and reburial of his brother and mother had "infuriated" the family."[266] The *Herald Scotland* reported that many Stonehouse inhabitants were angry at the pressure the investigation placed on the McInnes family. They quoted one resident as saying "The family are well liked and well-respected in the village. It is a tragedy for them. Our hearts go out to them."[267] Jimmy Hood, the Member for Clydesdale, accused the police of "creating a circus" and he called for them to "make a full and public apology". Hood said that, while unsolved murders clearly need to be investigated, "this case seems to be a text-book example of how not to go about it".[268]

In July 1996, the Lord Advocate stated that, although the file on Helen Puttock's murder would remain open, "there would be no further investigation into John McInnes.[269]

***

In her interview with Paul Harrison, Jeannie had said:

In recent times I've seen some of the folk put forward as Bible John; it is none of them. The man McInnes kind of looks similar. I'm told by press men that I apparently saw him in a police line-up and didn't pick him out. I've since studied the photographs of the man they dug up in Lanarkshire but I'm certain it's not him, but it's close, but close doesn't make it him![270]

Chapter 6.
Genealogy and a Name

There is always the chance that, eventually, a sample will be entered into the UK NDNAD which is such a close match to Bible John's DNA profile that it will lead investigators to the killer's identity. But, at this point in time, only those detectives still tasked with finding Helen Puttock's killer have access to the DNA profile extracted from the semen stain on her stockings. And these investigators do not appear to have connected the killer's DNA to any other family tree.

Without access to the killer's DNA profile, there appears to be only one avenue left open for those who might be trying to solve the Bible John murders – to return to the near match between the DNA profile derived from the semen stain on Helen Puttock's stockings and the DNA samples offered by the McInnes relatives. While Bible John was clearly not John McInnes, he was almost certainly related to him. The fact that permission was both sought and granted to disinter McInnes (and his mother) is testimony to the perceived strength of this DNA connection. And, as Superintendent Louis Munn had remarked in the cemetery on the day the family grave was opened, exhumation is *not* something that anybody enters into lightly.

It is difficult to know exactly what action investigators took, armed with the knowledge of the likely genetic link between members of the McInnes family and Bible John. It is possible, that they asked for DNA samples from all male relatives who fit the suspect's age range – from brothers, cousins and perhaps second or third cousins. But it seems more likely that investigators were so convinced of John McInnes's guilt that they looked no further along his family tree. Then, when confronted with the backlash over the disinterment, they "very swiftly shut the reinvestigation down" as journalist Audrey Gillan suggests in her podcast.[271] This means that the samples of DNA given by members of the McInnes family remain a vital and seriously underutilised connection to the past. Although the genetic relationship is clearly more distant than first presumed, their genealogy may well hold a clue to the identity of Bible John.

***

In September 2020, I sat down with Dr Stuart Boyer, who holds a PhD in molecular biology from the University of Western Australia. I wanted to know more about the process of DNA transmission and the means by which a profile match might be established. Dr Boyer explained that, in its simplest expression, profiles are created by heating a sample of DNA to separate the strands of chromosomes. Short segments, called primers, are then taken from the strands and scientists use chemical techniques to amplify them so they become readable. Then, by examining a large number of primers, scientists can discern patterns in the DNA, patterns which are unique to the individual.[272]

In 1996, when the DNA profile obtained from the semen stain on Helen Puttock's stockings was compared with the DNA samples given by the McInnes relatives, the press never offered any quantification of such shared patterns – only the imprecise and misleading phrases "a direct hit" and "a match". So, without access to the actual DNA samples, we have no way of determining the strength of the relationship between them. Nevertheless, investigators clearly believed they had found at least some sections of shared pattern along the DNA primers. And, as Dr Boyer explained to me, this does not occur when people are biologically unrelated. The shared patterns can only originate from a shared genetic inheritance.

What is more, DNA transmission is generational. The McInnes siblings, Janet and Hector, received their DNA from their parents, Robert Samson McInnes (1894-1954) and Elizabeth McClement Irvine (1896-1987). Dr Marie Cassidy, the forensic pathologist for the Crown in the McInnes exhumation, explains in her recent book, *Beyond the Tape,* that individuals derive half their DNA from their mother and half from their father.[273] Parents, in turn, receive their DNA from their parents, and so on through preceding generations.[274] So, for some patterns within the McInnes family DNA to match those of Bible John, there must have been an intersecting point in their family trees from which both parties inherited the shared DNA patterns. In other words, if we traced back through generations of McInnes ancestors, we would find that they had at least one ancestor in common with Bible John.

Of course, without knowing Bible John's identity, we would not necessarily recognise which McInnes ancestors are also present in the killer's family tree. Nevertheless, there is still much that we can do. For instance, we can begin by identifying the ancestors who contributed to Janet and Hector's DNA. This search will take us back through several generations of McInnes ancestry. Then, from the siblings' ancestors, we can identify the various branches of their family tree and trace them forward through time, along lines of family descendants. Eventually, we would return to the generation which included both the McInnes siblings and Bible John. This would enable us to identify any of the McInnes's male relatives who fit Bible John's age profile - establishing a cohort of men who both shared some of the McInnes siblings' DNA patterns and were within Bible John's estimated age range at the time of the murders. From there, the challenge would be to identify which of these cohort members fit witness descriptions of the killer. But first things first. We need to begin with the McInnes siblings' ancestors.

In moving forward, cold-case historians, as distinct from cold-case writers and criminologists, would turn to the vast and potentially rewarding field of genealogy. And it is important to note here that the information available to cold-case historians is not as narrow as people often presume. These records are not finite – generated only at the time of the Bible John murders. Genealogy has an ever-growing resource base. For example, our access to the information held in birth, marriage, divorce and death records is constantly expanding as the assigned periods of closure to the public expire. What is more, new records are created when people are born, marry, divorce and die. Held within these recently accessed and newly created records, are details of parentage and other family relationships which may not have been recorded elsewhere.

It must also be said that much of this information was not available to police in the years immediately following the discovery of the McInnes siblings' likely genetic link to Bible John in 1996. Potential suspects may not have married or divorced by that time, and they most likely hadn't died. In other words, records for many of these significant events had not even been created in 1996. And, to be fair, investigators are unlikely to have examined any of the genealogical evidence that was already in existence. Few detectives would have the time to search through birth, marriage, divorce and death records looking for some shared ancestry between the McInnes siblings and Bible John – a search which involves several generations.

These time-consuming tasks are made feasible nowadays by the existence of Scotland's vast online genealogical database, "Scotland's People". This database houses Scotland's birth, marriage, divorce and death records, among other incredibly useful genealogical data. Of particular note, are the database's census records which are currently available for the period 1841 to 1921. These censuses help us to reconstruct family relationships and understand familial connections to particular regions over time. Of course, these genealogical records may not contain all of the information we need to reconstruct the McInnes family tree but we can supplement our findings with information held in other traditional historical sources such as wills, valuation rolls, trade directories and cemetery headstones. And we can learn much from the family historians who have researched their own ancestry and entered their findings, and sometimes their sources, on websites such as Ancestry, MyHeritage and Family Search.

In constructing a family tree which focuses on generational DNA transmission, it is important to include parents who contribute to an individual's DNA but not necessarily the siblings who share it. If we want to understand how the McInnes siblings came by their DNA, it is enough to include their direct lineage; their parents, grandparents, great grandparents and so on. This ancestral representation, devoid of siblings, is usually referred to as a Generation Ancestor Chart rather than a family tree.

The siblings who provided detectives with their DNA samples, Janet and Hector McInnes, constitute the first generation of their Generation Ancestor Chart. The second generation consists of their parents, Robert Samson McInnes (1894-1954) and Elizabeth McClement Irvine (1896-1987). The third generation of the ancestor chart draws in the siblings' four grandparents - Hector McInnes (1871-1953), Elizabeth Murdoch Samson (1873-1948), John Irvine (1870-1938) and Janet Finnie (1872-1948). When we construct the fourth generation of the McInnes ancestor chart, we include Janet and Hector's eight great-grandparents and, in the fifth generation, we introduce the siblings' sixteen great, great grandparents. Fortunately, all of the McInnes ancestors included in these first five generations can be identified by cross-referencing Scotland's birth, marriage and death records.

The relationship between the McInnes siblings and these ancestors is represented in the following 5 Generation Ancestor Chart.

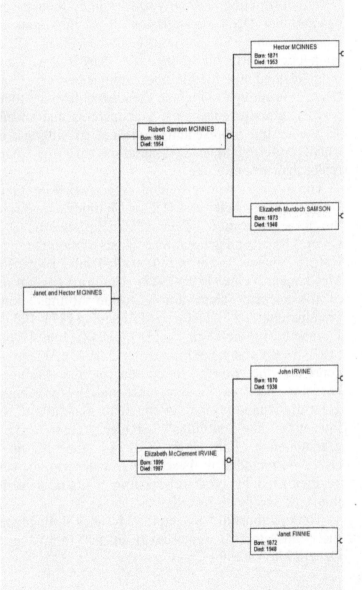

Janet and Hector MCINNES

Robert Samson MCINNES
Born: 1894
Died: 1954

Hector MCINNES
Born: 1871
Died: 1953

Elizabeth Murdoch SAMSON
Born: 1873
Died: 1948

Elizabeth McClement IRVINE
Born: 1896
Died: 1987

John IRVINE
Born: 1870
Died: 1938

Janet FINNIE
Born: 1872
Died: 1948

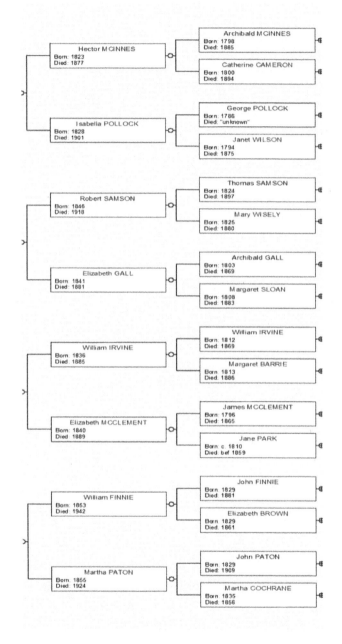

Hector MCINNES
Born: 1823
Died: 1877

Archibald MCINNES
Born: 1798
Died: 1885

Catherine CAMERON
Born: 1800
Died: 1894

Isabella POLLOCK
Born: 1828
Died: 1901

George POLLOCK
Born: 1786
Died: "unknown"

Janet WILSON
Born: 1794
Died: 1875

Robert SAMSON
Born: 1846
Died: 1918

Thomas SAMSON
Born: 1824
Died: 1897

Mary WISELY
Born: 1825
Died: 1880

Elizabeth GALL
Born: 1841
Died: 1881

Archibald GALL
Born: 1803
Died: 1869

Margaret SLOAN
Born: 1808
Died: 1883

William IRVINE
Born: 1836
Died: 1885

William IRVINE
Born: 1812
Died: 1869

Margaret BARRIE
Born: 1813
Died: 1886

Elizabeth MCCLEMENT
Born: 1840
Died: 1889

James MCCLEMENT
Born: 1796
Died: 1865

Jane PARK
Born: c. 1810
Died: bef 1859

William FINNIE
Born: 1853
Died: 1942

John FINNIE
Born: 1829
Died: 1881

Elizabeth BROWN
Born: 1829
Died: 1861

Martha PATON
Born: 1855
Died: 1924

John PATON
Born: 1829
Died: 1909

Martha COCHRANE
Born: 1835
Died: 1856

With each additional ancestral generation, the number of newly introduced family members doubles and so, by the end of our five-generational search, we have found a total of thirty McInnes ancestors (2+4+8+16). But, of course, there have not been thirty new surnames added in the 5 Generation Ancestor Chart, only fifteen. Each of the men retains their family surname. It is only the women, by way of marriage, who introduce new surnames to the ancestor chart. At this stage, these additional surnames include Irvine, Samson, Finnie, Pollock, Gall (sometimes spelled Gaul), McClement (sometimes spelled McClymont), Paton, Cameron, Wilson, Wisely, Sloan, Barrie, Park, Brown and Cochrane.

***

As noted earlier, we do not really know how close the DNA relationship is between the McInnes siblings and Bible John. True, in 1996 the press was claiming that Janet and Hector's samples were "a positive DNA hit" and investigators assumed the samples pointed to their brother, John McInnes, being Bible John.[275] But, in 1996, the science of DNA extraction and profiling was still in its infancy and so the relationship was overstated.[276] Although the "match" indicated that Janet and Hector McInnes were likely related to Bible John, it did not mean that the killer was their brother nor their cousin nor even their second or third cousin. The connection between them might have been more remote. So, in order to ensure that we reach the point of shared ancestry between the McInnes siblings and Bible John it seems sensible to construct the McInnes Generation Ancestor Chart for as far back as we reliably can go.

This is, at best, seven or eight generations. Searching any further back in time becomes too difficult because the historical records are incomplete.

In 1855, Scotland legislated the civil registration of all births, marriages and deaths, making it compulsory to record these life events. Prior to this, births or baptisms, banns or marriages, and deaths or burials were recorded by local churches – if, and only if, families chose to report them. Sometimes it was not practicable to record life events, particularly for families living in remote areas. And even when births, marriages and deaths were recorded in these very early years, the information written down was not always complete or reliable. Essentially, the older the church records, the lower the likelihood that parentage was recorded and the less consistent the spelling of surnames.

***

Generation six of the McInnes 6 Generation Ancestor Chart sees the introduction of another thirty-two ancestors. I have been able to trace most of these family members through Scotland's birth, marriage and death records, supplementing some of the information from the names, dates and relationships included in censuses, on cemetery headstones and in family history websites. In the table which follows, the column on the left is a repeat of the fifth McInnes generation, showing its relationship to the newly constructed sixth generation.

5th Generation	6th Generation
Archibald McINNES (1798-1885)	Colin McInnes (1760-) Effy **McLEAN** (1776-1864)
Catherine CAMERON (1800-1894)	Alexander Cameron (1774-) Euphemia **CAMPBELL** (1777-1850)
George POLLOCK (1786-)	William POLLOCK (1760-) Elizabeth **WALLACE** (1763-)
Janet WILSON (1794-1875)	John WILSON (c1767-1798) Janet **HAMILTON** (1772-1853)
Thomas SAMSON (1824-1897)	James SAMSON (1786-1886) Margaret **BROWNLEE** (c1776-1851)
Mary WISELY (1825-1880)	Joseph WISELY (1799-bef1841) Elizabeth **MURDOCH** (1789-1877)
Archibald GALL (1803-1869)	William GALL (1759-) Elizabeth **BREAR** (1762-)
Margaret SLOAN (1808-1883)	David SLOAN (1783-1859) Janet **BROWN** (1789-1825)
William IRVINE (1812-1869)	Samuel IRVINE (1765-bef1841) Margaret **SMITH** (c1771-aft1841, bef1861
Margaret BARRIE (1813-1886)	Dennis BARRIE (-) Unknown
James McCLEMENT (1796-1865)	James McCLEMENT (1774-) Ann **McCROW** (1775-)
Jane PARK (c1810-bef1859)	unknown PARK unknown
John FINNIE (1829-1881)	Hugh FINNIE (1782-1830) Margaret **CLARK** (1784-1861)
Elizabeth BROWN (1829-1861)	James BROWN (1787-1871) Margaret **FREW** (1790-1878)
John PATON (1829-1909)	Andrew PATON (1807-1870) Helen **CUNNINGHAM** (1808-1848)
Martha COCHRANE (1835-1856)	Andrew COCHRANE (1784-1841) Agnes **BROWN** (1794-1866)

Of the possible sixteen new female ancestors in this sixth generation there are two (marked "unknown") who I have been unable to identify. When Margaret Barrie (sometimes spelled Berry) died in 1886, her father's name was noted on her death certificate but, unfortunately, her mother's name was not. I have also found difficulty identifying the parents of Jane Park with any certainty. The name "Jane Park" appears both on her husband's death certificate and her daughter's marriage certificate. However, I cannot recognise which of the birth, marriage or death certificates might be hers. Her name is simply too common to allow for anything but guesswork.

Nevertheless, fourteen of the sixth-generation female McInnes ancestors can be identified. As you can see in the 6 Generation Ancestor Chart, their surnames include: McLean, Campbell, Wallace, Hamilton, Brownlee, Murdoch, Brear (or Brier), Brown, Smith, McCrow, Clark, Frew, Cunningham and Brown again. Many of these surnames are common in Scotland. They regularly appear in lists of the "top 100" Scottish surnames. For example, the National Records of Scotland include in their most common one hundred surnames: McLean, Campbell, Wallace, Hamilton, Brown, Smith, Clark and Cunningham.[277] The names Brear, McCrow and Frew are less common.

The McInnes 7 Generation Ancestor Chart sees the introduction of another sixty-four people, including thirty-two female ancestors who bring new surnames to the family tree. At this stage, there are a number of ancestors who cannot be traced. Their records are either missing or incomplete or their names, like Jane Park's, are too common for parentage to be identified amongst the many possibilities. The missing names for these ancestors are recorded in the following table as "unknown".

Nevertheless, most branches of McInnes ancestry can be traced back to the seventh generation. And it is in this generation that one of the newly introduced names stands out - the name "Margaret Templeton". Of course, we know from Jeannie's evidence that "Templeton" was the surname she thought Bible John gave that night in the Barrowland Ballroom. Jeannie told detectives that Helen's dance partner had introduced himself as John and later offered the surname "Templeton, Sempleson or Emerson".

When Margaret Templeton (1766-unknown) married Thomas Murdoch (1763-1841) in 1789, and became part of the McInnes 7 Generation Ancestor Chart, the surname "Templeton" was uncommon in Scotland. It was confined, for the most part, to Western Scotland. The surname became more prevalent over time, but it would not have been considered a common Scottish surname even in 1969, when Bible John claimed it for his own.[278]

So, the odds of finding the name "Templeton" among a total of sixty-three surnames introduced in any seven-generational search are remote. But the odds of finding the surname offered by Bible John among the ancestors of a family with a DNA connection to the killer, is well beyond remote. It is nothing short of extraordinary.

The following table records the name "Margaret Templeton" amongst the seventh generation McInnes ancestors. Again, the preceding sixth generation has been repeated in the column on the left to indicate the connections between the two generations.

6th Generation	7th Generation
Colin McINNES (1760-)	Hugh McINNES (1729-1792) m Katharine **CAMPBELL** (1739-1792)
Effy McLEAN (1776-1864)	Donald McLEAN (1755-1792) m Ann **McLEAN** (1753-1823)
Alexander CAMERON (1774-)	John CAMERON (1733-1776) m Mary **McARTHUR** (1736-1776)
Euphemia CAMPBELL (1777-	John CAMPBELL (1751-) m Katharine **McLEAN** (1755-1791)
William POLLOCK (1760-)	William POLLOCK (1732-) m Janet **STRUTHERS** (1743-)
Elizabeth WALLACE (1763-)	Henry WALLACE (1738-) m Janet **LISTON** (1740-)
John WILSON (c1767-1798)	Hugh WILSON (1745-) m Jean **COCHRAN** (1748-1766)
Janet HAMILTON (1772-1853)	John HAMILTON (-) m Janet **WATSON** (-)
James SAMSON (1786-1886)	Hugh SAMSON (1763-) m Mary **FISHER** (1762-)
Margaret BROWNLEE (c1776-	unknown BROWNLEE (-) m unknown
Joseph WISELY (1799-bef1841)	unknown WISELY (-) m unknown
Elizabeth MURDOCH (1789-1877)	Thomas MURDOCH (1763-1841) m Margaret **TEMPLETON** (1766-)
William GALL (1759-)	Archibald Gall (1730-) m Grizel **WRIGHT/BROWN** (1735-)
Elizabeth BREAR (1762-)	unknown BREAR (-) m unknown
David SLOAN (1783-1859)	William SLOAN (1754-1798) m Jean **PARK** (1759-1800)

Janet BROWN (1789-1825)	William BROWN (1769-1800) m Margaret **SCOTT** (1756-1798)
Samuel IRVINE (1765-bef1841)	unknown IRVINE (-) m unknown
Margaret SMITH (c1771-aft1841)	unknown SMITH (-) m unknown
Dennis BARRIE (-)	unknown BARRIE (-) m unknown
unknown	unknown m unknown
James McCLYMONT (1774-)	James McCLYMONT (1756-1801) m Elisabeth **McGARVIE** (1743-)
Ann McCROW (1775-)	John McCROW (-) m unknown
unknown PARK	unknown PARK (-) m unknown
unknown	unknown m unknown
Hugh FINNIE (1782-1830)	James FINNIE (1750-) m Mary **DEVLIN** (1750-)
Margaret CLARK (1784-1861)	James CLARK (1750-) m Jean **ORR** (1751-1791)
James BROWN (1787-1871)	John BROWN (1757-1806) m Elizabeth **McKINNEL** (-)
Margaret FREW (1790-1878)	David FREW (1761-1846) m Agnes **McCALLUM** (1765-1835)
Andrew PATON (1807-1870)	John PATON (1776-1844) m Ann **ALLAN** (1780-1855)
Helen CUNNINGHAM (1808-	Adam CUNNINGHAM (-) m Janet **RAMAGE** (-)
Andrew COCHRANE (1784-1841)	Alexander COCHRANE (1751-1804) m Mary **SMITH** (-1818)
Agnes BROWN (1794-1866)	Hugh BROWN (1770-) m Margaret **MIEKLE** (1766-)

The improbability of finding the surname "Templeton" in the McInnes Ancestor Chart is compounded as we delve deeper into the family's ancestry.

Margaret Templeton's birth certificate indicates that her father's first name was John. Her mother, Margaret Hunter (1732-1797), worked as a servant for a minister named Thomas Walker in Dundonald Parish. So too did her father, John Templetoune (1730-1800). The couple married in Dundonald in June 1759 and Margaret Templeton (spelled Templetoune in previous generations) was born some seven years later.

This means that Janet and Hector McInnes were in fact directly related to a man who shared the full name, not just the surname, that Jeannie thought she heard Bible John give in the Barrowland Ballroom on the night her sister was murdered. True, this John Templetoune had died in 1800, long before Bible John stalked the Glasgow dancehall, but it was common practice in Scotland for men to name their sons after both themselves and their fathers.

Further genealogical investigation indicates that John Templetoune and Margaret Hunter named one of their sons John (1761-c1833). They also had sons named Adam (1760-unknown) and James (1767-c1841). While I have been unable to trace Adam's descendants back down through the generations, Margaret's brothers John and James both named one of their sons John. Moreover, many of John and James's other sons also passed the name on.[279] In other words, the number of John Templetons increased with each subsequent generation and, if we follow them back down through lines of their descendants, there is a very good chance that we will find a John Templeton who was not only related to the McInnes siblings, but who also fit the age profile of Bible John.

***

So, what does all of this mean? It means that on the night of Helen Puttock's murder, there is every chance that Bible John gave his real name and that Jeannie heard it correctly. If we accept, at least tentatively, that Bible John was in fact telling the truth when he said his name was John Templeton, we would not be surprised to find that particular surname in the McInnes Ancestor Chart. On the contrary, we would expect to find it there. The killer's surname must have existed at some point in the McInnes family tree in conjunction with the shared DNA.

When Jeannie told detectives that her sister's killer gave his surname as "Templeton, Sempleson or Emerson", they may have thought he chose an unusual alias. But alias they would certainly have assumed it was. After all, what kind of killer tells a witness his real name?

So, although the surname "Templeton" is often acknowledged as Jeannie's first impression of the name she heard that night, it has rarely been discussed. What is potentially the most important of all clues, seems to have been considered so improbable that it has been largely overlooked.

It is important now that we ask ourselves again, what kind of killer gives his real name? The answer is most likely someone with a rigid sense of morality - a man who doesn't swear, doesn't smoke, doesn't drink. A man who doesn't lie. When Bible John introduced himself as "John" in the Barrowland Ballroom, Jeannie noticed that he was apprehensive. Remember, she told Paul Harrison: "When it came to Helen's partner, he seemed to pause for a second or two before giving his name as John, he seemed [to be] a bit apprehensive and it was the only time I saw him look less than confident because he seemed so certain of himself in every other way."[280] Bible John *was* apprehensive. He was apprehensive because he knew the danger of offering his real name. But, it appears, offer it he felt he must. And then when he did, when he said that his name was John, no-one believed him. What is more, Jeannie, Helen and Castlemilk John made it obvious they didn't believe him. Jeannie joked - "It seems everyone around here is called John!"[281] And they all laughed.

As David Wilson and Paul Harrison suggest, in *The Lost British Serial Killer*, "All four of them knew what [Jeanie] meant by the joke: you were lucky to be given a real name by either sex on 'Over-25s' nights at the Barrowland."[282] The killer couldn't let this slide. He continued to dwell on it. Jeannie told investigators that: "There was one point in the evening when he seemed reflective and was clearly thinking about something, then he suddenly announced his surname".[283] In other words, Bible John returned to the subject of his own volition, offering his surname to the whole group as though it would in some way dispel suspicion that he lied when he said his name was "John". He took the enormous risk of giving his surname in order to prove that he was no liar and, perhaps more importantly, to refute any insinuation that he was an adulterer.

***

While Joe Beattie appears to have hung on Jeannie's every word, investigating even the slightest detail she could remember, he showed little interest in the name she heard the killer give that night. In his book *Power in the Blood*, Donald Simpson writes of Joe Beattie: "In his career he investigated many murders which he solved and only three were never brought to court. In two of the three he knew the killers and never had enough evidence to bring them to justice. The third and last one was 'Bible John' of whom Mr. Beattie said, 'I did not even have a name to go on, it has always bugged me. I have never let go, my search has continued even in my retirement from the police. I know my instincts were correct, someday I'll have that name.'" [284]

It appears that, without realising it, Joe Beattie had the name all along. Jeannie had given it to him.

Chapter 7.
Establishing Our Cohort

Finding the surname "Templeton" among the McInnes ancestors changes everything. We no longer need to investigate all the descending branches of the McInnes family tree in our search for a man who fits Bible John's age profile and description. We appear to have found the point of shared ancestry between the McInnes siblings and Bible John. If Bible John did use his real name on the night he murdered Helen Puttock, and surely this possibility warrants investigation, then we have identified the likeliest of shared ancestors in the marriage of John Templetoune (1730-1800) and Margaret Hunter (1732-1797). This provides us with a starting point. We can now concentrate our investigation on the Templetoune branch of the McInnes family tree.

In my interview with Dr Stuart Boyer in September 2020, I asked whether it was possible that patterns in DNA could be transmitted through several generations. He answered, yes. Dr Boyer said that this strong transmission would be particularly likely in cases where some of the family genes and their expression patterns are dominant. Such dominant patterns, he explained, could carry all the way through multiple generations. In order to be clear in my own mind, I showed Dr Boyer the McInnes family tree and asked him whether patterns in DNA could have been transmitted from John Templetoune and Margaret Hunter to one or more relatives as far down the line of descent as the McInnes siblings – in other words, to them and at least one other relative from their generation. Again, Dr Boyer answered, yes.[285]

So, having traced back in time through generations of McInnes ancestors to the marriage of John Templetoune and Margaret Hunter, we can now use this couple as a base from which to move forwards again through generations of descendants, much like constructing a family tree in reverse. And now we are not constructing a Generation Descendant Chart but a whole family tree where siblings become relevant. Parents pass their genes on to all their children so we must follow each of the descending family lines - daughters as well as sons. It is not only male descendants who might have given the name "Templeton" to their children. There are many cases in the historical record where unmarried mothers pass their own surname on to the next generation. This means that we need to trace all the Templeton descendants, male and female. Theoretically, the process should lead us to a man named John Templeton who fits the age profile of Bible John.

This task of tracing forward in time along lines of Templetoune descendants is not as difficult as it sounds. As an example, we can follow one branch of John Templetoune and Margaret Hunter's descending family tree.

In 1794, John and Margaret's third son, James Templeton (1767-c1841) married Margaret Wilson (1776-1810). The couple had eight children. Robert Templeton (1807-1866), their sixth child, grew up to be a baker and he married Elizabeth Carswell (1815-unknown) in Cathcart in 1835. Robert and Elizabeth had a son named John (1848-1909). He became a shipwright and, in 1872, he married a domestic servant named Martha Howie (1853-1926). The couple had six children. The youngest of their sons, James Templeton (1890-1965), became a marine engineer. In 1907, he married a nurse named Martha Jane Muir (1895-unknown). James and Martha named their second son, John Muir

Templeton (1933-1998) and this John Templeton was thirty-five years old, turning thirty-six, in 1969.

While this birth year places John Muir Templeton outside Jeannie's estimate of twenty-five to thirty years of age, it is consistent with the broader estimation of other witnesses. He is, therefore, included in the cohort of John Templetons we are interested in – those aged between twenty-five and thirty-five. Most importantly, in the process of finding John Muir Templeton, we have established that John Templetoune and Margaret Hunter's lineage can indeed be traced forward, through generations of descendants to the generation in question. This proves that it is possible to find at least one man named John Templeton who is both related to the McInnes siblings and who fits Bible John's age profile. We now need to ask ourselves whether he is the *only* John Templeton who fits these criteria.

***

Of course, we could continue our investigation by tracing forward in time through generations of Templetoune descendants, searching for other John Templetons who fit Bible John's age profile. However, this is not necessarily a profitable way to proceed. We would need to be certain that we can trace *all* branches of the Templetoune family tree. Admittedly, we were able to identify John Muir Templeton by using this technique, but our success was due largely to the fact that the genealogical records for James Templeton (1767-c1841) are remarkably complete. The birth, marriage and death records for him and his wife, Margaret Wilson (1776-1810), and for their children and their children's children are intact and open to the public. Unfortunately, the same cannot be said about the records for all the Templetoune descendants.

We already know that there is at least one branch of the Templetoune family tree which cannot be followed in Scotland's genealogical record. John and Margaret's son, Adam Templeton (1760-unknown), can only be found in the birth records. There is no documentation of his marriage or his death. A search of the Ancestry genealogical website shows that Adam Templeton has been included in a number of family trees but none of the Ancestry members have been able to verify his marriage or death details. Some claim that Adam married a woman named Mary Jamison either before or after migrating to the United States. Unfortunately, these members offer scant information and no documentary evidence of this marriage. In other words, there is no way to verify that the Adam Templeton who married Mary Jamison is, in fact, *our* Adam Templeton. This is important because, if our Adam Templeton did not migrate to the United States, then he probably remained in Scotland. Indeed, there are Ancestry members who believe that Adam passed away in Auchinleck in 1832 and others who suggest that he passed away in Auchinleck in 1841. Again, there is no evidence to prove that either of these Adam Templetons is the son of John Templetoune and Margaret Hunter but, if one of them is, then there could be a large branch of the Templetoune family tree, still living in Scotland, who we cannot detect. And if the John Templeton that we're looking for is on Adam Templeton's line of descent, we will miss him.

It is also very difficult to find which, if any, of the Templetoune or Templeton daughters from these early generations had one or more illegitimate children. Indeed, I have not been able to identify any of John Templetoune and Margaret Hunter's early descendants who received their surname from their mother, but this does not mean there weren't any. Their births might not have been recorded or the documentation might be missing. Moreover, the birth records which were collected by the church before 1855 offer little information.

In some cases, there is only the mother and child's name, so we cannot be certain of the mother's family connections. This means that if the John Templeton we're looking for is on one of the descending female branches of the Templetoune family tree, we will very likely miss him.

The same problem arises if John Templetoune (1730-1800) had siblings who shared much of his DNA. The birth certificate of John Templetoune b.1730 gives his father's name as John but it does not record the name of his mother. This means we cannot identify his siblings. What is more, there are some family genealogists who claim that the John Templetoune who married Margaret Hunter was John Templetoune b.1732, the son of Adam Templetoune (c.1710-1795) and Margaret Lindsay (1719-1784). This John Templetoune had at least one sister and three brothers. But, regardless of which of the two John Templetounes married Margaret Hunter, he likely had siblings who sent their DNA forward through generations of their own descendants, together with the Templeton name. And, again, we might not find the John Templeton we are searching for if he is on one of these more remote branches of the Templetoune family tree.

***

Fortunately, there is a more reliable way of ensuring that we find the John Templeton we're looking for. We can use the Scotland's People database. Aside from being a repository for Scotland's genealogical records, this database offers an invaluable search capability. We can use the database to run a search of the birth indexes over a specified period of time. In other words, we can search for births of "John Templeton" between selected years. As mentioned earlier, if Bible John was estimated to be between twenty-five and thirty-five years of age in 1968 and 1969, then he was likely born between 1933 and 1944. But what if the killer looked a little older than he actually was and managed to slip into the over-25s nights before his twenty-fifth birthday? Alternatively, what if he looked a little young for his age? In order to cast a wide net, to be generous with these age limits, it seems sensible to add a couple of years either side of the witnesses' age estimates. This means we need to run a search of the database for the John Templetons born in Scotland between 1931 and 1946 inclusive.

As previously noted, in 1855 it became compulsory to register all births in Scotland. So, the records that we now need are not ad hoc or sketchy as they are for the very early years when churches were responsible for record-keeping. Nevertheless, just in case anything untoward happened to any of the birth records that we're looking for, we can also check the death records on Scotland's People. This can be done by running a similar search. Certificates of death, for this period, usually include a person's age at the time of their death. Therefore, we can run a search of the death records, based on the person's calculated birth year. This means that, if any birth certificates are missing, we can find our "John Templetons" in the death records, assuming of course that they have already died. This process of double-checking is just precautionary.

***

A search of the birth and death indexes on Scotland's People reveals thirty-two John Templetons who were born in Scotland in the years between 1931 and 1946, inclusive. [286] Of course, it is unlikely that all these John Templetons can be traced directly back to the marriage of John Templetoune and Margaret Hunter. Some of them will have descended from other seemingly unrelated Templeton families living in Scotland. But it is important, for the time being at least, that we assume all thirty-two John Templetons may have descended from John Templetoune and Margaret Hunter. We must think of them as potential relatives of the McInnes siblings because they may be connected to the Templetoune family along a line of descent that we have been unable to trace. As explained earlier, this would be true for the descendants of Adam Templeton (1760-unknown), for the children of Templeton women who were given their mother's surname, for the descendants of John Templetoune's siblings and for any Templeton child whose birth entry is simply not included among the records created before 1855.

The thirty-two John Templetons identified by searching Scotland's People all share the name that Jeannie heard the killer give on the night her sister was murdered. All of them may share patterns in their DNA with Janet and Hector McInnes. And crucially, all these John Templetons are also within the age range suggested by witnesses who saw the killer with either Jemima MacDonald or Helen Puttock.

It is these thirty-two individuals who make up our cohort.

Chapter 8.
The Process of Elimination Begins

While it may feel unsettling to investigate people who have been, or who perhaps still are, living in our own time it is important that we learn more about each of these John Templetons so we can compare them with what we already know about Bible John. This gives us the opportunity to rule out any possibility that they are the killer. And, although any effort to find personal information might appear clandestine, it is not plausible to approach relatives or friends to ask them about the John Templetons in our cohort. If by chance we are on the right track, then we must not jeopardize the official investigation by providing information to those who might know the killer. If the John Templeton we're searching for is still alive, and he may well be, any hint that he is being investigated might result in the destruction of the evidence he took, and possibly retained, from the three crime scenes.

Given that we cannot approach relatives or friends, we must confine ourselves to historical records and more current online sources such as community and family Facebook sites, assuming they are public rather than private sites. And there will undoubtedly be some cohort members whose family and social networks cannot be identified with certainty. It is then very difficult to learn anything significant about their lives. Hopefully, the John Templeton we're looking for won't be one of these cohort members.

***

So, we begin our search by returning to the indexes of Scotland's birth, marriage, divorce and death records. These indexes include fundamental details such as name, age and the location of the birth, marriage, divorce or death. They are immediately open to the public because access to this kind of personal information is not considered to infringe on people's privacy. We can also investigate some of the records that have already been opened; records which are beyond the prescribed period of time where restricted access is considered desirable.

Scotland's death indexes indicate that two of our thirty-two cohort members did not survive to adulthood. Indeed, for these two individuals, the full death records have already become available on Scotland's People. John Watters Templeton (1935-1935) died from "gastro enteritis" on 14th June 1935 at the age of only four months. John McCormack Templeton (1936-1936) passed away from pneumonia on the 11th October 1936 when he was only three months old. These two premature deaths eliminate John Watters Templeton and John McCormack Templeton from our cohort, reducing the number of those remaining to thirty. (30)

The indexes to Scotland's immigration records reveal that another member of the cohort, John Templeton (1934-), migrated to Canada in 1957 and there is no evidence that he ever returned to Scotland. What is more, the immigration records for this year are now open and they indicate that John Templeton (1934-) was a motor mechanic by trade. When Jeannie was interviewed by Paul Harrison in 2003, she described Bible John's hands in detail. She said that his "fingernails were well cared for, almost as if they had been manicured, and his hands weren't grubby or cut, they looked clean and well presented."[287] As a motor mechanic, John Templeton (1934) would unlikely have had the pristine hands that Jeannie remembered. (29)

After Helen Puttock's murder, much was made of the killer's accent. Joe Beattie believed that Bible John's accent originated "west of a line from Stirling to Lanark".[288] This presumption was based on the fact that Jeannie had not detected any marked difference in the killer's accent and she was attuned to Glaswegian or Western Scottish accents. But this clue is not as useful as it might seem. Of the twenty-nine John Templetons remaining in our cohort, all but five were born in Western Scotland. Even more problematic is the fact that, although someone's birthplace might be suggestive of their accent, there is always the possibility that they moved to another region while they were young. In other words, someone born east of Joe Beattie's imaginary line might well have moved west of it. And this certainly did happen. For instance, John Cunningham Templeton (1944-) was born in Aberdeen but his parents divorced while he was still an infant. Although his father remained in Aberdeen, his mother returned to Western Scotland, passing away in Kilmarnock in 1957. So, if John Cunningham Templeton grew up with his mother, he may well have crossed Joe Beattie's imaginary line while he was still a very young child.

At the end of the day, it is too risky to eliminate any of our John Templetons based on their presumed accent.

***

Our search must now move beyond the written record. One of the strongest clues we have, regarding the identity of Bible John, is his physical appearance. As discussed earlier, this was verified by numerous witnesses – some who saw the killer with Jemima MacDonald, some who saw him with Helen Puttock and still others who saw him on the number 6 night-service bus. After Jemima MacDonald's murder, the press reported that the killer was 6' to 6' 2" tall, slim in build, with a "thin pale face" and, alternately, with "fair, reddish hair" or "reddish, fair hair".[289] When George Lennox Paterson interviewed two of the witnesses in this case, he was told that the killer was very good-looking in the conventional sense. Then, on the night of Helen Puttock's murder, there were witnesses who were able to corroborate or qualify this description and add a good deal more detail. While they confirmed that Bible John had light-auburn or sandy-coloured hair and a long, thin face, they estimated his height at 5'10" to 6', rather than 6' to 6' 2".[290] And, to this description, witnesses (and especially Jeannie) added that the killer had blue-grey eyes, light eyebrows and a milk-and-roses complexion. He also had "nice straight teeth, with one tooth on the right, upper, overlapping another tooth" and one tooth missing at the position of a number four or five tooth on the upper right-hand side.[291]

Given the strength of these descriptions, it seems plausible to use them to narrow our cohort of John Templetons. In order to do this, we must use written descriptions or photographs, old or current, of the cohort members themselves. Anything that has been published in magazines or posted online is already in the public domain. Nevertheless, in order to minimize any intrusion on people's privacy, none of the photographs I have found will be reproduced here.

John James Templeton (1934-2023), was a farmer who competed in sheepdog trials, representing Scotland nearly forty times at an international level.[292] Even a cursory glance at a black and white photograph of him, taken in Hyde Park in 1964 and reproduced in *Farm Ireland*, indicates that he could not possibly have been Bible John. The images of the killer show thick locks of hair swept across his forehead. The photograph of John James Templeton reveals that he had a receding hairline some five years before Helen Puttock's murder. Moreover, John James Templeton had a deep dimple in his chin. Given Jeannie's keen eye for even the smallest of descriptive details, it is not plausible that she failed to notice either a receding hairline or a dimple in the killer's chin. (28)

John Ferguson Templeton (1937-) has played lawn bowls for Garrowhill Bowling Club and two, colour photographs of him were uploaded to the bowling club's website in 2015. These photographs indicate that John Ferguson Templeton's nose is considerably broader than that in the Bible John images. What is more, Bible John's ears apparently lay almost flat against his head while John Ferguson Templeton's ears do not. And Jeannie had described Bible John's eye colour as blue-grey but John Ferguson Templeton's eyes are a deep, definite blue. (27)

John F. Templeton (1941-2015) played cricket for many years for Stirling County Cricket Club and, in his later years, he became a well-liked and well-respected umpire of the game. When John F. Templeton passed away in 2015, his family donated a trophy, named in his honour. Stirling County played the inaugural match for the John Templeton Trophy against Stenhousemuir Cricket Club. At the time, Stenhousemuir posted a 2001 photograph on their club website which shows John F. Templeton alongside twenty-six other men and he appears to be one of the shortest; unlikely as tall as 5' 10". Indeed, in the Stenhousemuir article, he is referred to as "the great wee man". What is more, a colour photograph of John F. Templeton was recently uploaded to Ancestry.com which reveals that, as an elderly man, he retained traces of very dark hair. (26)

A colour photograph of John Shepherd Templeton (1943-1991) was also uploaded to Ancestry.com by a member constructing his own family tree. This photograph shows John Shepherd Templeton as a relatively young man with unmistakeably dark brown hair and brown eyes. Indeed, his colouring was so completely at odds with the light-auburn or sandy-coloured hair and blue-grey eyes described by witnesses in relation to Bible John, that John Shepherd Templeton can also be eliminated from our cohort of potential suspects. (25)

Two black and white photographs of John Templeton (1938-2017) were posted on Facebook by a granddaughter. One of these photographs had been taken before John Templeton was married and the other on his wedding day in 1961 – several years before the Bible John murders. In both photographs, John Templeton's hair, although it was very thick, was already receding from his temples (in a pronounced "M" shape). In other words, these photographs show a marked difference with the hairline so often attributed to Bible John. (24)

John Sim Templeton (1941-) has his own Facebook account and two of his profile pictures reveal that, despite his age, he still has salt and pepper hair. You can see that it was very dark in his youth. What is more, John Sim Templeton has a significant overbite and a distinct gap between his two front teeth. He also has additional spacing between his front teeth and the adjoining lateral incisors so there is little chance that he ever had one front tooth overlapping another. And it is important to remember here that the description of Bible John's slightly overlapping front teeth does not derive solely from Jeannie. The overlap was corroborated by the bite mark found on Helen Puttock's wrist. (23)

In 2021, one of the contributors to the public Facebook group "Pictures of Old Kilmarnock", posted a 1957-1958 sepia photograph of the 1st Kilmarnock Boys Brigade. When this photograph was taken, John Barrie Templeton (1941-) was a sergeant in the Brigade. He would have been about sixteen years of age and he clearly had very dark hair.[293] (22)

Two colour photographs of John Donnachie Templeton (1938-) have been posted on his granddaughter's Facebook page. They show a man who has very fine features and thick hair swept across his forehead to the right. However, these photographs, like John Donnachie Templeton's own Facebook profile picture, indicate that his hair is still dark brown. (21)

John Andrew Templeton (1939-1999) appears in a black and white photograph which his daughter posted on Facebook. This photograph, taken on his wedding day in 1958 shows John Andrew Templeton's hairline receding some eleven years before Helen Puttock's murder. It also indicates that he had what Jeannie referred to as "jug ears". (20)

John Brian Templeton (1941-1975) was born in Galashiels and died there at the age of thirty-three. Two black and white school photographs, dated 1949/1950 and 1953/1954, place him in Galashiels during his childhood. This means that he would have had a Borders accent. What is more, these photographs show that, as a child, he had dark hair.[294] John Brian Templeton's cousin changed her Facebook profile picture in 2019 to a colour photograph which she titles "Me and my cousin Brian in 1972". This photograph shows a young man with dark hair, dark eyebrows and a strong five o'clock shadow. (19)

A black and white photograph of John Alexander Templeton (1942-2015), taken in the year he passed away, was posted on Facebook as his daughter's profile picture. This photograph indicates that he had a markedly different facial structure to the images of Bible John. He had a small, round face rather than a long, thin face. One of his daughter's friends responds to the photograph, by writing "Awww, your wee Dad" and, in response to online comments about the photograph, John Alexander Templeton's daughter also refers to him fondly as "my wee dad". (18)

John James Templeton (1945-2017) clearly had dark hair in his youth. His wife posted a colour photograph of him in his later years on her Facebook page and his hair still showed strong dark traces, as did his eyebrows. (17)

John Cunningham Templeton (1944-) also appears in a recent colour photograph posted on his wife's Facebook page. Unfortunately, his glasses conceal his eye colour, but his nose was broader than that depicted in the images of Bible John and his hair continues to show dark traces. (16)

While the elimination of these John Templetons, based solely on their appearance, might appear too dismissive we must accept that the men's approximate height, hair colour, eye colour, the shape of their nose and the positioning of their ears and teeth are essential in any discussion of Bible John's identity. If we accept the most fundamental descriptors, and it is clear that we must, then none of the John Templetons whose photographs I have mentioned here could reasonably be considered a suspect. As a consequence, another thirteen John

Templetons can be eliminated from our cohort. This means that the number who remain now stands at sixteen.

**

The only other clue that we have with regards to Bible John's appearance is Jeannie's description of his hands.[295] As mentioned earlier, when Paul Harrison interviewed Jeannie in 2003, she described the killer's hands as particularly well-cared for, almost pristine.[296] And she compared Bible John with her own dance partner, who she said had "coarse, strong hands that were obviously used to manual labour".[297]

Unfortunately, it is difficult to ascertain the occupations of many of the John Templetons who remain in our cohort. While marriage and death certificates almost always record a person's occupation, the documents relating to our John Templetons are too recent to be open to the public. Old telephone directories sometimes yield information about people's occupations. They might, for instance, mention that someone is a builder, a general practitioner or a farmer. But, while some of the John Templetons who remain in our cohort have appeared in the British telephone books as farmers, none have appeared in connection with any other occupation.

At least five of the sixteen remaining members of the cohort may have grown up on family farms: John Dunn Templeton (1933-1992), John Templeton (1935-2019), John Drennan Templeton (1945-), John Muir Templeton (1937-2011) and John Templeton (1945-) from Glencairn. At first sight, this information seems promising. Young men who grow up on family farms have likely done a good deal of farm labour and their hands would show the effects, in which case we could perhaps eliminate them from our cohort. But we cannot be certain that these particular young men did any farm work at all. Their parents may have been able to afford to hire people to do most of the farm labour. The Valuation Roll for 1940-41 indicates that John Dunn Templeton's family employed at least one labourer at Carnochan Farm while he was growing up.[298] And the Valuation Roll for the same year for Dumfries indicates that John Muir Templeton's family hired a ploughman and an "oddman" on Muirhousehead Farm while he was young.[299] So we cannot assume that the John Templetons who grew up on family farms undertook any farm labour. Indeed, they might have kept their hands in very good condition.

Those John Templetons who became farmers themselves, however, would almost certainly have had strong hands, used to manual labour. One of these was John Dunn Templeton (1933-1992), who continued to work the family farm into adulthood. Indeed, when his older brother William passed away in 1967, John and his father were managing both Carnochan and Dallowie farms for some time.[300] After his father's death in 1972, John Dunn Templeton continued to work Carnochan Farm.[301] And John Drennan Templeton (1945-), born to the Templetons of Carnell Home farm went on to work the neighbouring Pocknave farm. As late as 2017, the *Ayrshire Journal*, shows Johnnie, his wife Margaret and son Robin with their Carnell herd.[302] And John Templeton (1945-) moved with his family from Dumfries-shire to Peebles-shire, where he still lives (and possibly works) on Colquhar Farm. The labour which these three John Templetons must have undertaken over many years would undoubtedly have shown on their hands by their mid-twenties to mid-thirties. (13)

Another cohort member whose occupation I was able to ascertain was John Stewart Templeton (1934-2021). John Stewart Templeton recently passed away in Perthshire at the age of eighty-seven and an obituary was placed in the *Herald Scotland*. It reads: "TEMPLETON – Dr John Stewart Passed away peacefully, in the tender care of Rivendell Care Home, Dunkeld, on Friday 30th April 2021..."[303] Clearly, John Stewart Templeton was a medical doctor but this does not mean we can eliminate him from the cohort. He would almost certainly have had pristine hands. What is more, medicine is one of the professions that D.C.S. Tom Goodall suggested would engender the degree of trust that Helen Puttock felt for her killer. Remember, Goodall told Joe Beattie that he believed the killer was someone who was "beyond the average person's suspicion", and likely belonged to one of a few respected professions which included, "the physicians, doctors, the medical profession".[304]

***

With thirteen John Templetons remaining in our cohort, it is now time that we move on from the killer's appearance. Afterall, Bible John left other clues behind. Of these, some of the most important and least often discussed are those which imply that Bible John grew up as a foster child in Glasgow, most likely in or near Scotstoun.

Chapter 9.
The Homies

Jeannie was able to recall much of Bible John's conversation in the taxi on the night her sister was murdered. She distinctly remembered the killer speaking about foster homes or foster children in what she assumed was an attempt to change the subject after he inadvertently mentioned his sister. But raising the subject of foster homes or foster children seems an odd way to redirect a conversation. What is more, when the taxi passed through Scotstoun, Bible John recognised a block of flats on Kingsway. Jeannie remembered him quietly muttering something about his father or another relative having worked there and then saying that the site was once occupied by a children's home. This repeated reference to fostering was not lost on detectives. According to David Wilson and Paul Harrison, this second mention was "accorded great significance." Indeed, detectives concluded that the killer had likely been a foster child himself.[305]

In *Bible John: Search for a Sadist*, Charles Stoddart argues that, with regards to the murder of Helen Puttock, "two particular incidents were quite crucial." The first was Bible John's recognition of the site of the former children's home. The second, was his paraphrasing of the story of Moses. Indeed, Stoddart says, it was "this passing biblical reference which was the basis of the nickname subsequently attached to the stranger".[306]

But the significance of the killer's biblical reference goes well beyond this. Police believed, from what Jeannie could remember, that the passage which Bible

John paraphrased was Exodus 2:3 – 2:4 – a passage in which a mother abandons her infant son (albeit in an attempt to save his life).[307]

> *And when she could no longer hide him, she took for him an ark of bulrushes, and daubed it with slime and with pitch, and put the child therein; and she laid it in the flags by the river's brink. And his sister stood afar off, to wit what would be done to him.*

While Bible John appears to have referred to Verses 3 and 4 which see Moses abandoned by his family, those which follow, Verses 5 through to 8, show him being taken in, or fostered, by another. In these later verses, Moses is found by the Pharoah's daughter who spares his life, allowing his sister to find a "nurse of the Hebrew women", to care for the child *for her*. If detectives paid heed to this fostering reference in the chapter which Bible John chose, above all others, to paraphrase, it could only have strengthened their belief that he was once a foster child himself.

What is more, if investigators were right and Bible John had been a foster child, then his immediate recognition of the Kingsway flats as the site of the old Scotstoun House Children's Home indicates that he was likely connected to that particular children's home. Afterall, he recognised the site without hesitation, despite the fact that Scotstoun House was demolished in 1962, some seven years before he passed by in the taxi with Helen and Jeannie.[308]

***

The Scotstoun House Children's Home, known locally as "the homies", opened in 1919 and did not

132

change function until the closing years of the 1950s when, according to a former employee, it offered only short-term institutional care for children under five years of age.[309] This means that Scotstoun House operated as a children's home for the early years of all the John Templetons in our cohort, born as they were between 1931 and 1946.

Of course, an examination of the records of this or any other children's home would not have helped detectives working on the Bible John murders at the time. Even though they suspected that the killer grew up as a foster child and even though they recognised his likely connection to the Scotstoun House Children's Home, there was no way for them to identify him from the personal records of the many children who passed through the homies in the 1930s and 1940s – not without a name.

However, the situation is quite different for us. We have a name. Our difficulty lies instead in the fact that the personal records for individuals who were admitted to the children's home are closed to the public for one hundred years so we cannot simply search the Scotstoun House Children's Home registers for a child named John Templeton. We need to use a different approach. To begin with, we can establish which, if any, of the thirteen remaining members of our cohort grew up with their birth families.

The most obvious historical sources for tracing family or household composition are the census returns. The Scottish government has gathered census information every ten years since 1841 but, like the children's home records, these are closed to the public for one hundred years. Given that the latest available census was compiled in 1921, there is no way we can use it to explore family composition in the 1930s and 1940s. Another obvious source for tracing family relationships is wills. But unfortunately, these are only open online up until 1925. None of our John Templetons had even been born then.

Luckily, there are alternative sources which might show lasting, continuous family relationships for some of our remaining thirteen John Templetons. In many instances, it is possible to use the place names recorded in birth, marriage and death records as evidence suggestive of enduring birth-family relationships. There are also cemetery headstones and obituaries which testify to the longevity of these bonds. And regional Facebook chats often include reminiscences which provide evidence about an individual's long-term friendships, family relationships and community ties.

***

We originally traced John Muir Templeton (1933-1998) by moving through years of descendants from his ancestors, John Templetoune (1730-1800) and Margaret Hunter (1732-1797) and their third son James Templeton (1767-c1841). John Muir Templeton was born in Ardrossan and he married there in 1964, settling in the neighbouring town of Saltcoats. When his father died in 1965, John Muir Templeton was still very much in contact with his birth-parents. Indeed, he signed his father's death certificate as a witness so it seems unlikely that he spent his young years in the Scotstoun House Children's Home or that he was ever fostered out to another family. (12)

John Templeton (1935-2019) was born into the Templetons of Willoxton (or Willockstone) Farm. His parents settled in Mauchline after marrying in 1933 and John Templeton continued to live in Mauchline until he passed away in 2019. After his death, he was buried with his father and mother in the same grave in Mauchline Cemetery. Their headstone reads:

In loving memory of John Templeton – Willoxton – Died 28th May 1961 Aged 64 Years Beloved Husband of Janet C. Pollock Also the Above Janet Craig Pollock Died 20th September 2002 Aged 92 Years Also Their Son John Died 10th June 2019 Aged 84 Years[310]

John Templeton's obituary also testifies to his close birth-family relationships. It reads, "dear brother of Ellen and the late Jimmy and a dear uncle and great-uncle".[311] Given the evidence of these enduring family ties, it seems unlikely that John Templeton (1935-2019) grew up in a children's home or as a foster child. (11)

John Muir Templeton (1937-2011), as distinct from our earlier John Muir Templeton (1933-1998), was born in Dumfriesshire to the Templetons of Muirhousehead Farm in the Applegarth Estate. According to the British phone books, his family were still living on the farm in the 1960s. While none of this proves that John Muir Templeton grew up with his family at Muirhousehead, we know that he married Catherine Hannestad in 1965 in Dumfriesshire. Moreover, John and Catherine had three children who were all born in Dumfries and John Muir Templeton died, in Dumfries, in 2011. This evidence of geographical continuity is supported by the fact that John Muir Templeton's children keep in contact on Facebook with members of their extended Templeton family network.[312] This retention of extended family relationships suggest that John Muir Templeton almost certainly spent his childhood on Muirhousehead Farm with his birth family. (10)

John Shearer Templeton (1942-2022) was born the eldest of three sons. He was named after his father, John

Shearer Templeton (1921-2014) and his father before him, John Shearer Templeton (1891-1933). This succession of the family name, from grandfather to father to son, suggests that John Shearer Templeton was very much part of his birth family. And this is supported by the inscription on his parents' headstone in Strathaven Cemetery. At the bottom of this headstone are the words: *"Loving mother father of John, James and Ronald"*.[313]

John Shearer Templeton passed away recently in Hamilton, where his brother Ronald had died two years before him, and his obituary in the *Hamilton Advertiser* mentions his loving relationship with his surviving brother, James. Clearly, John Shearer Templeton's birth family ties endured throughout his lifetime. (9)

Like John Shearer Templeton (1942-2022), John McCloy Templeton (1946-) was named after his father and grandfather, John McCloy Templeton (c1891-1963) and John McCloy Templeton (1922-2014). And again, this succession of the family name suggests there was a strong birth family connection. John Templeton (1946-) was born in Kilmarnock, as was his brother David Stevenson Templeton (1950-2017). Indeed, Kilmarnock was home to the extended Templeton family. John McCloy Templeton (1946-) appears in the British phone books in 1972, at the age of twenty-six, still living in Kilmarnock. It seems very unlikely that he had been fostered to a home in the area while his parents and extended family continued to live there. (8)

John Kerrigan Templeton (1943-2006) features in some of the online reminiscences on the Facebook chat "Being West Kilbride". He was given the childhood nickname "Spaniard" and, according to the reminiscences of the group's members, he and his brother James (nicknamed "Coodles"), were so much part of their community that they are referred to nowadays as "West Kilbride characters".[314] (7)

John Templeton (1943-) was born in Stevenston, where he still lives.[315] His daughter, Shirley, contributes to the Facebook group, "Stevenston Ayrshire, Now and Then". Her reminiscences often involve her father and members of his immediate family. For instance, Shirley mentions that her father's parents owned an ice cream van and she recalls with sadness that her grandfather Sam "was a foreman in the acids" and "finished up with no lungs".[316] Shirley describes how her father worked day and night, renovating his sister's shop and other locals remember his role in this renovation.[317] All of these recollections are testimony to the close generational bonds in the Templeton family. When his mother died, John Templeton (1943-) was mentioned in her obituary, which was published in the *Irvine Times* in 2012. It reads: "At home on the 18th February 2012, Eliza (Lila) Anderson, aged 90 years. Beloved wife of the late Samuel Templeton and dear mother of John, Matt, Anne, Margaret and of the late William". (6)

As noted earlier, John Stewart Templeton (1934-2021) was a medical doctor. He would undoubtedly have required significant funding for the duration of his medical degree. While it is possible that he had been fostered by a wealthy family, it seems more likely that the funding for his education came from his birth family. John Stewart Templeton's father was a successful confectioner. The Valuation Rolls of 1940 indicate that the family lived in Eastwood and paid rates on both a "House and Garden" and a "Garage" with a combined gross annual value of £59 which far exceeded the working-class annual accommodation values of £12-£20.[318] It is also worth acknowledging that, as the son of a relatively affluent family and as a doctor who had been practising for many years prior to 1969, John Stewart Templeton would unlikely have worn cheap "Woolworth-type" cufflinks like the one found near Helen Puttock's body. (5)

The elimination of these John Templetons, who clearly had ongoing ties with their birth-families, leaves only five remaining in our cohort.

Chapter 10.
Closing In

I suggested earlier that we would very likely encounter roadblocks during our search for Bible John. This was never truer than for some of the remaining John Templetons in our cohort. For two of these John Templetons there is little information either about their parentage or their lives in general. This makes it difficult to draw any meaningful conclusions about whether they spent their young years living with their birth-families.

For example, I have been unable to identify the parents of John Paterson Templeton (1944-) with any certainty. His birth certificate is of course still closed to the public. There was a John Paterson Templeton (1905-1974) who, in 1943, married Grace Smith (1911-2005), a laundry-worker based in Cambuslang. On their wedding certificate, John Paterson Templeton indicated that he lived, and presumably worked, on Whitlawburn Farm in Cambuslang. But Cambuslang is a considerable distance from Douglas, where John Paterson Templeton (1944-) was born. What is more, there were other Templeton children in Douglas around the same time so it is possible that he was born to a family in Douglas rather than to the Cambuslang Templetons.

John Templeton (1937-1993) was born in Kilmarnock to John Templeton (1906-1977) and Margaret Wright Dickie McIvor (c.1911-2000). The couple also had a daughter named Elizabeth Hyslop Templeton (1939-2017) and twins, James and Thomas, who were born prematurely and survived for only a few days. But, unfortunately, I can find no evidence that John Templeton (1937-1993) ever married, although he may well have done. Given that he has no middle name, it is difficult to trace his relationships and movements. What is more, when his sister Elizabeth Hyslop Dearie (nee Templeton) passed away in 2017, there was no mention of her siblings in her obituary, only her husband, children and grandchildren. All I can find, is that John Templeton (1937-1993) died in Kilmarnock at the age of fifty-six. Although this indicates at least some level of geographical continuity with his birth-family, it is not really enough to establish that he grew up with them – albeit it seems likely that he did.

***

For the other three John Templetons the problem lies, not with a shortfall of information, but rather with the fact that the information I have been able to gather indicates that they may indeed have been foster children – at some point in their lives.

One of these three cohort members, John Templeton (1945-), was born in Aberdeen Northern District on the 11th November 1945. His mother, Margaret Jane Templeton (1921-2017), was single at the time and she gave her son her own surname. On his birth certificate, Margaret Templeton entered her "usual residence" as 46 High Street in Grantown-on-Spey. While her mother, Janet McPherson Younie (1895-1932), had passed away years before, Margaret's father, Walter Templeton (1891-1948), lived with her at the High Street property.[319]

In Scotland in the 1940s few single mothers could afford to stay at home to care for their infant. The luckiest would have had family members who were both willing and able to assist them financially or to mind the child when the mother returned to work. Other single mothers might have used their wages to pay for a nanny or for temporary foster-care. But there was no government assistance available to single mothers. Any relief they might receive through the Poor Laws, or Public Assistance, was locally determined and could result in them being separated from their child and sent to the workhouse. It wasn't until the passage of the 1948 National Assistance Act that single mothers received any government assistance.[320]

While Walter Templeton was still alive, he worked as a butcher and may have been able to provide for his daughter and grandson on his earnings. But when Walter passed away in May 1948, John Templeton was only two years old. Margaret indicated on her son's birth certificate that she had been working as a housekeeper. It is possible that she continued in that role and may even have been allowed to keep her son with her. Margaret had an older half-sister but it is unlikely that she was able to help with any child minding. The word illegitimate had been written on her birth certificate in 1916 and she was sent to Kinloss to be raised by another family. Nevertheless, Margaret also had a younger sister named Roseanna (1925-). Roseanna would have been about twenty when John was born and she may have been able to help look after him in his early years. Otherwise, Margaret might have been left with no option other than to pay for John to stay with a nanny or in foster care, at least until government assistance became available.

Although there is no evidence which connects John Templeton (1945-) to Glasgow, let alone to the

Scotstoun House Children's Home, it is important that we find out more about him if we can. The possibility that he was once a foster child is simply too significant to ignore.

***

One avenue of investigation open to us is to construct the family's Generation Ancestor Chart. Evidence of a direct link back to the marriage of John Templetoune (1730-1800) and Margaret Hunter (1732-1797), would at least indicate shared patterns in DNA between John Templeton (1945-) and the samples provided by the McInnes siblings.

The first few generations of this Ancestor Chart are well documented. We can say with certainty that John Templeton was the son of Margaret Jane Templeton (1921-2017) and that, in turn, she was the daughter of Walter Templeton (1891-1948) and Janet McPherson Younie (1895-1932). Margaret even shares her parents' headstone in Grantown Cemetery. But there are also reliable records which predate this. According to the couple's marriage certificate, Walter Templeton's parents were Alexander MacIntosh Templeton (1847-1924) and Jessie Duguid (1854-1919). And Alexander McIntosh Templeton is easy to identify on Scotland's People as the son of James Templeton (1817/1820-1892) and Ann Margaret Falconer (1820-1896).

However, from this point on, there are some considerable anomalies in the historical record. For instance, James's death certificate states that he was seventy-two years old when he passed away in 1892, indicating that he was born c.1820. The 1851 census also records that he was born in 1820. And yet more than a hundred family trees on Ancestry give James's birth year as 1817. What is more, James's death certificate states that his father was a farmer named Thomas Templeton and that his mother's name was Agnes Adamson. But in the indexes of Scotland's People, there is no record of any Thomas Templeton marrying an Agnes Adamson, only one who married a Margaret Adamson in 1808 and, according to Margaret's death certificate, he was a shepherd.

While I have my reservations, most Ancestry members accept that the James who married Ann Falconer was born in 1817 to Thomas Templeton (1789-1852) and Margaret Adamson (1789-1873). Perhaps Margaret used Agnes as her preferred name and Thomas was a sheep farmer, an occupation which, in the old records, was often referred to as shepherding. Even so, we are still left with the difference in James's birth year.

Most Ancestry members also claim that Thomas Templeton (1789-1852) was the son of Thomas Templeton (1748/1751-unknown) and Ann Hamilton (1752-1811). Again, I can find no records to confirm this parental link. Nevertheless, I have shown these seven generations of John Templeton's possible family in the following 7 Generation Ancestor Chart.

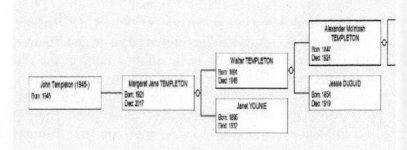

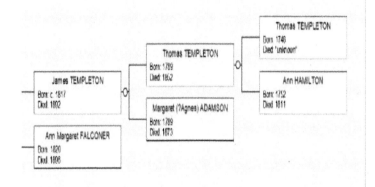

Thomas TEMPLETON
Born: 1789
Died: 1852

James TEMPLETON
Born: c. 1817
Died: 1892

Margaret (?Agnes) ADAMSON
Born: 1789
Died: 1873

Ann Margaret FALCONER
Born: 1820
Died: 1898

Thomas TEMPLETON
Born: 1748
Died: "unknown"

Ann HAMILTON
Born: 1752
Died: 1811

This 7 Generation Ancestor Chart, reaching back as far as Thomas Templeton's birthyear of 1748/1751, shows no direct link between John Templeton (1945-) and the marriage of John Templetoune (1730-1800) and Margaret Hunter (1732-1797). However, given the anomalies and lack of evidence regarding parentage, it is possible that a link does exist. It might be that the Thomas who fathered James was the son of someone other than Thomas (1748/1751-unknown). For all we know, this may have been Adam (1760-unknown), John (1761-c1833) or James (1767-c1841) but, of course, we have no evidence of this either.

What is more, we acknowledged earlier that we knew little about the parents of John Templetoune (1730-1800). It is very likely that he had a number of siblings who we cannot identify – possibly even a much younger brother named Thomas. Interestingly, most Ancestry genealogists who include John Templetoune (1730-1800) and Margaret Hunter (1732-1797) in their family tree, claim that John Templetoune fathered a son named Thomas Templeton (1756-1820) some three years before he and Margaret were married. And, although there is no record of this relationship in the birth, marriage or death indexes of Scotland's People, Thomas Templeton, son of John Templetoune (1730-1800), may have existed. As noted previously, the early church records are far from complete.

But, even if John Templetoune did father a son named Thomas before he married Margaret Hunter, there is no hint of any ancestral relationship between John Templeton (1945-) and John Templetoune (1730-1800). The birthyears and the birthplaces for the two Thomas Templetons simply don't match up. According to Ancestry members, the father of Thomas Templeton (1789-1852) was either born in Muirkirk in 1748 or

146

Carmichael in 1851. The Thomas Templeton whom many Ancestry genealogists claim is the son of John Templetoune (1730-1800), was born in Wigtownshire in 1756. In other words, even with what is potentially a whole new line of Templetoune ancestors, there is no clear link between John Templeton (1945-) and John Templetoune (1730-1800). This means that the construction of this 7 Generation Ancestor Chart, while not actually disproving anything, lends no support at all to the theory that John Templeton (1945-) is Bible John.

***

Of course, none of this is sufficient to eliminate John Templeton (1945-) from our cohort. Afterall, we know that there are a number of branches of the Templetoune family tree which cannot be traced. So there seems to be only one course of action left open to us and it is a contentious one. I mentioned earlier that I believed it was not plausible to approach relatives or friends to ask them about the John Templetons in our cohort. However, while I was researching the Generation Ancestor Chart of John Templeton (1945-), I noticed three public member trees on Ancestry which include Margaret Jane Templeton (1921-2017). Each of these family trees is managed by a different Ancestry member. I decided to press on, albeit very cautiously, by making a general inquiry about the family without providing any explanation. People often seek information about distant family members from those managing family trees. Ancestry is set up to enable such communication.

In a bid to learn more about John Templeton (1945-) I sent a brief message to each of the three Ancestry members seeking any information they could provide about Margaret Jane Templeton and her son, John. I did not offer any information myself, nor did I indicate that I was researching the Bible John murders. Thankfully, two of the Ancestry members responded to my inquiry and were happy to help me without requesting any explanation or information in return.

One of these Ancestry members knew nothing about either Margaret or John that would further our investigation. The other told me that she knew Margaret Templeton "fairly well". In fact, her mother was Margaret's first cousin and the two women had been quite close when her mother lived in Scotland and, since then, they had seen each other on occasion. This Ancestry member recalled that Margaret was in the British Armed Forces but gave no indication of when or where Margaret served.[321]

She then mentioned that Margaret had married a man known as "Webbie" in England. I checked the Marriage Index for England and Wales and found that Margaret married John P. Webb (1918-c.1980) in 1967 in Northumberland.[322] By that time, John Templeton (1945-) was twenty-one years old. This Ancestry member said that John Templeton (1945-) also married in England and she believed he was still living there with his wife, Cath, and a daughter named Deborah.[323]

The information about John's life in England was particularly valuable. I returned to my Facebook app, knowing that I was searching for a John Templeton who lived in England, rather than Scotland, and who might be connected through his Facebook friendships to a Cath or Deborah. Armed with this information, I found that John Templeton (1945-) had recently opened his own Facebook page, on which he states that he was born in Grantown-on-Spey. His daughter "Debbie" is among his Facebook friends. In 2012 she posted a colour photograph of her father and, although this revealed that he has blue-grey eyes and features not dissimilar to those in the images of Bible John, it shows that John Templeton (1945-) must have had dark hair in his youth. In 2012 there were still traces of this colouring in both his hair and his eyebrows. Clearly, John Templeton (1945-) could not be Bible John. (4)

Chapter 11.
A Likely Foster Child

Another of the three John Templetons who may, at some stage, have been a foster child is John McAdam Templeton (1939-). This John Templeton was born in Muirkirk on the 27th March 1939, the son of a twenty-one-year-old single woman named Margaret Barr Martin Ness Smith Templeton (1918-2002).[324] At the time of his birth, John McAdam Templeton (1939-) was given his mother's surname which carried over from her late father, a coal miner named Alexander Templeton (1893-1919). Alexander Templeton had been born in a mining cottage in Laurieland Row, Crosshouse, and according to his death certificate, he died from tuberculosis at the age of twenty-six, the year after his only child, Margaret, was born.[325] Margaret Templeton's mother, re-married in 1920 and, when Margaret gave birth to her son John, in 1939, she gave him the middle name "McAdam", after her step-father, John McAdam (1897-1966).

In 1940, the year after John McAdam Templeton was born, Margaret Templeton married a coal miner named Andrew Frew (1922-1953).[326] According to her marriage certificate, she was working at the time in Douglas as a "farm servant". Margaret Templeton and Andrew Frew set up home near Muirkirk, in the small village of Glenbuck and, within a year, they had a daughter who they named Martha Barr Martin Smith Frew (1941-1989). In 1942, they had a son named William Wyllie Frew (1942-2018) and the following year, they had twin daughters, Joan McAdam Frew and Mary McSephney Robertson Keggans Frew (1943-

1943). The twins were born prematurely and passed away only hours after their birth.[327]

From 1944 through to 1949, the couple had another six children: Mary McKinnon McKenzie Frew (1944-), John McAdam Frew (1945-1988), Margaret B. N. M. Frew (1946-), twins who they called James Frew (1948-) and Elizabeth Murdoch McAdam Frew (1948-2008) and Andrew Frew (1949-).

In May 1953, at the age of thirty-one, Andrew Frew (snr.) was killed in an accident at Kames Colliery.[328] Two years later, Margaret Templeton married a power-station attendant and widower named Daniel McIsaac (1920-1959). In 1956, they had a daughter who they named Catherine McIsaac (1956-), after Daniel's mother. Then, in 1958 they had another daughter named Isobella Clifford McIsaac (1958-).

The following year, Daniel McIsaac died from "Carcinoma of Bronchies".[329]

In 1960, Margaret Templeton married David Wilson, in Muirkirk. There is no evidence that the couple divorced, but the divorce indexes only begin on Scotland's People after 1984. Clearly, though, something happened to end this relationship because, in 1976, Margaret Templeton married her fourth husband, a widower named William Stewart Burns (1916-1998). William Burns was eighty-two years old when he died some twenty-two years later, in 1998.[330]

Margaret Templeton passed away in 2002 at the age of eighty-four. She was buried in a grave she shares with her first two husbands, Andrew Frew and Daniel McIsaac. Her headstone does not mention any of her children by name. It reads:

In loving memory of Andrew Frew Killed at Kames Colliery 7th May 1953 Aged 31 Years Beloved Husband of Margaret Templeton Also Daniel McIsaac Died 25th May 1959 Aged 44 Years Also the Above Margaret Templeton Died 31st January 2002 Aged 84 Years Beloved Wife of the Above Loving Mother, Grandmother and Great Grandmother Always in Our Thoughts and Always in Our Hearts "Till We Meet Again"

While Margaret had far too many children for them to be listed on her headstone, it would have been interesting to see if her first child, John McAdam Templeton, was named among them.

***

There is certainly some indication that John McAdam Templeton did not live with the young Frew family. For instance, in 1945, when John McAdam Templeton was six years old, Margaret Templeton and Andrew Frew named their second son, "John McAdam Frew". While the couple used many names more than once, they did this only for their children's middle names. To give a child the two and only two Christian names which have already been given to a previous child was something only ever done in families when the first child died at an early age. John McAdam Templeton is still very much alive. So, the act of naming "John McAdam Frew" suggests that Margaret Templeton's first-born child was unlikely to have been living in the Frew household.

And there is some corroboration of this. As in many Scottish towns, the people of Muirkirk have a current Facebook group where they often reminisce about past places and people and, thankfully, they have made this

Facebook group accessible to the public. In "Muirkirk, East Ayrshire", people who grew up in the area often discuss events from their childhood and upload old school photographs to share with others. One of John McAdam Templeton's half-siblings, Margaret B is a member of "Muirkirk, East Ayrshire". In fact, she often contributes to the site, fondly mentioning her immediate family members and identifying them in school photographs. Other "Muirkirk, East Ayrshire" members also identify the Frew and McIsaac children in these historic photographs. But, what is particularly interesting, is that all of the Frew and McIsaac children have been discussed, at some point in time, by one or more members of the Facebook group. Indeed, with the exception of Mary Frew (referred to by Margaret as "May"), all of Margaret Templeton's children appear in at least one school photograph – all except John McAdam Templeton.[331] There is not a photograph, nor even a mention of him, on "Muirkirk, East Ayrshire".

In some of her responses to member posts for this Facebook group, Margaret B refers explicitly to the number of children in her family, most often in relation to the timing of her father's death. In 2012, when a member of "Muirkirk, East Ayrshire" mentions Andrew Frew's mining accident, Margaret replies, "there were 8 of us at that time". She is quite specific, saying: "Martha was the oldest at that time and Andrew was the youngest about 2-3 yrs."[332] There was no mention of John McAdam Templeton and he certainly was not afforded his position as the oldest child in the family.

When Andrew Frew died in May 1953, the family were intending to move to a nearby house at 129 Henderson Drive.[333] Despite the tragedy, Margaret and the children settled into their new home and, shortly afterwards, they had a family photograph taken there.[334]

This photograph was found only recently by a member of "Muirkirk, East Ayrshire" and she uploaded it to the group's Facebook page. She appealed to other members: "Anyone know this family from 129 Henderson Drive?" Margaret B responded: "This is my family (Frew) taken just after our father was killed in the Kames pit, when we moved into our new home in the scheme."[335]

The photograph shows Margaret Templeton with eight children, four boys and four girls. John McAdam Templeton was not among them. The Frew family photograph includes only the children that Margaret B referred to when she said that, at the time of her father's death, there were eight children in the family. The implication, again, is that John McAdam Templeton was not living in the Frew household. And yet, at the time of Andrew Frew's death, in May 1953, John McAdam Templeton had only just turned fourteen.

***

When children left council-run homes, around the age of fifteen, they were sometimes given their birth certificate. If John McAdam Templeton spent his early years in a children's home or with a foster family, it is possible that he was given his birth certificate when he left. After 1919, the word "illegitimate" was no longer scrawled on birth certificates under a child's name. Nevertheless, these children were often registered under their mother's maiden surname and usually only their mother's name was recorded on the certificate.[336] This means that, if John McAdam Templeton was given his birth certificate, he would have known at least two things – that he was born before his mother married and that his mother had a very distinctive name.

There is some indication that John McAdam Templeton may have met with his mother, or perhaps even joined the Frew family, soon after Andrew Frew's death. Some of Margaret B's conversations in "Muirkirk, East Ayrshire", are puzzling. As noted earlier, she says in 2012 that there were eight children in the family in 1953. And yet, in a previous conversation in 2009, she says that, when her father was killed in the accident at Kames Colliery, he left her mum "with 9 weans".[337] And, during a conversation in 2014, she includes the two McIsaac children in her count, saying "there was 11 of us and I was in the middle".[338] People don't miscount the number of children in their family, not even in large families. Nor do they mistake their own position in the family. This means, there must have been another child who Margaret B was not counting, for whatever reason, in some of her comments - a child who was not included in the family photograph. It might be that Margaret Templeton was pregnant at the time her husband was killed in Kames Colliery. She might have given birth to a "ninth" Frew child late in 1953 or early in 1954, but I have not been able to find any record of this birth and none of the Frew family members who are on Facebook ever mention another Frew sibling. And yet, at some point in time, another sibling has been added to Margaret B's count.

If Margaret Templeton had given birth to another child between May 1953 and the time of her marriage to Daniel McIsaac in 1955, Margaret B would have been the fifth of eleven surviving children (with four older and six younger siblings). If, on the other hand, an older child had returned to claim a place in Margaret Templeton's family, then Margaret B would have been the sixth surviving child and, as she herself said, the middle child of eleven children. Margaret B's use of the phrase "nine *weans*", suggests that, if John McAdam Templeton had indeed joined the family, then he likely did so while he was still young enough to be considered a "wean". This would mean that he returned to his mother soon after the Frew family photograph was taken c.1953, when he was fourteen or fifteen years old.

There can be no doubt that, by 1960, John McAdam Templeton knew who his mother was and he knew what was going on in her life. Indeed, by then, he certainly considered himself to be part of her family. In 1960, when he was twenty-one years old, John McAdam Templeton married a woman named Agnes Shields Sayers (1939-2015) in the nearby town of Catrine. This was the same year that Margaret Templeton married her third husband, David Wilson. And remarkably, at his own wedding, John McAdam Templeton registered his marriage under two different surnames, Templeton and Wilson. Clearly, he knew that David Wilson was his new step-father.

In 2018, Margaret B posted a photograph on "Muirkirk, East Ayrshire" of her family gathered at her brother James's wedding in 1967. Of course, I cannot ask her to name the family members in this photograph, but there is one couple who do not number among the ten Frew and McIsaac siblings. If this extra couple is John McAdam Templeton, with his wife Agnes Sayers, then it is safe to say that John McAdam Templeton had dark hair when he was young. Only one of the men in the photograph had light-coloured hair and that was William Frew. But we cannot eliminate John McAdam Templeton from our cohort on this evidence alone, because we have no proof that he and Elizabeth were the additional couple in the wedding photograph.

***

It is important, once again, that we construct a Generation Ancestor Chart to see if John McAdam Templeton's genealogy can be traced back to the marriage of John Templetoune (1730-1800) and Margaret Hunter (1732-1797). As mentioned earlier, this would indicate a direct link to the DNA samples provided by the McInnes siblings and therefore to the semen stain on Helen Puttock's stockings.

To begin with, Margaret Barr Martin Ness Smith Templeton (1918-2002) was born in 1918 in Crosshouse, the only child of Alexander Templeton (1893-1919) and Martha Barr Martin Smith (1899-1983). Alexander Templeton (1893-1919) was one of six sons born to a coal miner named James Rutherford Wallace Templeton (1859-1916) and a domestic servant named Margaret Ness (c.1857-aft.1919).[339] He and Margaret Ness were married in Kilmarnock in 1882 but lived in Crosshouse.

James Rutherford Wallace Templeton's parents, or John McAdam Templeton's great-great grandparents, were James Steven Templeton (1831-1897) and Margaret Gilmour (c.1836-aft.1897). James Steven Templeton was also a coalminer.[340] He married Margaret Gilmour in Kilmaurs in 1854 and, like their descendants, the couple lived in Crosshouse.

James Steven Templeton's father was William Templeton (1808-1871), a coalminer born in Dundonald.[341] William married Elizabeth Wallace (1809-c.1881) in Riccarton in 1829 and the couple remained in Riccarton for several years before moving back to Dundonald and then eventually settling in Crosshouse.

William Templeton (1808-1871) was the son of another coal miner, John Templeton (1781-aft.1851) and his wife

Jean Brown (c.1788-aft.1851). While there has been some controversy among Ancestor members about who John Templeton (1781-aft.1851) actually married, the connection to Jean Brown is clearly indicated by the fact that, in 1833, William Templeton and Elizabeth Wallace, named their first-born daughter Jean Brown Templeton. John Templeton (1781-aft.1851) and Jean Brown (c.1788-aft.1851) had married in Dundonald in 1808 and, again like their descendants, they settled in Crosshouse. According to the 1841 and 1851 censuses, they were still living in Crosshouse in their elderly years.[342]

Unfortunately, the connection between John Templeton (1781-aft.1851) and his father, John Templeton (1761-c.1833), is difficult to prove because the birth record for John Templeton (1781-aft.1851) is incomplete. While his father is named as John Templeton, his mother's name was not recorded on his birth certificate. Nevertheless, most family genealogists accept that John Templeton (1781-aft.1851) was the son of John Templeton (1761-c.1833) and Mary Andrew (1763-c.1829) and this seems plausible. Certainly, the link between father and son is made credible by their common connection to the village of Dundonald. John Templeton (1761-c.1833) had been born in Dundonald and, as already mentioned, John Templeton (1781-aft.1851) married Jean Brown there in 1808, before settling down in Crosshouse.

We came across John Templeton (1761-c.1831) earlier when we first mentioned the children of John Templetoune (1730-1800) and Margaret Hunter (1732-1797). John Templeton (1761-c.1831) was one of their three or potentially four sons (if we include the Thomas who was reportedly born to John Templetoune in 1756, three years before he married Margaret). This means that we can trace John McAdam Templeton's lineage all the way to the point of shared ancestry with the McInnes siblings. While Janet and Hector McInnes descended from John Templetoune and Margaret Hunter's daughter, Margaret Templeton (1766-unknown), it appears that John McAdam Templeton descended from their son, John Templeton (1761-c1833).

These familial relationships are expressed in the following 9 Generation Ancestor Chart.

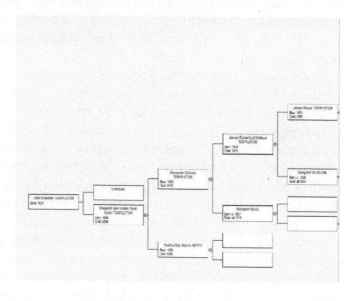

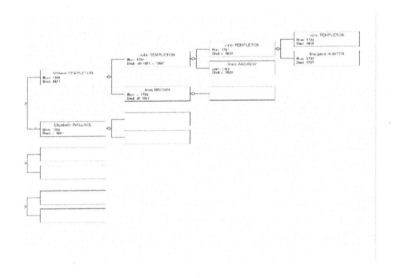

***

It is now important that we take a closer look at John McAdam Templeton's life and examine anything that he may have held in common with Bible John. To start with, we know that John McAdam Templeton was born on 27th March 1939. This means that he was twenty-eight years old when Patricia Docker was murdered in February 1968. He was thirty years old when Jemima MacDonald and Helen Puttock were murdered. This puts him in the centre of the age-range suggested by witnesses, although admittedly on the upper edge of Jeanne's estimate.

Joe Beattie thought that Bible John was likely either a serviceman or an ex-serviceman and it is very likely that John McAdam Templeton enlisted in one of the forces in order to complete his two-years of National Service. The U.K. National Service Act, 1949 required that all healthy men undertake military service between the ages of seventeen and twenty-one unless they were prepared to work for a period of eight years in the essential services of coal mining, farming or the merchant marine.[343] This system was in place through the 1950s but it was being wound down in the 1960s. It was decided that only men born before 1st October 1939 would need to complete their National Service.[344] Given his birthday of 27th March, John McAdam Templeton would have been required to undertake National Service by a margin of some six months. Unfortunately, National Service records are not yet open to the public. They will be invaluable to researchers when they are because service records not only indicate the date on which a conscript signed up and the base to which they were sent, but also a description of them in terms of their hair and eye colour and their height.[345]

In terms of the currently accessible written record, John McAdam Templeton does not appear again until his marriage in Catrine in 1960, when he was twenty-one years old. Agnes Sayers's family had been based in Catrine for generations. Indeed, Agnes was born there in 1939.[346] The only other evidence relating to John McAdam Templeton's whereabouts in the 1960s comes from the birth of his son, John Templeton (1962-2015), who was born in Catrine some two years after the couple married. After this, it is not until 1977 that John McAdam Templeton again appears in the written record. Then, he is included in the British phone books, under the name "J. Templeton", living in the same street in Catrine where he still resides.[347] So, while we cannot be absolutely certain, it appears that John McAdam Templeton was likely living in Catrine from at least the time of his marriage in 1960 through to the present.

If John McAdam Templeton actually is Bible John, then his residence in Catrine might explain why detectives found it so difficult to trace clues about the killer's haircut, suits and teeth. Police investigations had concentrated on Glasgow. It might also explain why, as David Wilson and Paul Harrison suggest, "someone who was so obviously different from the crowd" could not be identified by those living in the suburbs of Glasgow.[348]

However, the village of Catrine is a long way from the three murder scenes and it is unlikely that Bible John could have returned home on the nights of the last two murders. Admittedly, he used a car on the night he murdered Patricia Docker, which would have allowed him easy passage back to Catrine, but he was dependent on public transport on the nights he murdered Jemima MacDonald and Helen Puttock. If Bible John had left his car at the Barrowland on those nights, he would have needed to double back to collect it before driving to Catrine. This theory is particularly problematic in the case of Helen Puttock. Bible John would not have alighted the number 6 night-service bus near the corner of Gray Street if he intended to return to the Barrowland to fetch his car. He would have continued travelling east along Argyle until he reached the city. Moreover, if the killer did not use a car on those two nights, then he would have been stranded in Glasgow. There were no buses leaving Glasgow for Catrine in the early hours of the morning and there were certainly no trains. In fact, the local train station of Mauchline had closed in 1965. The killer may have sought short-stay accommodation in Glasgow, but no landlord ever came forward to identify him despite the extensive newspaper and television coverage of his description.

***

Perhaps the most frustrating aspect of the search for information about John McAdam Templeton, relates to where he grew up. Given that it seems unlikely he spent his childhood in Muirkirk with his birth family, the implication is that he grew up either in a children's home or with a foster family. Unfortunately, I have been unable to find anything to connect him directly to Scotland's foster-care system and certainly not to the Scotstoun House Children's Home.

As mentioned earlier, the records for all children's homes and foster families are closed to the public. This means that the only hope we have of connecting John McAdam Templeton to the homies, or at least to the Scotstoun area, would be through his attendance at one of the local primary schools. There was a legal requirement for children from the homies, like all children in institutionalised care, to have access to education. The Education Act of 1872 made schooling compulsory in Scotland between the ages of five and thirteen and the leaving age was raised to fourteen in 1883.[349] However, a number of children's homes provided what they deemed to be an adequate education on site. So, while children who were living with a foster family would have attended their local primary school, there would have been some children living in institutions, who might never have attended an offsite school. These children would not appear in any of Scotland's education records.

There is no information available about education at the homies so we cannot know for certain whether the children who lived there were educated on or off site. But, if John McAdam Templeton really did grow up in the Scotstoun House Children's Home, there is a chance that he was educated at one of the local primary schools. The schools closest to the homies, Scotstoun Primary School and Bankhead Primary School, both remained open during the war years and so it is possible that John McAdam Templeton was enrolled at one of them.[350] Given that he was born on the 27th March 1939, he would most likely have commenced his schooling in the August of the year after his fifth birthday – in other words, in August 1944.

According to www.glasgowfamilyhistory.org.uk, while many of the education records for Scotland's country areas are incomplete, "an excellent set of records for Glasgow" is held in the Mitchell Library's Glasgow City Archives. Fortunately, the Admission Registers for both Scotstoun and Bankhead Primary Schools for 1944, and for the few years either side of this, are held in these archives.[351] When covid restrictions prevented me from returning to Scotland, I asked my research assistants, Gordon and Margaret White, to examine the Admission Registers for both Scotstoun and Bankhead Primary Schools. They searched each of the Registers to see if a "John Templeton" had been admitted to either Scotstoun or Bankhead in 1944 or in the period immediately preceding or following this year.[352] They did not find one child with that name in the registers. Clearly, John

McAdam Templeton did not enrol as a student at either Scotstoun or Bankhead Primary Schools.

So, at the end of the day, we might not be able to eliminate John McAdam Templeton from our cohort but we have nothing which connects him to the Scotstoun House Children's Home. Indeed, we have nothing to connect him to Glasgow at all.

Chapter 12.
A New Suspect

Now we come to the third John Templeton – one who definitely did not grow up with his birth family. John Templeton (1945-2015) was born in Glasgow on the 27th March 1945, making him one of the youngest in our cohort. He was the son of a single mother named Emma Dresser Johnston (1911-1990). When John Templeton was born, Emma Johnston was thirty-four years of age. Her parents, John Johnston (1881-1939) and Alice Jane Kerr (1879-1940) had both passed away. And although Emma had an older brother, he was living in Kent. In other words, Emma had no immediate family members who were able to help her raise her child.

Just before she gave birth to John Templeton in Glasgow's Maternity Hospital, Emma was working as a short-hand typist and living at 4 Sinclair Street, Helensburgh. But she had been born in Dumfries and lived there at least until 1939, by which time she was twenty-eight years old. According to the Valuation Rolls, Emma's father rented "2 Saughtree House" on Annan Road throughout the 1930s. He passed away at that address in April 1939 and it was Emma who signed his death certificate.[353] The following year, Emma's mother died in her home at 1 Moorfield Street, Gourock.[354] This time it was Emma's brother, William Alexander Johnston, who signed the death certificate, despite the fact that he lived in Kent. The implication is that Emma was not likely living with her mother at the time. She may still have been living in Dumfries or have moved to Helensburgh by then.

Given that John Templeton (1945-2015) was born in 1945, his birth certificate is not yet open to the public. But the information it contains is so vital to our search, that I contacted a private investigator in Edinburgh and asked him if he was able to help me. Again, I did not reveal that I was researching the Bible John murders, even though this particular John Templeton had already passed away. The private investigator successfully applied for access to John Templeton's birth certificate through whatever channel was open to him. He then forwarded a copy of the certificate to me.

According to this birth certificate, John Templeton's father was a munitions inspector named William Templeton (unknown-unknown) but there is no indication, either on the certificate or in the records held on Scotland's People, that Emma Dresser Johnston and William Templeton ever married. Indeed, at the time of their son's birth, Emma Johnston stated that her usual residence was in Helensburgh while William Templeton lived at "Maybank", Lovers' Walk, Dumfries. It is possible that Emma knew him from there.

Although we know that Emma Johnston travelled from Helensburgh to Glasgow when it was time for her to give birth, we cannot be certain that William Templeton joined her there. Admittedly, his name is on the birth certificate, but it was entered in handwriting which appears to be indistinguishable from Emma Johnston's. What is more, the word "present", which usually accompanies a father's name on the birth certificate, was not included in the space provided.

***

In order to trace John Templeton's lineage, we need to know who William Templeton's parents were. Unfortunately, no middle name was included for William Templeton on his son's birth certificate. All the certificate indicates is that he was working as a munitions inspector when Emma Johnston knew him and that, in 1945, he lived or had recently lived at "Maybank", Lovers' Walk, Dumfries. And this Dumfries address does not appear to be an indication of William Templeton's birth place. The Valuation Rolls for the late 1920s through to the mid-1930s, reveal that "Maybank" was occupied by a woman named Jean Ramsay Brown and in 1940, even after the war had begun, the proprietor and occupant of the property was named in the Valuation Roll as George Alexander Campbell. So, "Maybank" could not have been William Templeton's family home. He only moved to "Maybank" sometime after 1940, possibly because started work at the Drungans munitions factory which was commissioned in January 1941.[355]

In a later document, John Templeton mentions that his parents were both Scottish by birth but, given that "Maybank" was not William Templeton's family home, he may have been born anywhere in Scotland.[356] This makes tracing his ancestry extremely difficult. Admittedly, Emma Johnston was born in 1911, so it seems reasonable to assume that William Templeton was born somewhere between say 1890 and 1920. But a check of Scotland's People indicates that one hundred and fifteen William Templetons were born in Scotland in this period. Of this one hundred and fifteen, approximately thirty died before 1944. It is possible to trace the ancestry of many of the remaining eighty-five and some of them can be directly linked back to the marriage of John Templetoune (1730-1800) and Margaret Hunter (1732-1797). But this does not prove that any of these William Templetons was the father of John Templeton (1945-2015).

The fact that William Templeton was working as a munitions inspector might indicate a connection to the Home Guard. A number of women from the Auxiliary Territorial Service worked as ammunition inspectors in the United Kingdom during the Second World War.[357] Some of the men who worked as munitions inspectors may also have enlisted in the reserve army, in the Home Guard. According to the *Home Guard List 1941: Scottish Command* and the military records held at www.forces-war-records.co.uk, there was a 2nd Lieutenant "W. Templeton" enlisted in the Home Guard's 2nd Dumfriesshire Battalion. While his residential address was recorded as Dumfries (without a house number or street name), he was stationed in Glasgow during the war.[358] It is possible that 2nd Lieutenant W. Templeton was the William Templeton we're searching for but the available records offer no more information about him. We do not even know for certain that his first name was William.

There is also a possibility that William Templeton was not enlisted in either the Home Guard or the armed forces. He may have been a government employee. Certainly, men who were unable to sign up, for whatever reason, were sometimes employed by the government as munitions inspectors.[359]

So, unfortunately, without finding additional information about William Templeton, it is impossible to trace his ancestry. This means that we can neither prove nor disprove a direct ancestral connection between John Templeton (1945-2015) and the marriage of John Templetoune and Margaret Hunter.

***

Luckily, I have had much more success finding records which tell us about John Templeton (1945-2015). I was able to establish, for instance, that he left his mother's care when he was very young, definitely before the age of five. Indeed, when John Templeton started school in August 1950, he was already living with a foster family. At that time, he was, in fact, a foster child growing up in the very area of Glasgow that was so familiar to Bible John.

As noted earlier, the records pertaining to Scotstoun House Children's Home are still closed to the public but we are able to search Scotland's primary school records and, in particular, the Admission Registers for the schools within walking distance to the homies – Scotstoun Primary School and Bankhead Primary School. We already found that at least some of the Admission Registers for these two schools are intact and accessible to the public. My research assistants, Gordon and Margaret White, examined them when they were trying to establish whether John McAdam Templeton had been enrolled at either of the primary schools. Together with the staff of the Glasgow City Archives, they then broadened their search to cover the available Admission Registers from the mid-1930s through to the mid-1950s.

While they found that no "John Templeton" had attended Scotstoun Primary School during the whole of this period, their search of the Bankhead Admission Registers proved more fruitful. Admittedly, the collection was less complete because the school's early records were destroyed when Bankhead Primary School was bombed in March 1941. Nevertheless, the Glasgow City Archives holds the Bankhead Admission Registers that were created after the bombing.[360] A search of these later records revealed that a "John Templeton" did indeed attend Bankhead Primary School. His name appears in the volume, "Bankhead Primary, Boys and Girls, 1944-1951".[361]

According to the Bankhead Admission Register, John Templeton was admitted to the primary school on the 28th August 1950, when he was five years old.[362] His date of birth was recorded as 27th March 1945, so there can be no doubt that this John Templeton is John Templeton (1945-2015). The Bankhead Admission Register also records the name of his "parent or guardian" and a contact address. According to the Register, John Templeton's guardian was a woman named "Mrs Fransman" and his contact address was given as, "c/o Mrs Fransman, 1965 Dumbarton Road".[363] This was not the address of an institution. The Valuation Roll for 1940 indicates that the structure on 1965 Dumbarton Road was a terraced apartment block, a residence where many families lived.[364]

The Glasgow Electoral Registers, reveal that a family named Trausman was first registered as living in the apartment block in 1955. At that time, there were three eligible voters in the family, William and Eliza Trausman and their daughter Elizabeth. These names were repeated in the Electoral Roll for 1956. In 1957, William and Eliza were still registered as living at 1965 Dumbarton Road but Elizabeth was not. The couple's second daughter, Doris, had reached the voting age of twenty-one so the names in the Electoral Register were recorded as William, Eliza and Doris Trausman. In the Register for 1960, these three names appear as William, Eliza and Doris Fransman.

It is not clear exactly when John Templeton became part of the Fransman family. The entry in the Bankhead Primary School Register was made on his admission in August 1950 and, at that time, the Fransmans were living at 14 Polnoon Avenue, only a block away from Bankhead Primary School. In fact, the family had only moved to Polnoon Avenue in 1948 or 1949, from their previous address at 126 Boreland Drive. They had chosen a house which was only a four-minute walk to Bankhead Primary School, suggesting that they may well have fostered John Templeton before they moved to Polnoon Avenue and definitely before he enrolled at the school in August 1950. John Templeton then moved with the Fransmans to 1965 Dumbarton Road late in 1954 or early in 1955. The fact that the entry in the Bankhead Primary School Admission Register gives the later address, indicates that it was updated when the family moved.

What these three addresses show is that, from the time John Templeton was born, the Fransmans lived continuously within walking distance and certainly within working distance to the Scotstoun House Children's Home. Admittedly this proximity might be coincidental, but it seems more likely that John Templeton arrived at the homies soon after his birth and, from there, was fostered by the Fransmans, at least a year or two before he began school in August 1950.

So, what the early School Admission Registers and the Electoral Rolls from the 1940s and 1950s tell us is that there actually was a man named John Templeton who grew up in, and was therefore familiar with, the area around Knightsbridge, Scotstounhill and Scotstoun. Even more remarkably, this man was a foster child, just as police suspected. He also fits the age profile of our cohort. Certainly, John Templeton (1945-2015) was among the youngest of our John Templetons. Born in March 1945, he would have been twenty-four years old when witnesses saw Bible John with Jemima MacDonald and a few months shy of twenty-five when the killer was seen with Helen Puttock. Perhaps he looked a little older than he was. But we must also consider the role played by the power of suggestion. One of the two key witnesses who saw Bible John with Jemima MacDonald and most of those who saw him with Helen Puttock had been in the Barrowland Ballroom at the time. They were attending an over-25s night. It probably didn't occur to them that someone younger than twenty-five was in attendance on those particular nights. An estimation of twenty-five was the obvious starting point.

***

Over the years, a number of writers and former detectives have claimed that Joe Beattie placed far too much stock in Jeannie's evidence. Even recently, Detective Inspector Billy Little of Strathclyde Police suggested that, "there's maybe too much importance put on what was said in the taxi generally." But this is simply not the case. We already know that Bible John offered his real name that night at the Barrowland Ballroom rather than lie to Helen, Jeannie and Castlemilk John. We also know that he genuinely recognised the site of the homies and that his comment about foster children or foster homes was likely grounded in his own experience. What is more, Bible John's references to the buses and Blue Train services north of the River Clyde, which show a good deal of local knowledge, were never considered anything other than accurate.

In *Bible John: Search for a Sadist*, Charles Stoddart recalls Jeannie's account of the taxi conversation. She said that, when she and Helen tried to make light chatter, John "refused to be drawn out; whenever he was asked a direct question, he changed the subject or didn't answer at all."[365] Clearly, he was using strategies of avoidance in preference to telling outright lies. So, it appears that, when the killer did impart any information, he did so truthfully. And, if he really was being compulsively honest, then there is no way that too much importance has been placed on what was said in the taxi. On the contrary, the killer's comments were all vital clues.

This being said, we now need to investigate whether the other clues that Bible John so liberally left behind, fit with what we know about John Templeton (1945-2015). There are no historical sources that I can think of to assess some of the clues, such as the suggestion that Bible John's family holidayed in a caravan in Irvine or that his cousin had recently achieved a hole-in-one (although John Templeton certainly did have foster cousins). But there are ample sources available which might help us to check other clues, especially the remarks Bible John made about his family.

***

John Templeton's foster father, William Fransman (1889-1968), was born in Amsterdam on 2nd October 1889 but he moved to Australia when he was young, enlisting in the Australian Imperial Force in 1915 at the age of twenty-five.[366] He was a Private in the 5th Pioneers when he married Eliza Mackay Moir (1896-1977) in Edinburgh in December 1917. At the time, Eliza was twenty-one years old and living with her family in

Edinburgh. Eliza continued to live in her family home while William served in the AIF and indeed until he returned to Edinburgh in or before 1921.[367]

William and Eliza Fransman had three children and, although I cannot find a birth entry for any of them in the indexes of Scotland's People, under either "Fransman" or "Trausman", these children appear in other records. The couple's oldest child, Elizabeth Robertson Fransman (1923-1995), was born in Edinburgh in January 1923. Approximately three years later, around the time the young Fransman family moved to Glasgow, Eliza gave birth to William George Moir Fransman (1926-1999). Some ten years later, William and Eliza then had a second daughter who they named Doris Moir Fransman (c.1936-).

The precise structure of the Fransman family is important because, on the night that Helen Puttock was murdered, Bible John made a number of small but significant comments about members of his family. When he was in the taxi, Bible John initially described himself as an only child and, for John Templeton (1945-2015) this is true. He was the only child of Emma Dresser Johnston. But Bible John then mentioned having a sister. Indeed, he gave Jeannie the distinct impression that he was, "one of a family of two, his sister and himself".[368] Jeannie felt certain that this was an important clue because she considered it to be an unintentional admission. She even thought that Bible John quickly redirected the conversation in order to divert attention from the slip.

At first sight, the structure of John Templeton's foster family appears to be a poor fit with the statements that Bible John made. We know that William and Eliza Fransman had three of their own children before fostering John Templeton, so he actually belonged to a four-child family. But John Templeton did not grow up with all these foster siblings. His eldest foster sister, Elizabeth Robertson Fransman, was working as a nurse and she was away for lengthy periods of his childhood. According to the General Nursing Council for Scotland, Elizabeth registered to study nursing in June 1944 at Ruchill Hospital in Glasgow and she qualified on the 22nd November 1946.[369] A few years later, on the 6th June 1950, the United Kingdom outward passenger lists show her leaving the United Kingdom, via Liverpool, for Montreal. On the passenger list, Elizabeth gave her most recent address as 17 Welbeck Mansions in London.[370] Elizabeth Fransman returned to the United Kingdom in August 1952 but she disembarked in Greenock, rather than Glasgow.[371]

This may have been because she was continuing her professional education in Greenock. Despite spending another five months in Montreal in 1955, Elizabeth qualified as a midwife on the 7th November 1957, from the Royal Infirmary, Greenock.[372] Although Elizabeth is recorded as resident at 1965 Dumbarton Road in the Electoral Registers from 1954 to 1956, she was moving between Greenock, short-term rental accommodation in Hillhead and Montreal at this time. She then returned to England. So, for virtually all the years that John Templeton was growing up as a foster child in her parents' home, Elizabeth was absent.

The same can be said of George and Eliza's son, William George Moir Fransman. He appears to have left home either before or soon after his parents fostered John Templeton. William jnr. married Jane Cunningham Dickson in Partick in 1949. According to the Electoral Registers, he had been living with his parents in Polnoon Avenue in 1949 but, after his marriage, he was no longer registered at that address. Indeed, for some time he and Jane were not registered at any address. The couple first appear in the Glasgow Electoral Registers in 1955, living in Saxon Street, Scotstoun and, in 1959, the Registers place them in Merryton Avenue, Scotstoun.

In contrast, the Fransman's youngest daughter, Doris Moir Fransman, lived with her parents, both in Polnoon Avenue and later in Dumbarton Road. In fact, Doris remained living with her parents, and of course with her foster brother, until she married Ian Mackenzie McCulloch (1935-1998) in 1961. By that time, John Templeton was in his final year of high school. This means that Doris lived with John Templeton as his sister, and indeed as his only sibling, for almost the whole of his childhood, from the time he was fostered until the time he joined the workforce at the age of sixteen.

It is certainly plausible then that John Templeton would have mentioned only one sister in his conversation. Perhaps he considered himself to be an only child on the one hand and from "one of a family of two, his sister and himself" on the other.

***

Jeannie also recalled Bible John quietly mumbling that "his father or another relative" once worked at the site of the Kingsway Flats. As mentioned earlier, the Fransmans lived within walking distance to the site throughout John Templeton's childhood. And by the time construction on the Kingsway Flats began in 1962, William Fransman was seventy-three years old.[373] If he had worked at the Kingsway site, it was likely in the 1940s or 1950s, while it was still occupied by the

Scotstoun House Children's Home. Perhaps, he first saw John Templeton there as a very young child.

When William Fransman enlisted in the Australian Imperial Force, his occupation was recorded as "labourer" and the Census of 1921 describes him as a general labourer.[374] According to the Valuation Rolls of 1925, 1935 and 1940 he worked as a "machine man". But, in 1957, when William Fransman was included in *The Edinburgh Gazette*'s naturalisation list, his occupation was recorded more specifically as 'Assistant Machine Man (Printers)'. This is consistent with his death certificate, some eleven years later, in which he was described as a retired "printer's labourer".[375] The fact that his brother-in-law, Robert Moir, was a letterpress printer who lived nearby in Maryhill, suggests that William may have been employed by Robert as an assistant machine man or a printer's labourer. But, given the varied work experience of his early years, it is conceivable that he was employed part-time, in the 1940s and 1950s, at the homies as a general labourer or an odd jobs man.

Having said this, when Jeannie recalled the taxi conversation, she was unsure exactly which of his relatives Bible John was referring to. Jeannie could only tell police that the killer's "father *or some other relative*" had worked at the site of the Kingsway flats. Afterall, the killer had been mumbling, as if to himself, at the time. Instead of the word "father", perhaps Jeannie caught the tail end of the word "mother". The last syllable sounds the same and, if prefaced by the word "my", it would have been safe for Jeannie to assume that Bible John was referring to a relative. While there is no occupation recorded for Eliza Fransman on any census or on her marriage certificate, it is possible that she worked part-time when Doris was school-aged. The homies certainly did employ local women. One of the contributors to "Scotstoun memories" said that her mother "worked there in the kitchen".[376] Perhaps Eliza also worked in the kitchen or maybe she volunteered her time as one of the "Aunties" who visited the children.[377]

It is even possible that Bible John said the word 'sister' when he was referring to the relative who once worked at the Kingsway site. It might be that the Fransman's eldest daughter, Elizabeth, was employed at the homies as a nurse in the late 1940s. As mentioned earlier, Elizabeth qualified at the end of 1946 and although the London Electoral Registers indicate that she was living in Hampstead in 1947, she moved around a great deal from year to year. Elizabeth is absent from the London Electoral Rolls of 1948 and 1949, reappearing in 1950 at a different Hamstead address. Perhaps, she had returned to stay in Glasgow for a year or so to be near her family. And, nurses were definitely employed on site at the homies. One of the contributors to the Facebook group "Scotstoun memories", who lived opposite the children's home, recalled the grounds at Kingsway with its "field full of cows and nurses playing in the grounds with proper uniforms and white starched hats."[378] A former nurse, who had lived in Anniesland while she worked at the homies, suggested on "Scotstoun memories" that staff, "all must have stayed nearby when they worked at Scotstoun House" unless, of course, they had a room there.[379]

***

In his book *Goodbye Beloved Brethren*, Norman Adams suggests that Bible John may have been a member of the exclusive brethren. Even Charles Stoddart argues that Jeannie's impression that the killer had a strict, religious upbringing, "might lead one to think of a minority religious group rather than the established Church."[380] And media revelations of Bible's John's references to the scriptures, together with the moniker Bible John, fuelled speculation that the killer might even be a priest or a monk.[381]

In an attempt to dispel the myth that the killer was some Bible-thumping zealot, Detective Inspector Ricky Mason said, in his 2005 interview for the documentary *Unsolved*, that: "These Bible quotes weren't specific Bible quotes that you would need to know a lot about the Bible to speak about. These were quotes that somebody might say in everyday normal sort of language. There's nothing unusual about them."[382] While I doubt that, in the late 1960s, many people referenced biblical passages in their "everyday normal sort of language", D.I. Mason makes a valid point. What he appears to be saying, is that Bible John paraphrased passages from the Bible rather than quoting them. And, if Bible John had belonged to an evangelical sect or if he was religiously obsessive in the churchgoing sense, he would not have paraphrased biblical verses - he would have recited them.

Jeannie was raised as a Catholic and attended chapel every Sunday. If the killer had quoted passages from the Bible, she would almost certainly have recognised them. But she didn't. Indeed, Bible John's biblical references were so vague that, although Jeannie felt she recognised the subject matter, detectives were left to deduce that the killer had been referring to Exodus 2:3-2:4.[383] What is more, according to former Detective Superintendent Robert Johnstone, the killer questioned whether Helen and Jeannie knew what happened to the adulterous wife. "Did you read it in the Bible?", he asked them and, when the sisters indicated that they had not, he said, "She gets stoned to death".[384] But, in the Bible, the adulteress is brought before Jesus (John 7:53- 8:11) and, despite the fact that Mosaic Law prescribes stoning for adultery, he responds to the woman's accusers with the words: "He that is without sin among you, let him cast a stone at her." When everyone departs without having cast a single stone, Jesus tells the adulteress to go and sin no more. So, although Bible John may have been familiar with Mosaic Law, he seems to have been unaware that the adulteress in the Bible is *not* stoned to death.

And the phrase "den of iniquity" which is often cited as evidence of the killer's deeply religious beliefs, is not actually a biblical quotation. Although the use of the word "den" to reference a specific site of crime or immorality can be traced back to the King James Bible when Jesus speaks of a "den of thieves", the term "den of iniquity" was popularised in American literature in the 1940s.[385] And, if the term had been commonplace in religious circles in the 1960s, again Jeannie would likely have been familiar with it. But she wasn't. Indeed, according to Charles Stoddart, she immediately noticed the oddness of the expression and was so taken aback that she wasn't even able to respond.[386] Stoddart says, "Jeannie hadn't a clue what he (or his father) meant. Dens of iniquity?"[387] But, then, Jeannie would not likely have encountered the phrase in its literary context.

Even the police findings support the theory that Bible John was not particularly religious, at least certainly not in terms of church attendance. Afterall, none of the investigations into religious institutions proved fruitful. As mentioned earlier, Joe Beattie claimed that: "Every church and kirk in Glasgow of all denominations was visited with priests, ministers and members of the clergy being interviewed about their congregation and their own people."[388]   And, as Norman Adams suggests, in *Goodbye, Beloved Brethren,* detectives questioned brethren families in Central Scotland in relation to the Bible John murders. [389] But no suspects came from any of these investigations. It seems that Bible John was not known in Scotland's religious circles.

The implication from all of this is that Bible John's knowledge of the scriptures was quite rudimentary. Perhaps what we're seeing is, at most, a relatively loose connection to the established church – definitely not a deep immersion in some religious sect. In other words, the killer may have belonged to a church where it was possible to have a relatively casual attendance or he may not have belonged to a church at all. Afterall, you can be moralistic without being especially religious. At the end of the day, the moniker Bible John was perhaps not only a misnomer, but a seriously misleading one at that.

***

So, could the Fransmans have been the strict family that Bible John was referring to? When William Fransman joined the Australian Imperial Force in 1915, he recorded his religion as Church of England. Two years later, he and Eliza Moir married in a Church of Scotland ceremony in St Michael's Parish Church in Edinburgh. In other words, there is no indication that either William or Eliza belonged to any alternative or minority religious group. They were mainstream Protestants.

Although it is difficult to ascertain the depth of the Fransmans' religious commitment, there is some indication that at least one of the Fransmans might have had a stronger than usual connection to the Church of Scotland. During her twenties and thirties, William and Eliza's eldest daughter,

Elizabeth Fransman, relocated at least twice, for five-or-six-month periods, either to Montreal or to somewhere near Montreal. These journeys were recorded in the UK outward passenger lists for 1950 and 1955. Then, in September 1959, Elizabeth Fransman left the United Kingdom for Colombo, Sri Lanka. According to the UK outward passenger list, Elizabeth was by this time a qualified midwife.[390] What is more, she may not have been travelling alone. Three English nurses also boarded the S.S. Leicestershire bound for Sri Lanka. Like Elizabeth Fransman, these nurses were single women who intended to be resident in Sri Lanka for at least a year.[391] Interestingly, there was also a young, single woman aboard the ship who was a school teacher. She too intended to be in Sri Lanka for at least a year.[392]

In the 1950s, the Church of Scotland had strong connections with both Montreal and Colombo. There was an established presence in the form of the Church of St. Andrew and St. Paul in Montreal and in the form of St Andrew's Presbyterian Church (formerly, "St Andrew's Scots Kirk") in Colombo. Certainly, St Andrew's Church was central to Colombo's Scottish ex-pat community, even after Ceylon gained independence in 1948.[393] Moreover, the Church of Scotland had long dominated missionary activity in India and this continued after independence, increasingly expressed as humanitarian aid. It seems plausible that Elizabeth Fransman undertook her journey to Colombo in the capacity of a medically-trained missionary.

But even if this suggested a stronger than usual family connection to the Church of Scotland, it would not really explain the intensity with which Bible John spoke about adultery or, more specifically, adulterous women. Nor would it explain his reluctance to drink alcohol. So, perhaps the origin for these moralistic preoccupations came from the killer's own family background, rather than from any experience with mainstream religion.

There was, for instance, something in William Fransman's past which perhaps engendered a family culture both deeply critical of adultery and heavily invested in the social stereotypes of good and bad women. William Fransman's service hospital records indicate that he, like some 65,000 of his unlucky fellow diggers, contracted venereal disease while he was stationed in France.[394] In 1918, he was repeatedly hospitalised with gonorrhoea.[395] Then, when the war ended, he was reluctant to return to his wife in Edinburgh. William Fransman's army records include a series of letters which allude to some of the difficulties that he and Eliza were experiencing in the early years of their marriage. On the 8th August 1919, Eliza wrote to the "Officer in Charge", explaining that she had received "a most unpleasant letter" from her husband on his return to Australia earlier that year. Eliza says that, in this letter, William told her he was not going to send her any money, that he was unwell and that the best thing for her to do was to get a divorce. Eliza told the Officer in Charge that she was "a very respectable girl" and that it was hard for her to be treated in such a way.[396] The officer forwarded William Fransman's address, as Eliza had requested, and the couple were reunited in Edinburgh by 1921. But, although they resumed married life, the discovery of her husband's adultery and the resulting sexually transmitted disease may have hardened Eliza's attitudes towards adultery. She may have forgiven William for his role in what transpired and transferred all responsibility to the "adultress". And for his part, William may have continued to blame this woman for giving him gonorrhoea. Remember, it was

William, not Eliza, who warned his foster son about the Barrowland being a "den of iniquity".[397]

And the issue of alcohol consumption might also have taken on particular relevance in the family culture of the Fransmans. Eliza's father, George Moir, worked in a number of alcohol-related occupations and his drinking habits may have contributed to his ill health and eventual death. According to the census of 1891, George Moir was proprietor of the King's Arms Hotel in Irvine and, when the family moved to Greenock, where Eliza was born, he owned a "Spirit Dealer" shop. By the time of the 1901 Census, Moir had become a "traveller wine merchant" and, according to the 1911 Census, he was a "barman". George Moir died in 1913 after suffering for eighteen months with "general paralysis". His wife and children may well have attributed his protracted illness to his alcohol-related occupations. It would certainly be interesting to know if George Moir's illness and death gave Eliza and her husband the kind of "severe parental attitude towards drink" that Bible John alluded to.

***

John Templeton (1945-2015) remained at Bankhead Primary School until 27th January 1958, when he was twelve years old. The Bankhead Primary Admission Register was again updated, indicating that he was going on to Victoria Drive Higher Grade Public School, referred to by its former students as Victoria Drive Secondary School.[398] And, according to the Victoria Drive Secondary School Register, John Templeton was a student there until 1st September 1961, by which time he was sixteen years of age.[399]

In the years that followed, John Templeton moved into the print industry like his foster father. But while William Fransman worked as a printer's labourer, John Templeton entered a lengthy apprenticeship to become a compositor or typesetter. Compositors were apprenticed for around seven years and they usually supplemented their learning with part-time study at the Glasgow College of Printing.[400] In the 1950s, compositors worked in various publishing houses or for newspapers, type-setting individual letters, one line at a time. Some of them used hot-metal typesetting where molten lead was poured into a cast which might be used for whole lines of text. However, by the 1960s, when John Templeton was serving his apprenticeship, these techniques were giving way to the more modern process of phototypesetting or photocomposition. Indeed, Glasgow was at the forefront of this radical technological change and photocomposition machines, first used commercially in 1956, had been installed in many of Scotland's publishing firms by the mid-1960s.[401]

Jeannie told detectives that she was certain Bible John was not a labourer. His pristine hands and his milk-and-roses complexion suggested as much. As a compositor, John Templeton was certainly no labourer. Moreover, he would have spent his working-life indoors, giving him the complexion that Jeannie described. But, in the taxi, Bible John had specifically said that he worked in a laboratory and we know that he was, at the very least, reluctant to lie. So, could it be said that, as a compositor, John Templeton worked in a laboratory?

In Glasgow in 1969 compositors who worked for publishers or print establishments of any size were almost certainly using the latest photocomposition machines. They would have been familiar with the science of cathode ray tubes, lens arrangements and photo multipliers. I found some original footage from the short documentary *Linotype: The Film*, which shows compositors using the Linotron 505 in 1969. In this documentary, compositors who worked in the processing stage examine character grids under microscopes and develop exposed plaques in a series of chemical baths. Even more importantly perhaps, the footage shows that, for the duration of these activities, compositors wore white laboratory coats.[402] So, there can be no doubt that compositors who worked at least in the processing stage of photocomposition could accurately have described their workplace as a laboratory.

***

When she was describing her sister's killer, Jeannie compared him to the other men who attended the Barrowland Ballroom, saying that he "was a cut above the others," a "wee bit better class". And Jeannie insisted that he was "well spoken". According to Charles Stoddart, she said that he was "polite and well-spoken" and that he was "well-spoken without being lah-de-dah or Kelvinside".[403] Jeannie used the latter phrase to indicate that she didn't believe Bible John was upper-class or wealthy. And yet, in the taxi, the killer had said he had plenty of money.[404]

But there is not necessarily any contradiction here. If, as indicated earlier, Bible John grew-up as a member of the working-class and became upwardly socially mobile, through apprenticeship and education, then he might genuinely have considered himself to be well-off. Bible John clearly believed that he was superior to the Barrowland's clientele and this was not only a moral superiority. His clothes and manners testify to his sense of class. The way he addressed the manager of the

Barrowland Ballroom, intimating that he would raise his concerns with the local Member of Parliament, also speaks of his assumed entitlement. Indeed, it appears that Bible John considered himself to be middle-class, rather than working-class, and he wanted his social status to be recognised.

John Templeton had gone into a trade which paid very well. Although many workers in the print industry received only an average wage, compositors earned significantly more. So, John Templeton was certainly not "old-money" wealthy but he did have plenty of money. What is more, he belonged to an elite group within the print industry who had very specialised skills, especially in terms of the requirements of literacy.[405] As one former compositor suggested, "they became excellent at their language and particularly in grammar and spelling. Compositors also became very knowledgeable in a wide variety of subjects".[406] With a job like this, John Templeton would certainly have been "well-spoken". Perhaps not "lah-de-dah or Kelvinside", but definitely well-spoken. He might also have been well-acquainted with many literary phrases. Perhaps the phrase "den of iniquity" would not have been jarring to him, as it so obviously was to Jeannie.

What is more, as a compositor, John Templeton was definitely upwardly socially mobile. He had come a long way from his humble beginnings as a foster child, homed with a working-class family. William Fransman worked in a number of jobs, always in an unskilled capacity. But, through years of training and study, John Templeton had risen well above his foster father's social standing. In a brief biography of his time as a London compositor in the late 1950s, Isidore Cannon, writes: "The compositor was in an ambiguous class situation. Compositors were relatively

189

affluent and high in status, and one would have expected them to be just the kind of people likely to be undergoing what would later be called embourgeoisement: adopting a more middle-class way of life ..."[407] In response to Cannon's article, a number of past compositors and their children confirmed his finding that their life-style was "more 'middle-class' than skilled workers generally".[408] One respondent, "Aleydis" said that her father had been a compositor and "he always drew the distinction between himself and mere "printers", his being the higher status occupation."[409] Another respondent explained that he had grown up in working-class Dublin in the 1950s and became an electrician. A friend of his, "a very bright lad", had become a compositor and his job "seemed like a profession" whereas being an electrician "was a trade".[410]

But perhaps there was even more to John Templeton's rise in social status than his being a compositor. He worked for a publishing firm at Anniesland Cross which was responsible for making the composites for Glasgow University's examination papers.[411] And this connection to the university, in combination with his high-status employment, might well have reinforced John Templeton's middle-class identity. Not only had he risen to the ranks of the middle-class, he was doing important, confidential work for the university.

As mentioned earlier, D.C.S. Tom Goodall believed that Bible John was someone who was "beyond the average person's suspicion". He was someone people trusted unreservedly and this trust emanated from the position he held in the community. Goodall felt that they were looking for a man who belonged to one of a few respected professions – "solicitors, the police, the legal profession, physicians, doctors, the medical profession, firemen, priests, the church and the press."[412] Although Goodall never got a lead suggestive of any of these professions, he might well have been on the right track. As a compositor, John Templeton was a member of the press.

So, what was the piece of paper or card that Bible John showed Helen Puttock which seems to have put her at ease? Jeannie hadn't been able to see the card or paper but she said that it was pink and looked official, like some form of identification card. And although she couldn't hear the conversation clearly at the time, she thought that Helen's John might be "trying to prove that he was really employed as such-and-such, or had been to some place or other."[413] Perhaps it was a combination of these things. Bible John might have produced the card in order to prove that he worked at or for a particular place – that he was connected to, and trusted by, Glasgow University. The fact that he was tasked with making composites for university examinations, would certainly have been both a mark of his respectability and evidence of his trustworthiness.

***

On the 24th May 1968, nearly seven years after John Templeton left school, William Fransman passed away and it was John Templeton who witnessed his death certificate. According to this certificate, William Fransman died in his home at 1965 Dumbarton Road. But the death certificate was not witnessed by his son William or his daughter Doris – even though they were both living in Glasgow at the time. Instead, it was witnessed by John Templeton in his capacity as foster son. At the time, John Templeton was still living in his foster parents' home at 1965 Dumbarton Road and so he signed the document on the day his foster father died.[414]

191

District No. 644-7	Year 1968	Entry No. 454	Record Lineage

DEATH REGISTERED IN THE DISTRICT OF... Glasgow
.... in the Burgh of Glasgow.

(1) Name(s) and Surname	William Fransman.		(2) Sex M.
(3) Occupation	Printer's Labourer - Retired.		
(4) Marital Status	Married	(5) Date of Birth -/-/-	(6) Age 78 years
(7) Name, Surname and Occupation of Spouse(s)	Eliza Moir.		
(8) When and Where Died	1968, May Twenty-fourth, between 12.30m A.M. and 7.0m A.M. 1965 Dumbarton Road, Glasgow		
(9) Usual Residence (if different from Place of Death)			

(10) Name(s), Surname and Occupation of Father	(11) Name(s), Surname(s) and Maiden Surname of Mother
John Fransman Stevedore (Deceased)	Jonsen Fransman m.s. (Deceased)

(12) Cause of Death	1 (a) Cerebrovascular accident (b) Arteriosclerosis (2) II
Name and Qualifications of Medical Practitioner	J. McFarlane M.B.
(13) Informant's Signature and Qualification	John Templeton Foster-Son
(14) When Registered	1968, May 24th	(15) Registrar's Signature	W.H.G.Dunning Asst. Registrar
R.C.E.			

William Fransman's death certificate - available on Scotland's People.

Clearly, John Templeton had lived in the Knightsbridge-Scotstoun area from before the age of five through to his early twenties. He would certainly have been familiar with the Blue Train services north of the River Clyde, with the buses which travelled along Dumbarton Road and with the bus stop which serviced the North Terminal of the Govan Ferry. It would not be surprising to find that he also knew many of the pubs in the neighbouring suburb of Yoker. But, even more importantly, John Templeton would have been relatively up-to-date with this knowledge because he had retained his local connection. Indeed, later documents prove that John Templeton continued to live at 1965 Dumbarton Road until the beginning of August 1969, approximately two weeks before Jemima MacDonald's murder and just under three months before the murder of Helen Puttock.

Jeannie told detectives that, in the taxi, there was some discussion about the cost of public transport and she recalled that Bible John was very familiar with the fares for transportation north of the river Clyde.[415] At the time, Jeannie recognised that this was an important clue. As Paul Harrison suggests, she "felt he knew *too much* information about such things".[416] Indeed, if Donald Simpson is right, in *Power in the Blood*, Jeannie thought the killer had a detailed knowledge of the times as well as the fares for the buses and blue trains.[417] Either way, Jeannie not only recognised that Bible John knew a good deal about the local area, she realised that his knowledge was up-to-date and this is very significant.

Only someone with a very recent connection to the area could have known about the changing public transportation times and fares. In fact, a new edition of the City of Glasgow Corporation Transport Time-Table was published in July 1969 and it included not only the times of Glasgow's buses, but also the night services, fare stages and scale of fares.[418] Only someone who had travelled on public transport north of the River Clyde in July 1969 could have remained abreast of these changes.

What is more, Glasgow City Transport continued to increase fares as a counter to rising wages in the industry.[419] In August 1969, the Glasgow municipal transport committee recommended a new fare structure, increasing the 5d bus fare to 6d and replacing the 10d and 1s 3d fares with a flat rate of 1s 6d.[420]. So, for Bible John to have known of these fare changes, he was surely still living north of the river Clyde in August 1969, not south of it, and yet we know that John Templeton left 1965 Dumbarton Road in early August of that year.

***

In *The Lost British Serial Killer*, David Wilson and Paul Harrison argue that there is one aspect of the investigation into the Bible John murders "that seems to have been given insufficient weight". This aspect, they believe, "might have been an enormous clue in guiding the police to where Bible John lived". It was, of course, the last sighting of the killer – as he alighted the number 6 night-service bus on Argyle Street near the corner of Gray Street. Wilson and Harrison argue that Bible John was very likely going home.[421]

As mentioned earlier, detectives assumed from the outset that the killer alighted the number 6 night-service bus at the Gray Street bus-stop because it was near the Northern Terminal of the Govan Ferry. And certainly, as Charles Stoddart suggests, from the corner of Gray Street it would have been only a short walk down Kelvinhaugh Street, on to Pointhouse Road, to the terminal at the bottom of Ferry Road.[422] However, this route would have involved some backtracking – backtracking which could have been avoided if the killer had alighted the number 6 night-service bus a stop or two earlier, while it was close to the River Kelvin. In other words, Bible John could have alighted significantly closer to the ferry terminal.[423]

What is more, as already discussed, the two ferrymen did not remember seeing anyone who fit Bible John's description boarding the ferry on the night Helen Puttock was murdered and the Clyde ferries were by no means large vessels. Yet, despite these significant inconsistencies, Joe Beattie appears to have stuck to his original assumption. He showed little if any interest in exploring other exit routes that the killer may have taken. But what if Bible John did not live south of the River Clyde? What if he had never intended to catch the Govan Ferry? Then, surely, we need to ask ourselves what alternative exit route he may have had in mind.

A witness described Bible John as "walking quickly … in a determined manner along the Dumbarton Road".[424] And, when he boarded the night-service bus, one of the passengers noticed that he was "breathless".[425] The killer was obviously in a hurry. Given his conversation in the taxi, Bible John was aware of the new Corporation time-table. He knew that the night buses ran only on the hour and that the number 6 night-service bus had left the outer terminal of Garscadden at 2am.[426] Bible John had to walk a considerable distance from where he murdered Helen Puttock in Earl Street to where the bus would turn onto Dumbarton Road from Crow Road and, if he missed that bus, there would not have been another one until after 3am.[427] So, he was determined to catch that bus, almost certainly because it would deliver him to a place on route to his home.

Charles Stoddart is convinced that the killer did not live in Glasgow's eastern suburbs. In *Bible John: Search for a Sadist*, he reasons that, if the killer "had been heading for the east side of the city after the murder, then surely he would have stayed on the bus until it reached its terminus in George Square…"[428] And, in *The Lost*

British Serial Killer, David Wilson and Paul Harrison argue that we can be certain "the killer did *not* live in Scotstoun, or in any of the other western districts, such as Drumchapel, Yoker … Knightswood or the more upmarket Bearsden", given that he had chosen to travel east along Dumbarton Road.[429] Both arguments are sound. So, if Bible John was not trying to head west or east, and if he hadn't been intent on catching the Govan Ferry in order to travel to Glasgow's southern suburbs, there is only one possible direction left – the killer most likely alighted the number 6 night-service bus at the Gray Street bus-stop intending to travel northwards.

Charles Stoddart concedes that, "it was, of course, possible that Bible John lived on the north side of the river near where the bus stopped", but he goes on to muddy the waters, suggesting that, "if he had been heading for the north side or Maryhill area, he surely would have alighted at the foot of Bryers Road, then to strike northwards on foot."[430] But why would the killer take Bryers Road if he wanted to travel northwards on foot? Bryers Road was then, as it is now, a main artery. Although it would have been an obvious route for someone travelling by car, Bryers Road would have afforded a pedestrian no cover. The killer was clearly in a dishevelled state, with a fresh scratch under his eye. Witnesses had noticed him walking quickly along Dumbarton Road and those on the bus had paid particular attention to him. Perhaps the attention he received on the bus made him more cautious and he decided to take a less conspicuous route home. Then again, maybe he remained on the bus as it passed Bryers Road so that he could alight at a stop which was even closer to his home.

From the Gray Street bus-stop, the killer might well have proceeded on foot through Kelvingrove Park. That would explain why no one saw him after he left the bus. He would have been able to walk undetected all the way through the park to the suburb of Kelvinbridge or, by walking a little further, to the eastern-most part of Maryhill, now known as North Kelvinside.

***

As mentioned earlier, by 30th October 1969, the night that Helen Puttock was murdered, John Templeton was no longer living at 1965 Dumbarton Road. He had moved out of his foster mother's home less than three months previously. His former address was clearly west of Helen Puttock's murder scene. There is no way that he could have caught the number 6 night-service bus, travelling in an easterly direction, in order to return to 1965 Dumbarton Road.

But when he left his foster mother's home, John Templeton moved into a rental apartment which was still north of the River Clyde but closer to the city centre. According to the 1969 Register of Electors, John Templeton's new address was 3/1, 24 Melrose Gardens, North Kelvinside.[431] This means that Bible John had, in fact, caught the number 6 night-service bus as it travelled eastwards along Dumbarton Road towards John Templeton's new apartment. Indeed, the killer had alighted the bus at the stop closest, on that particular route, to 3/1, 24 Melrose Gardens. From that stop, it would have taken John Templeton less than 25 minutes to walk home – for the most part along the dark, tree-lined Kelvin Way.

3/1, 24 Melrose Gardens

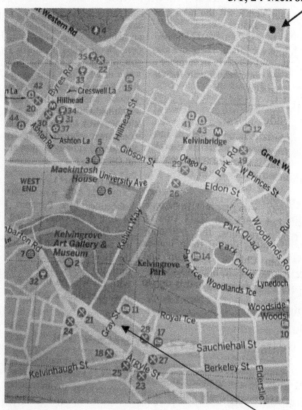

Suspect alighted here

Map from *Lonely Planet: Scotland*, 1999, 2019, p.114.

David Wilson and Paul Harrison suggest that "a man fitting Bible John's description boarded a bus at Gardner Street ... and got off at the junction of Dumbarton Road [named Argyle east of the River Kelvin] and Gray Street". They immediately follow this statement with the most obvious of questions – "Did he live around there?"[432] The answer very much appears to be "Yes".

Chapter 13.
What Happened to Bible John?

In 1967, a year before the Bible John murders began, John Templeton met a sales assistant named June who worked at Copeland and Lye's Department Store. Looking at a photograph of June taken in that year, you can't help but notice that she was very pretty with a slim build and dark-brown wavy hair, cut in a medium short style. On 2nd August 1969, after dating for two years, the couple married in a Church of Scotland ceremony in the Glasgow Cathedral. The wedding ceremony was officiated by Frank Myers, the Minister of June's local church.

Again, John Templeton's marriage certificate, having being created less than seventy-five years ago, is not open to the public. But the private investigator, who I contacted earlier, was able to access the document and forward a copy to me. The marriage certificate confirms the date and place of the marriage. It also gives John Templeton's birthdate as 27th March 1945, his address as 1965 Dumbarton Road and it includes the names of his parents - Emma Dresser Johnston and William Templeton. But what is perhaps most striking about the document is that a correction was entered at a later date, in the section marked RCE (Record of Corrections Etc) at the bottom of the page. In the period before 1984, a statement of divorce was sometimes entered on a marriage certificate in the form of a correction. The wording noted on John and June's marriage certificate is: "RCE 292/1977/Glw Decree of divorce against June .... (formerly ...... or ....)". [433]

When I saw this correction, I applied for the couple's divorce records under the Freedom of Information (Scotland) Act 2002. The Scottish Courts and Tribunals Service accepted my request and forwarded copies of the relevant divorce-court papers. These records indicate that it was John Templeton who filed for divorce, not June, and that, as the RCE on the marriage certificate suggests, the court found "against June".

The divorce-court papers reveal that John and June Templeton separated some six years into their marriage when June moved out of their Melrose Gardens apartment. At this time, John Templeton was convinced that June had been having a long-term extra-marital affair. In the court summons, John Templeton alleged, through his solicitor, that "the marriage was happy until about September 1974 when the defender, without warning, left the pursuer."[434] John Templeton believed "that the defender and co-defender, without his knowledge, began an adulterous relationship in about July 1973", some four and a half years into their marriage and fourteen months before June chose to leave the Melrose Gardens apartment. In the court documents, John Templeton's lawyer argues that June and the co-defender had, in fact, "been living together as man and wife … since about July 1975". On 23rd July 1976, June and her new partner allegedly "admitted their adultery to private investigators" acting on John Templeton's behalf and the divorce application was lodged less than two months later, on the 17th September 1976.[435]

June did not contest the allegations of adultery and, given that she and John had no children, the court had little to debate. The Templeton's divorce was decreed on 21st January 1977.[436] June then remarried on 7th July that year.

***

There have been many crime writers who believe that Helen Puttock was not Bible John's last victim, that he went on to kill again after 1969. In *The Lost British Serial Killer*, David Wilson and Paul Harrison suggest that Bible John may have become a commuter killer. They write: "we can be sure that he learned to change his behaviour, because he was organised and sufficiently clever to appreciate that he would be caught if he continued to 'maraud' around the Barrowland Ballroom. In all likelihood, he became a 'commuter' – in space and time, and in terms of his development as a killer."[437] Wilson and Harrison go on to suggest that Bible John developed tactics to avoid both detection and capture, "blending in rather better than he did in 1968 and 1969."[438] Of course, this suits their theory that Bible John was actually Peter Tobin and that, after murdering Patricia Docker, Jemima MacDonald and Helen Puttock, he went on to kill Vicki Hamilton, Dinah McNicol and Angelika Kluk. But we already know that Peter Tobin was not Bible John.

A number of other writers have suggested that Bible John, after lying low for several years, resumed his killings in Scotland in 1977. They cite the fact that, in the two-year period from 1977 to 1978, there were six young women murdered in Scotland, who might also have been his victims. In *Bible John: Hunt for a Killer*, Alan Crow and Peter Sampson argue that, after the reopening of the Bible John inquiry in the 1990s, detectives "looked closely" at the unsolved murders of Anna Kenny, Hilda McAulay Miller, Agnes Cooney and Mary Gallacher.[439] Charles Stoddart and Georgina Lloyd suggest that Bible John was perhaps not only responsible for these murders, but also the 1977 double-murder of Christine Eadie and Helen Scott in East Lothian.[440]

While the timing of John Templeton's divorce, granted as it was in January 1977, would certainly tie in with the timing of these 1977-1978 murders another man, Angus Sinclair, has now been convicted of murdering three of these women. Sinclair was already serving a life sentence for countless rapes and indecent assaults and for the murder of eight-year-old Catherine Reehill when he was convicted, in 2001, of murdering seventeen-year-old Mary Gallacher in Glasgow in November, 1978.[441] Then, in 2014, Sinclair was also convicted of the double-murder of Christine Eadie and Helen Scott, known locally as the World's End murders.[442]

Two of the other three cases bear little resemblance to the Bible John murders. Anna Kenny and Agnes Cooney were both young, single women. Anna Kenny had been buried in a makeshift grave a hundred miles from home.[443] Agnes Cooney was stabbed twenty-six times after being held captive for up to twenty-four hours.[444] The case most similar to the Bible John murders, in terms of both victim profile and *modus operandi*, is that of Hilda McAuley Miller. Hilda was a thirty-six-year-old divorcee with two children who went out dancing once a week. On the night she was murdered, she had been to the Plaza Dance Hall. Hilda's battered body was found almost naked the following day, left in a wooded area just off Lovers' Lane near Langbank in Renfrewshire. Witnesses came forward saying they had seen Hilda at the Plaza with a man aged between thirty and thirty-five. They described this man as being approximately 5'8" tall with dark hair, a sallow complexion and prominent lips. This is a far cry from the description of Bible John as a tall man with sandy or light-auburn hair and a milk-and-roses complexion.[445] Indeed, the description of Hilda's killer resembles Angus Sinclair.[446]

In 2018, Guy Birchall, from the *Sun*, suggested that: "When Scottish detectives visited the FBI's Behavioural Science Unit in Quantico, Virginia, agents agreed the same killer was involved in all the 1977-1978 Glasgow cases."[447] The following year, the BBC claimed that detectives suspected that Angus Sinclair murdered Anna Kenny, Agnes Cooney and Hilda McAuley Miller, "but did not have enough evidence to charge him."[448] Apparently, all of the evidence from the unsolved Glasgow murders "had been lost". [449] But the consensus seems to be that the prime suspect is Angus Sinclair. Bible John is no longer considered in connection with any of these murders.

***

As mentioned earlier, in the documentary "Unsolved", Detective Inspector Ricky Mason says that he believes there never was a serial killer stalking Glasgow – that Patricia Docker, Jemima MacDonald and Helen Puttock were killed by two or three different men. He reasons that: "If they were separate murders then you would expect the killings to stop and if it was a serial killer as it has been portrayed, but we're treating it as three separate [cases], then you'd expect that person to go on and continue killing."[450] However, there is a problem with this logic. In her article for the *New York Times*, Jan Hoffman argues that the common assumption that serial killers are incapable of stopping is unjustified - that the reality is very different.[451] Sometimes serial killers simply stop killing.

Professor in Psychiatry at California University, J. Reid Meloy, argues that serial killers are not "compelled" to rape and murder. These acts "are intentional and predatory. There is choice, capacity and opportunity that is exercised."[452] And this is borne out by the many serial killers who chose to stop killing long before their arrest. For example, Joseph James DeAngelo Jr. (the Golden State killer), committed at least thirteen murders and fifty rapes between 1973 and 1986 and then killed no-one else before he was apprehended in 2018. Dennis Rader (the BTK killer), was convicted of ten murders between 1974 and 1991, ceasing long before his arrest in 2005. And Jeffrey Gorton, committed his first murder in 1986 and his second, which was also his last, in 1991, before he was apprehended in 2002.[453]

The fact that killers sometimes choose not to continue to kill was brought home to me by one of Western Australia's most notorious cold cases. In September 2020, a man referred to locally as the Claremont serial killer was convicted in the Western Australian Supreme Court of murdering two of the three women who disappeared from the Claremont entertainment strip in a fourteen-month period between January 1996 and March 1997. The Court found that Bradley Robert Edwards had murdered Jane Rimmer and Ciara Glennon, but believed there was insufficient evidence to convict him of the murder of Sarah Spiers, whose body has not yet been found. After murdering Ciara Glennon in March 1997, Bradley Edwards stopped killing. He was arrested in 2016, some nineteen years later, still living in Perth.[454]

Unfortunately, there have been few studies which ask why serial killers stop killing.[455] In her article for the *New York Times*, Jan Hoffman quotes homicide detective Eric Witzig when he says: "There has never been a survey of serial killers asking them why they stopped ... All we have are anecdotal hunches". The killer might think, "I don't want to do this anymore because I might get caught ... or I want to stop and reflect on the carnage I wreaked in the past."[456]

Perhaps, if Bible John did stop murdering women after 1969, it was because he felt deeply affected by a speech which Helen Puttock's husband, George, gave soon after her murder. According to the *Scottish Daily Express*, the thirty-year-old Corporal made a heart-felt appeal for community assistance to find his wife's killer. The newspaper reported that, while he was sitting in the courtroom above the Marine Police Station, he said: "I would like people to think of me and my two little sons. In two seconds, this man ruined my life and career, and ruined the life of my children."[457]

But, given the pattern of Bible John's behaviour, it seems unlikely that he was moved by the impact his murders had on George Puttock and his sons. After he killed Jemima MacDonald in August 1969, the *Evening Times* reported that her three children were "being cared for in a Glasgow Corporation home."[458] Ironically, because of Bible John's actions, these children were forced to live in an institution or perhaps later in a foster home. Without doubt, the killer would have read about this in the newspapers. And yet, within weeks, he went on to murder Helen Puttock. He certainly did not stop killing because of the pain he inflicted on Jemima MacDonald's young children.

If Bible John stopped killing after 1969, and it does appear that he did, it was more likely due to self-interest. He simply didn't want to be caught. The insouciance he demonstrated so clearly during all three murders, may have deserted him after the third. As David Wilson and

Paul Harrison suggest, "… he must have realised that he gave away far too much during the taxi ride with Jeannie and Helen."[459] And there was intense publicity about the suspect after Helen Puttock's murder. The newspapers and television stations ran huge campaigns asking the public for information.[460] This publicity continued well into the following year. The BBC even made a thirty-minute documentary which they aired in prime time on the programme "Current Account" on the 18th September 1970.[461] This documentary included a re-enactment of the time leading up to Helen Puttock's murder with look-alike actors standing in for Helen, Jeannie and the two Johns. The programme then discussed the police investigation into Helen Puttock's murder with Detective Chief Superintendent James Binnie assuring the public that police efforts would continue until Bible John was caught.[462]

***

John Templeton never re-married after he and June divorced. The Electoral Rolls from 2002 to 2015 are accessible online and a background report from 192.com suggests that, for these years at least, John Templeton lived alone at the Melrose Gardens apartment. He died there from a heart attack late at night on the 27th October 2015. His death certificate was signed by a woman named Margaret, who described herself as his "partner". But Margaret had not been living with John Templeton. She gave her home address as South Scott Street in Baillieston which is quite a distance from North Kelvinside.

John Templeton's funeral service was conducted by Reverend Peter Davidge from the Church of Scotland's

Gallowgate Parish Church. My research assistant, Gordon White, discovered that he was cremated at Maryhill Crematorium on the 4th November 2015. Moreover, according to the crematorium records, John Templeton's ashes were collected by someone, rather than being scattered within the grounds. Any further information was considered too sensitive to be released and so Gordon was unable to find out who it was that collected John Templeton's ashes. Perhaps it was his "partner", Margaret.

***

During the course of writing this manuscript, I contacted one of the members of "I went to Victoria Drive Secondary School" and asked her to see if anyone from the Facebook group could remember John Templeton. A small number of former students responded to her inquiry. All but one said they didn't know John Templeton and the respondent who did, replied "I think he was in the same year as me at Victoria Drive. Don't know anything else after that."[463]

Then, in August 2021, I contacted the private Facebook group "I Went to Bankhead Primary school", asking if anyone there could remember John Templeton.[464] I was hoping that someone would be able to describe him to me or, better still, identify him in a school photograph. There has been absolutely no response to my post. It appears that, although John Templeton attended Bankhead Primary School for some seven years, no-one on the Facebook site remembers him. The situation reminded me of Charles Stoddart's words: "No-one knew the killer. He appeared, committed the crime, and disappeared just as quickly. A real loner, he was to vanish into thin air."[465]

***

So, what has now become the most important task in our search for Bible John, is yet to be accomplished. We still don't know what John Templeton (1945-2015) looked like. And there are very few people who do. John Templeton's partner, Margaret, may still be alive, as perhaps is his foster sister Doris Fransman. But in February 1968, when Bible John murdered Patricia Docker, John Templeton was already dating June. By the time that Jemima MacDonald and Helen Puttock were murdered, John and June were married and living together in the apartment in Melrose Gardens. This means that it is June, above all others, who would likely know about this period in John Templeton's life.

I discovered that June was living near Glasgow and obtained her telephone number. Hopefully, it would be possible to get a description of her ex-husband without ever mentioning the Bible John murders. In May 2022, I asked my daughter Kayla to call June. I couldn't summon the courage to ring her myself. I feared that June would say her ex-husband had been short, with dark hair and brown eyes. This would mean, not only that I was mistaken about who had murdered Patricia Docker, Jemima MacDonald and Helen Puttock, but that my reliance on historical methods and sources was perhaps not viable for cold case research.

My daughter asked me what evidence suggested that John Templeton (1945-2015) was likely Bible John. I gave her my list:

- Bible John used the name John Templeton on the night he murdered Helen Puttock
- The name John Templeton exists among the ancestors of Hector and Janet McInnes, siblings whose DNA samples share patterns with the DNA profile extracted from the semen stain on Helen Puttock's stockings
- John Templeton (1945-2015) fits the age profile of Bible John
- John Templeton (1945-2015) was born and raised in Glasgow and would have had a Glaswegian accent
- John Templeton (1945-2015) was definitely a foster child, as police suspected Bible John was
- John Templeton (1945-2015) had been fostered by a family who lived within walking distance to the Scotstoun House Children's Home, the site which Bible John identified as he passed by in the taxi
- John Templeton (1945-2015) grew up with one sibling, a sister, just as Bible John implied he had done
- John Templeton (1945-2015) worked in a laboratory setting, just as Bible John said he did
- John Templeton (1945-2015) was still living in Scotstoun when the new transportation timetables and fare schedules came out in July 1969. Bible John was familiar with these north-of-the-river transportation timetable and fare changes
- John Templeton (1945-2015) moved into an apartment in North Kelvinside less than three months before Helen Puttock's murder. This apartment was within walking distance from where Bible John alighted the number 6 night-service bus on the night he murdered Helen Puttock

I found my list reassuring. We needed to contact June. Her description of John Templeton (1945-2015) would surely match that of Bible John.

So, my daughter made the phone call and to my relief June did not describe her ex-husband as short, with dark hair and brown eyes. On the contrary, she said that, although it was difficult to recall exactly, she believed he was approximately 5' 10" tall, with hazel eyes and "sandy" hair. My anxiety had been unfounded. June's description, for the most part, echoed the words Jeannie had spoken, both to Charles Stoddart and Audrey Gillan. Bible John, Jeannie told Stoddart, "was tall, about 5 feet 10 inches … He had sandy hair, not really red but not too far off it …".[466] And Jeannie had also used the word sandy when she was interviewed by Audrey Gillan. She had said: "To me in the dark you would take him for fair-headed but when you seen him in the light it was kinda sandy-fair, you know with the kind of light eyebrows."

After hearing June's description of her ex-husband, and with Covid restrictions lifting, I felt it was time I returned to Scotland.

Chapter 14.
Meeting June

Before leaving Australia, I telephoned June myself and she agreed to meet with me. She told me to ring again when I arrived in Scotland to arrange a time to visit. I phoned June on Sunday, the day after I arrived in Edinburgh, and she said she hadn't been well. She asked if I would call again on Wednesday. I got the feeling that June did not really want to meet with me. Perhaps she assumed that I wanted to quiz her about family history and she was too unwell to manage that. In a last-ditch effort to meet her, I decided to come clean. On the Wednesday morning I phoned again and told June, for the first time, that I was interested in speaking with her about John Templeton in connection with the Bible John murders. If I had expected any sign of surprise, I would have been mistaken. There was none. June did not ask how my interest in Bible John led me to her ex-husband. She simply agreed to meet me and gave me her address.

I found June to be welcoming and very generous with her time. After explaining a little about the process which had led me to her, I asked if she could tell me about John Templeton's early years - whether he had ever spoken about his birth parents. June said that he only ever mentioned his mother, a woman whom he believed was unmarried when he was born, a woman named Margaret. June told me that, while John didn't seem to be very sure about his parentage, he believed that his mother was born in Helensburgh, a seaside town. His father, he thought, was a butcher. June told me that Margaret worked for John's father, "and that was the connection there." She said, "That's all I know. That's all [John] knew as well."

I was puzzled by this account. I suspected that whoever spoke to John Templeton about his birth family had been referring to another family altogether. While they were correct in identifying John's connection to Helensburgh, they had somehow confused his birth family with that of John Templeton (1945-), one of the other two cohort members who may have been fostered at some point in their childhood. I only knew this because I had asked the private investigator to provide me with a copy of both men's birth certificates, so that I would be certain which one was which. John Templeton (1945-) was born in Aberdeen Northern District on the 11th November 1945. As mentioned earlier, his mother's name was Margaret and her father (not his) was a butcher named Walter Templeton who lived in Grantown-on-Spey.

It was clear from June's comments that John Templeton had not been given his birth certificate. When June first met him, he was completely unaware that his parents were Emma Dresser Johnston and William Templeton. June explained that it wasn't until she and John got married that he first saw his birth parents' names reproduced on his marriage certificate. At the time, he would also have learned that his parents were not married. As mentioned earlier, his mother had been working as a shorthand typist in Helensburgh just before his birth and his father was a munitions inspector, not a butcher. And yet when I spoke with June, it was clear that she had not corrected the earlier misinformation about John's parentage in her own mind. She had continued to believe that his mother's name was Margaret and that his father was a butcher. Perhaps she had not processed the new information because she saw it on her wedding day and John might not have spoken to her about his birth parents afterwards.

When John Templeton signed his marriage certificate, he would also have seen that the word "deceased" had been entered under William Templeton's name. But there was no such word written under his mother's name. Evidently, Emma Dresser Johnston was still alive. So, John must have known then, if he hadn't already been told, that he did not grow up with the Fransmans because his mother died when he was young. On the contrary, his mother had most probably taken him to the children's home. Of course, John Templeton would have known little, if anything, about Emma Johnston's situation or reasoning. And it appears that, even after learning her name, he made no attempt to contact her. He never sought to establish a relationship with her. June told me that she had not met Emma Johnston. What is more, she was certain that John had never tried to find her. According to June, for John "it was a case of well she didn't want me so I don't want to know her."

I asked June whether John ever spoke about a children's home. She said "No, he never did. He seemed to be in that family quite young because she wanted a wee baby, you know the Dutch people. She wanted a baby and they got him quite young as far as I know." And even into adulthood John retained his close connection with his adopted family. June said that, while she and John were courting, he was still living with the Fransmans. Indeed, she used to visit him at their house twice a week. And, after William died in May 1968, she and John continued to see Eliza.

When I asked June whether John considered the Fransmans to be particularly strict as parents, she immediately referred to their age. June said, "well, actually they were quite old when they got him so I think there was an age gap. There was a big age gap." As I understood it, June was intimating that there had been a generation gap between John and his foster parents and yes, she said, John considered them to be strict. I asked whether John's strict upbringing might also have been due to the Fransmans religious beliefs but June indicated that it was not. When I asked her whether John's foster parents had been very religious, she replied, "No, they seemed to be just Protestant. I never saw any other reference, same with John." So, it would seem, that neither the Fransmans nor John were particularly devout.

***

June told me that she first met John Templeton in 1967. She said, "we met at a dancehall" and then she went quiet, trying to remember the name of the ballroom. I asked her if it had been the Barrowland and she was insistent, "Not Barrowland. No, never. It was called Majestic and that's where we met". In the late 1960s, the Majestic was considered more upmarket than the Barrowland Ballroom and June's comment, "Not Barrowland. No never" suggests that she was well aware of the different status of the dancehalls and didn't want to be thought of as Barrowland clientele.[467] Nor did John. He was definitely no Barrowland regular.

In reference to their early days at the Majestic, June said "we had great fun." But she followed this statement with, "the only thing that goes wrong is when you get married. I become his mother." When I asked June what she meant by becoming John's mother, she explained:

Well, he couldn't seem to do anything constructive. He didn't want to sort of look towards the future – you know, let's save, let's get money in the bank, let's do this and that. He would save and stick it in a little box under the bed and I said to him, what in the name of God is wrong with you? Put it in a bank – joint account. Mind you, when we divorced, he was quick enough to empty the joint account. He wasn't handy with anything, you know. Anything that had to be done, I had to do. So, you ended up kind of like his mum.

The fact that John Templeton kept his money in a box under the bed struck me as being particularly odd and clearly, at the time, it struck June that way too. At first, it occurred to me that John may have kept his income under the bed, rather than put it into a joint account, in order to control access to it. Unless, June was prepared to raid the box under the bed, his wages were stored as his money and his alone.

Then I wondered whether something even more disturbing could have been going on. While it is purely speculative, I couldn't help thinking that the box might also have contained the meagre sums taken from Bible John's victims – indistinguishable to anyone else as they would have been. We know that Bible John used some of the ten shillings that would have been in Helen Puttock's red purse to pay for his bus fare, but what happened to the rest of her money? And the killer also stole from Patricia Docker and Jemima MacDonald – taking, among other things, their handbags. Presumably these handbags contained the women's purses. When Patricia Docker's handbag was retrieved from the water cart, detectives never said whether her purse, or the money that should have been inside it, was also retrieved. And Jemima MacDonald's handbag was never found, which means that any money she had in her purse on the night she was murdered also disappeared. If the missing money, no matter how small the amounts, had been stored in the box beneath John Templeton's bed, it would have served as a readily accessible trophy, an enduring reminder of each of the three murders.

It would have been difficult for the killer to keep any other trophies from the murders. While Bible John had stolen all of Patricia Docker's clothing, Jemima MacDonald's handbag and Helen Puttock's red purse, it would have been very risky for him to take any of these possessions home. Unlike the money, these items would have been difficult to conceal and virtually impossible to explain. Indeed, given the press coverage, the items would have been easily identifiable.

In what was probably a more direct question than any which preceded it, I asked June whether she ever found anything in the Melrose Gardens apartment which might have belonged to another woman. She responded, quite vehemently, "No. I would have kicked up merry hell because that's the kind of woman I am." Then she reiterated that she had found "nothing at all".

***

June told me that John did not smoke cigarettes and, when I asked her whether he drank alcohol, she replied, "No, not much at all. It would go through him pretty quick if he mixed a beer with a spirit … he couldn't hold it. He couldn't drink a lot." So, while John Templeton was not a teetotaller, it was clear that he rarely drank.

During our conversation, I also asked June whether John ever mistreated her and she replied, "Oh no, never in the least. He'd have got thumped." June explained that, even when John was angry, he was not vicious. In arguments, he would grimace but he always remained polite. Very occasionally, if he was particularly angry, he would swear – something which he almost never did. I asked June whether John's treatment of her changed as their marriage broke down. She replied, "He just accepted it," and added, "I stayed with my grandmother for eighteen months before the divorce." I later puzzled over this response. Clearly, John Templeton had not flown into a rage when he recognised June's adultery. Perhaps, instead, he dealt with her rejection in much the same way as he had done when he found out who his birth mother was - as a case of well she doesn't want me so I don't want her.

I had earlier noticed that, in the divorce papers, John Templeton's lawyer said he lived "most of his life" in Scotland and so I asked June whether John had ever lived anywhere else. She replied, "No, as far as I know. He didn't even like to go on holiday." I then turned my attention to the couple's honeymoon. I knew that the location and timing of their honeymoon was especially important because Jemima MacDonald had been murdered on the 16th August 1969, just two weeks after John and June were married. I asked June where they went on their honeymoon. She replied, "I can't remember where we did … I cannae remember a thing about it. We were moving into the flat so I don't think we probably went very far and it would have been just local so we could keep on with what we were doing with the house." I double-checked. "So, you didn't go away for a long time?" "No, no."

June said that she and John went to Spain some time afterwards but John "didn't like that at all" so they didn't go away much after that. June explained that, after their trip to Spain, they only holidayed locally up north. She told me that, after they married, John wanted to stay home most of the time. They rarely went out together to socialise and have fun as they had done in the days when they were courting. June understood this to be just one expression of a much larger problem for them. To her, John seemed content with his lot. He was satisfied staying at home in their Melrose Gardens apartment. He didn't strive for more.

Looking back on their time together, June said of John, "He was a nice lad. He was good natured but we had to move on. I met someone else and we were married for forty-five years." Indeed, her husband had only recently passed away. June explained that, while he was never good looking, as she believed John most certainly was, her husband was a "go-getter". She felt that John, on the other hand, had no ambition and she explained that it was his lack of drive which was foremost in her mind when she left him. June said, "I had to have a future. He didn't want to move on. He was quite happy when he was settled and it wasn't enough. It was tenements off Maryhill." Keen to provide examples of John's lack of ambition, June described how he was once approached by Glasgow University to do some overtime, making composites for the answers to their examination papers but, despite being offered a significant sum of money, he said "no, thanks". Nor would he agree to work any night shifts, June said, despite the fact that compositors could earn twice as much for these shifts. It seemed to June that John had accepted his social position and wasn't at all interested in trying to advance any further. "And yet", June said, "he was clever and he liked to be the gentleman all the time".

I didn't get the chance to ask June what she meant by the phrase "he liked to be the gentleman all the time" because she went straight on with an example. She said, "you know, like he preferred his cricket and his rugby rather than football or anything like that kind of thing." Her comment immediately reminded me of the killer's "derisory conversation about different classes of people" in relation to football. It was also consistent with Wilson and Harrison's suggestion that, "in a city where football dominated working class culture, [Bible John] couldn't be bothered with either Rangers or Celtic".[468] He had made it very clear that he preferred middle-class pastimes and, according to June, so did her ex-husband.

When I asked June about John's use of language, she immediately said that he was "very well spoken" and she considered him to be, "very careful with his speech. Very polite." I followed up by asking about John's manners. June told me that he had very good manners. She said that he would always open the door for her and he would gather her things and pass them to her. June reiterated that he didn't swear and then she recalled one occasion when John had visited her while she was still living at her parents' house. June said, "It's funny because one night he came in and my mother laughed, looking around, and she said your dad said he doesn't know whether he wants to be the king of the castle or the butler or either the way he talks. He was using Mr and Mrs S.... and all this kind of thing." I asked whether John's speech and behaviour were the same whether he was in private or in public and June replied that both were the same. John, she said, was "always polite". Indeed, she met him one day, after the divorce had been finalised, and, even then, he was polite to her.

***

At the time of the Bible John murders, detectives repeatedly appealed to the public for assistance. After the murder of Helen Puttock, they encouraged the press to circulate images of the suspect, continually asking "Do you know this man?" When the leads dried up, detectives became convinced that someone was shielding the killer. D.C.S. Dalglish told the press: "I would go so far as to say there is a possibility that someone, somewhere, for reason of loyalty, or desire for non-involvement, may be shielding this man."[469] In the *Evening Times*, John Quinn titled his article "Don't shield killer, pleads C.I.D. chief".[470] And, in her later years at least, Jeannie also came to believe that someone had sheltered her sister's killer. In an interview with Magnus Linklater in 1994, Jeannie reasoned, "he must have been scratched by those long nails of Helen's. He must have been well marked, that's why I know somebody's covering for him."[471]

But there was not necessarily someone covering for Bible John – a wife that realised her husband was the killer and refused to say. I imagine it would have been very difficult for June to suspect that the killer she kept hearing about was the man she had married. When I admitted to June that I believed John Templeton and Bible John were possibly one and the same man, she looked concerned and said, "Oh, because we'd have been married by then." I took the opportunity to ask her directly whether she ever considered that John might have been the killer. She replied, "Oh no, no, never. I mean he would go out and then go out with his friends but not often. Not often. He'd say go a wee walk. Oh, now that's another thing, go a walk. But it's all hazy now, a long time ago." Then, in a later telephone conversation,

June told me that John often went for long walks alone at night. I asked her what he wore on those occasions and she said, trousers. Predictably, he had not gone out walking at night dressed in a suit.

And what of the few times, early on in their marriage, when John went out with his friends? June considered that these friends were polite and nice and she said they shared John's interest in rugby. But June hadn't wanted to go out with them so she stayed at home on those nights. As she said, it wasn't often, but in the very early years of their marriage she and John still went out occasionally and there was only so much socialising she wanted to do. So, on the few nights that John went out to meet his friends, he went out alone. I asked June what John wore on those particular nights and she replied, "Oh, a nice suit and an overcoat in winter". I couldn't help recalling that Bible John had been well-dressed in a good-quality suit on the night he murdered Jemima MacDonald but none of the witnesses mentioned him wearing an overcoat. That was in August, in Scotland's summer. The killer had worn a "nice suit" and a coat, made from either tweed or gabardine, some six weeks later, at the end of October, when he murdered Helen Puttock.

I asked June where John purchased his suits and she told me that he didn't purchase them. She organised John's suits for him. She would buy good-quality fabric and take it to various tailors who worked in shops which no longer exist. Perhaps the fact that it was June rather than John who organised the suits, together with her reliance on a number of tailors rather than a regular one, explains why none of the 240 tailors interviewed by police, ever connected John Templeton with the descriptions of Bible John's suits. But, according to June, John's suits were both good quality and tailor-made.

They would have been well-fitted and there would have been no turn-ups on the trousers.

***

But what about all the other people who knew John Templeton? Did anyone have an inkling that he may have been Bible John? Joe Beattie was once asked by a reporter about the type of man he thought the killer might be. Beattie replied that he thought the killer was likely a loner who "possibly occupies some place in society where he has a little authority."[472] But, when he was pressed about the possibility that such "a superficially clean-cut and socially upstanding figure", must have at least some social contacts, Beattie replied: "Yes, he does have social contacts. They are aware of him but, unfortunately, they are eliminating him in their mind because of this clean-cutness that you speak of."[473] Even Jeannie had found it difficult at first to believe that the man she met at the Barrowland that night could have been a killer. When she learned of Helen's murder, she thought that perhaps George had killed her. She said in her interview with Audrey Gillan, "I mean I didn't even get the impression that John could do a thing like that. He just didnae look the type."[474]

And perhaps this focus on Bible John's clean-cutness had far reaching consequences. June told me that the police "did know the Templeton name". In fact, two plain-clothes detectives had arrived at the couple's Melrose Gardens apartment looking for John some six months or so after Bible John murdered Helen Puttock. June remembered that she was outside hanging up washing at the time. The detectives asked her if she lived with a man named John Templeton, explaining that they

222

wanted to speak with him. June took them inside and the detectives indicated that they wished to speak with her husband alone so June went into another room. She certainly knew that the detectives were interviewing John in relation to the Bible John murders. June understood that the police were interested in her husband for two reasons – firstly because they attributed significance of the name John Templeton and secondly because he had lived for some time in the Scotstoun area but had relocated before Helen Puttock's murder. In June's words, John and his foster family "lived in the area of Scotstoun which was quite near where that woman or some of the girls were murdered ... but then, when we got married, we moved to Maryhill which meant anyone in the district who wasn't there any more they were keeping an eye on and that's how they followed him sort of through to where we lived."

I asked June how John responded when the detectives arrived and she half-laughed and said, "actually they talked about cricket". June explained that, "they talked away for quite some time" and then she overheard them all laughing and talking about cricket. June was certain that neither of the detectives who came to their apartment that day was Joe Beattie. They were both young and it appears that John Templeton had charmed them with his middle-class banter. They no doubt found him to be friendly, even charismatic. June told me that, after their visit, "they never seen him again". I asked her whether the police ever took John in for an identity parade. She replied, "No, never anything like that."

It appears that Jeannie had been right. The police never had her sister's killer in a line-up. In her interview with Audrey Gillan, Jeannie said:

I think he slipped through the net and the reason he slipped through the net is because somebody, some police, some detective, has actually gone and interviewed him and they've said no theirselves. I mean there must be a lot that they've seen and I've not seen.[475]

So, although Joe Beattie paid some heed to the name John Templeton, it was not enough. He certainly wasn't convinced that the killer had given his real name that night in the Barrowland and he clearly didn't recognise the significance of the Melrose Gardens address. If he had, he would likely have gone to the apartment himself. Perhaps he would even have asked Jeannie to take a look at John Templeton. Instead, he sent two young detectives to question him and they appear to have fallen for the clean-cutness that Beattie himself acknowledged.

At the same time, it must have given John Templeton a terrible shock to realise that the police investigation had come so close – that detectives had noted his name and were aware of his former and current address. As mentioned earlier, in *The Lost British Serial Killer*, David Wilson and Paul Harrison argue that Bible John probably stopped killing (or became a commuter killer) after he "realised that he gave away far too much during the taxi ride with Jeannie and Helen."[476] Perhaps the realisation that the information he gave away had led detectives to his doorstep, frightened him just enough to put an end to the murders.

***

I couldn't help feeling that, after meeting June, after all the questions and responses, I had been unable to move much beyond her conviction that John Templeton was a nice lad with a good nature. And yet I was even more convinced that John Templeton was Bible John. There had never been a time in our conversation when June said anything which might indicate otherwise. She had not provided John with an alibi for any of the murders nor had she described any behaviours which contradicted those attributed to the killer. She had not even expressed any incredulity or disbelief given my suspicion that her ex-husband was a serial killer. Indeed, everything that June told me was consistent with what we know about Bible John.

Of course, there were the obvious parallels in Jeannie and June's descriptions of various behaviours. In June's own words, John Templeton was "very well spoken" and "liked to be the gentleman all the time". He didn't smoke, rarely swore and hardly ever drank alcohol. In a later telephone conversation, June described John as "very mannerly" and she immediately reiterated that "he liked the cricket and the rugby, not the football." What is more, in all of June's observations, and in her very phrasing of them, you can hear Jeannie's description of her sister's killer.

Moreover, June offered a few examples of John Templeton's behaviour which give us a closer look at the similarities. For instance, Jeannie told police that she and Helen had "excitedly laughed" at Bible John's display of manners – the fact that he pulled out Helen's chair whenever she returned to the table and stood up when the women went to the toilet. Jeannie later said that she and Helen had laughed because it wasn't the sort of thing that happened to them or the kind of behaviour they were used to. In other words, Bible John had made a show of manners which didn't really fit the social situation, so much so that it was comical. Then, when I asked June about John Templeton's manners, she recalled an occasion which resembled the sisters' experience in the Barrowland. June's mother had quite literally laughed at John's display of manners. When John Templeton visited June's parents at their house, he addressed them with a formality they found unwarranted, even inappropriate. Indeed, his speech led June's father to conclude that John didn't know whether he wanted to be the king of the castle or the butler. At a guess, John Templeton wanted to be the king of the castle. It's just that he used the role of the butler, the art of deference, to prove that he knew the rules of polite society. In other words, John Templeton, like Bible John, employed manners which were incongruous in working-class circles as a tool with which to demonstrate his now middle-class status.

Jeannie had also described the way Bible John expressed his anger over the faulty cigarette machine. She told Paul Harrison: "He wasn't outraged or shouting, he was collected and calm but very assertive. It was like a schoolteacher speaks to a young child, he was giving the manager a real dressing down without losing his temper."[477] This sounds very much like the man that June described when I asked her how John behaved when he was angry. In an argument, June had said, John might grimace but he would always remain polite. Indeed, June repeatedly insisted that John was "always polite". Even when she met him after the divorce, he was polite.

Before I left, I asked June whether John ever mentioned wanting to have children. "No, he didn't want children", she said. There had been no hesitation. Her response was emphatic. I asked her whether he had given any reason for not wanting to have children and she said, "he was always on about I don't like the look of my face and my nose. I wouldn't like a kid to have a big nose. He didn't have a big nose. I don't know where he got this from … There was nothing wrong with his nose." Clearly, June had struggled to make sense of John's excuse because she considered him to be not only good-looking but also very good with children. Still, if June ever pressed him for a more convincing excuse and received an answer, she never told me. She simply repeated that John certainly didn't want to have children of his own. Perhaps it never occurred to June that what John was really trying to say was, I don't want to have children because they might grow up, not to *look* like me, but to *be* like me.

Chapter 15.
Unmasked

Although I was convinced by this time that John Templeton (1945-2015) was Bible John, I still didn't know what he looked like. All I knew was that, at the time of the murders, he had sandy-coloured hair and was about 5'10" tall. I wasn't too worried about June's description of his eyes as hazel rather than blue-grey. They were clearly light in colour. But I knew I needed more to go on. As I was preparing to leave, June handed me a black and white photograph of herself and her then date, John Templeton. The photograph had been taken at the Copeland and Lye's Staff Dance at the Plaza in 1967, the year before the Bible John murders began. The place and date were recorded on the back of the photograph.

When you examine this photograph alongside George Lennox-Paterson's portrait of Bible John, it is not difficult to see how effective Jeannie had been in conveying her recollections. The portrait was, as Lennox Paterson said of his earlier sketch, essentially "[his] idea of her idea of his face."[478] Yet despite this necessary mediation, the elements of the portrait bear an uncanny resemblance to those of the 1967 photograph of John Templeton. For instance, the photograph shows his hair as thick, cut short and very neat. It was not thinning or receding but draped across his forehead, very much as the killer's hair is depicted in the images we have of Bible John. There is only one marked point of difference when you compare John Templeton's hair to these images of Bible John - the photograph shows his hair as parted on the right and swept to the left while Bible John's hair was parted on the left and swept to the right.

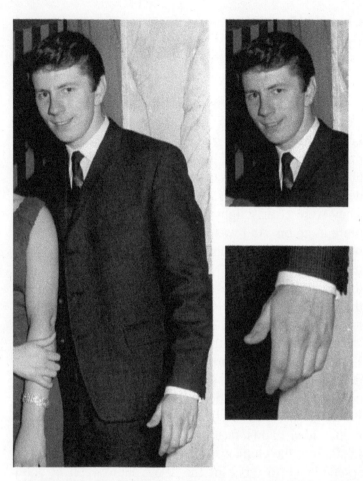

Photograph gifted by June and annotated on the back – "June and John, Plaza – Copeland's Staff Dance – 1967". Close-up of John Templeton's face and one of his well-manicured hand.

It is also clear from the photograph that John Templeton's jawline, the length of his chin, the distance between his mouth and the tip of his nose and the length of his nose are all comparable to Lennox Paterson's portrait of Bible John. The proportions are roughly the same. What is more, the size and positioning of John Templeton's ears and the shape of his face resemble those depicted in Lennox Paterson's portrait.

John Templeton's left hand is visible in the photograph and, as Jeannie said of the killer's hands, it looks pristine. As mentioned earlier, Jeannie told Paul Harrison that the Bible John's "fingernails were well cared for, almost as if they had been manicured, and his hands weren't grubby or cut, they looked clean and well presented."[479] They were not coarse and strong like the hands of a manual labourer. John Templeton's left hand certainly fits Jeannie's description. But perhaps this is not surprising, given that he worked as a compositor. He was engaged in light work, not heavy labour, and he worked indoors so his hands were not weathered. Nor incidentally was his skin. In the photograph, John Templeton appears to have the "milk and roses" complexion that Jeannie described.

***

When Jeannie was first interviewed after her sister's murder, she was very specific in her description of Bible John's teeth. And, as Paula Murray writes in her 2021 article for the *Scottish Daily Express*, "The dental clue was seen as vital by Detective Superintendent Joe Beattie". [480] As noted earlier, Beattie even had a replica of the suspect's teeth made up.

Recently, forensic artist Melissa Dring Little has been working on a new sketch of Bible John. When she was interviewed in *The Hunt for Bible John*, Dring Little explained: "What I'm trying to do is make a copy of [Lennox Patterson's] drawing but open the mouth to depict these teeth."

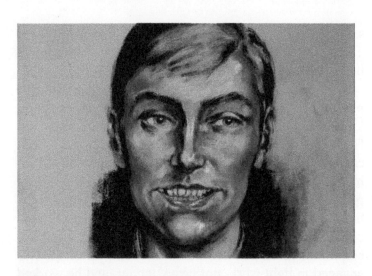

Melissa Dring Little's sketch published in the *Scottish Daily Express*, 20th November 2021.

Although I accept the importance of including all aspects of the witnesses' description in the sketch, the inclusion of the suspect's teeth in this instance dominates the drawing. It looks as though he has a mouth full of crooked teeth. Indeed, the word "crooked" has snuck into descriptions of Bible John's teeth over recent years – so much so that it's been included in a number of newspaper headlines – such as the *Scottish Daily Express* title, "New sketch of serial killer Bible John's crooked teeth revealed in BBC documentary" and the *Daily News* title "New sketch of killer: Bible John's 'crooked teeth' shown in fresh BBC documentary". But Jeannie never once used the word crooked in her description of the killer's teeth. Nor was it true to her recollection.

On the contrary, newspaper reports which immediately followed Helen Puttock's murder, reported Jeannie's description of Bible John's teeth as *nice and straight*, with the exception of one front tooth overlapping another.[481] For example, on the 3rd November, the *Evening Times* described Bible John as having "good straight teeth, with one tooth on the right upper side overlapping the next tooth."[482] On the 4th November 1969, the *Daily Record* suggested that he had "nice strait teeth. But one tooth on the right upper overlaps the next."[483] The same day, the *Scottish Daily Express* claimed the killer had "nice straight teeth, with one tooth on the right, upper, overlapping another tooth" and the *Glasgow Herald* described him as having "nice straight teeth with one tooth on the upper jaw overlapping the next tooth".[484] As mentioned earlier, Jeannie told Charles Stoddart that, when she was standing next to Bible John in the Barrowland, "her height brought her only to the point where her eyes were level with his mouth, and she saw that he had two front teeth which *overlapped very slightly*."[485]

Fortunately, some original footage of an interview with Joe Beattie has been included in the documentary *The Hunt for Bible John* and this footage includes images of the replica teeth which Beattie had made up at the Glasgow Dental Hospital.[486] During the interview, Beattie takes the replica teeth out of his desk drawer and rotates them in front of the camera. The images below have been reproduced from this footage.

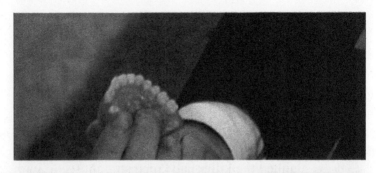

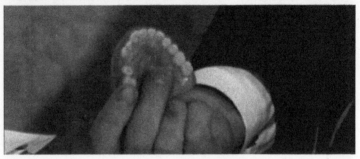

Original footage included in the BBC documentary *The Hunt for Bible John*, screened in 2021.

These images show what Jeannie intended them to show, relatively straight upper teeth with the exception of one front tooth overlapping the other. The images indicate some overcrowding in the front and a definite, although not dramatic, overlap of the right front tooth over the left. Any crossover between the teeth appears to be close to the lower edge or tip of the teeth – which is consistent with Jeannie's suggestion that the overlap was only slight.

So how does this compare with the 1967 photograph of John Templeton? It seems from the photograph that John Templeton had nice straight teeth. Unfortunately, it is difficult to determine whether he had one front tooth slightly overlapping the other. His smile is simply not full enough to reveal the lower edge of his upper teeth. In June 2022, I had the original photograph scanned using a high-resolution scanner in order to produce a close-up image of John Templeton's teeth. I took this image, together with the original photograph, to the Principal Dentist at Kings Dental, Dr Jeremy Keating. After studying both the photograph and the close-up, Dr Keating suggested that there appeared to be some crowding involving the two central incisors and the adjoining lateral incisors, but there was insufficient evidence to ascertain whether this overcrowding involved a slight overlap of any teeth. While there might have been such an overlap, Dr Keating said, he couldn't be certain because John Templeton's lower lip was concealing the lower edge of his upper teeth.

However, Dr Keating noticed that the left central incisor looked slightly wider than the right. On his suggestion, I asked one of my tech-savvy friends to use Photoshop to compare the width of the central incisors at the point closest to the lower lip. While this gave us only a rough approximation, it appears that Dr Keating was correct. In the photograph, the left central incisor is a little wider than the right. But, again, Dr Keating was careful not to read too much into this. He suggested that the difference might be due either to the fact that the photograph was not taken perpendicular to the front teeth or to a slight overlap, with the left tooth appearing to be wider because it was slightly overlapping the right.

If there was such an overlap, Dr Keating suggested, it would have been only slight.

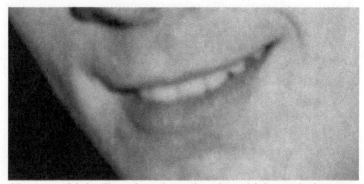

Close-up of John Templeton's teeth, using a high-resolution scan from the original photograph.

In *Bible John: Search for a Sadist*, Charles Stoddart claims that Jeannie told detectives that her sister's killer had a tooth missing and this is clearly shown in the replica that Joe Beattie requested. According to Jeannie, the missing tooth was, "on the right-hand side, a tooth which in dental terms would be described as a number four or five." [487].

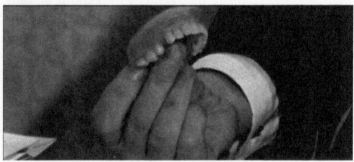

Original footage included in the BBC documentary *The Hunt for Bible John*, screened in 2021.

When I showed Dr Jeremy Keating the close-up of John Templeton's teeth, he said: "It looks like he's missing his, what we'd call, tooth 2,4." Dr Keating explained that the first of these digits refers to the corner of the mouth and the second refers to the tooth number counting from the centre out. So, 2, 4 simply means the fourth tooth in corner 2, or, in lay terms, in the upper left. What Dr Keating saw was that John Templeton was missing a number four upper tooth, just as Bible John was.

But clearly, there is a problem with this. Although the 1967 photograph indicates that John Templeton was missing a tooth in the number position that Jeannie specified, it was missing from the upper left-hand side, not the upper right. The same problem was evident when Dr Keating suggested that John Templeton's left central incisor appeared a little wider than the right. If this had been due to any overlap, then it was John Templeton's left front tooth which overlapped the right, not the other way around as Jeannie had observed. And, of course, it is the same problem that we found with John Templeton's hair. According to the photograph, his hair was parted on the right and swept to the left, while all the images of Bible John indicate that the killer's hair was parted on the left and swept to the right.

While Dr Keating and I were looking at the photograph of John Templeton, he suggested that perhaps the negative had been reversed in the process of printing and that what we were looking at was in fact a reversed image. It made sense. I knew that, if Dr Keating was right, then John Templeton would have been missing a tooth in the precise position that Jeannie indicated – a number four tooth from the upper right-hand side. What is more, if there had been a slight overlap in John Templeton's two front incisors, it would have been the right tooth slightly overlapping the left, as Jeannie had suggested. And John Templeton's hair would have been parted on the left and swept to the right just like Bible John's.

There was no way to discern from the photograph alone whether it had been printed correctly or in reverse so I telephoned June. I asked her whether she was able to picture John in her mind's eye, not as she had seen him in the photograph, but as though he was standing in front of her. Then I asked her whether she could tell me on which side his hair was parted. June replied: "Hmm, it wasn't much of a parting. Wait a minute. Wait a minute. If I'm looking at him, it would be his left-hand side." I wanted to be certain, so I restated her answer, "parted on the left and swept towards the right?" "Yes," she said. I told June that I was asking her about the part in John's hair because I thought the photograph that she had given me might have been printed from the negative in reverse. She said, "Yes, that's true," but, unfortunately, she no longer had the negative.

While June and I were still on the phone, I asked whether she could remember the name or location of John's dentist. She replied: "No. I can honestly say I don't. I don't because I don't remember him going to the dentist." Again, I repeated her statement as a way of asking her to confirm it. "You don't remember him *ever* going to the dentist?" "No," she replied, "He had a nice set of teeth. He had a nice smile." So, at least in the years that June was married to John Templeton, he did not have a regular dentist. Indeed, he did not have a dentist at all. This means that there almost certainly had been no dental records anywhere in Glasgow for detectives to find. Clearly, John Templeton was not among the 5300 or so men who, Charles Stoddart claims, were "given a personal visit by the police" because dentists reported that their "particular tooth formation" resembled the description of Bible John's. And, of course, these 5300 men were all eliminated from the investigation.

***

The image below has been flipped from the original photograph in order to show what John Templeton actually looked like.

In an interview for the 2005 documentary "Unsolved", former Detective Superintendent Robert Johnstone reflected on Joe Beattie's leadership in the investigation of the Bible John murders. He said:

> It's a lonely job. You're on your own. Everybody in the public thinks you're wonderful if you clear the crime up, you're an idiot if you don't. But you do need the luck and I would say, thinking back to when Joe Beattie was working there almost twenty-four hours a day in fact seven days a week, he didn't get that lucky break that you really need.

Nevertheless, there can be no doubt that Joe Beattie came close in his hunt for Bible John. Afterall, detectives were sent, presumably on his instructions, to interview John Templeton. What is more, they were interested in him, not simply because of his name, but because he had once lived in Scotstoun, which they knew would explain his familiarity with the area, and because he no longer lived in Scotstoun, which would explain why he caught the night service bus as it travelled away from Scotstoun on the night he murdered Helen Puttock. Joe Beattie had clearly identified some of the most important of clues.

Yet it took him some six months after Helen Puttock's murder to investigate John Templeton (1945-2015). And, even then, he sent two young police officers to interview him rather than go himself. Had Joe Beattie been more convinced that the killer used his real name and had he concluded that the killer perhaps lived close to where he alighted the number 6 night-service bus, the outcome would almost certainly have been different, not only for Beattie and for the killer, but for all the people affected by the Bible John murders. Instead, Beattie appears to have been only routinely checking men with the name John Templeton, while remaining convinced that the killer moved from Scotstoun to Glasgow's southern suburbs or beyond. He continued to believe that Bible John alighted the bus at the Gray Street bus-stop in order to take the Govan Ferry across to the south-side of the River Clyde.

***

All the same, there can be no doubt that what retired Detective Superintendent Robert Johnstone said is true. You do need the luck. And, at certain junctures in my research, I had a good deal of luck. I was fortunate to find well-documented genealogical records for the McInnes family. Although these records weren't completely intact, there were enough entries in the database at Scotland's People and sufficient surviving headstones in the cemeteries of western Scotland to enable me to find the surname Templeton among the McInnes ancestors. It was only then that I realised the killer had likely used his real name when he introduced himself to Helen, Jeannie and Castlemilk John that night in the Barrowland Ballroom. It was only then that I recognised the connection between Bible John's moralistic behaviours and the compulsive honesty of his conversation.

And I was lucky too to find that John Templeton (1945-2015) had been fostered by a family who lived near the Scotstoun House Children's Home. If the Fransmans had lived further afield, then John Templeton might not have attended Bankhead Primary School and I may not have found him in the primary school records. It was the Bankhead Admission Registers which unlocked a trail of information concerning John Templeton's early life with his foster family.

But perhaps most of all, I was lucky that John Templeton's ex-wife, June, was alive and well and that she was prepared to meet with me. In fact, her candid conversations have proved invaluable. What is more, the fact that June still possessed a photograph of John Templeton as a young man and was generous enough to give it to me is more than I could have hoped for. Thankfully, John Templeton was smiling in that photograph, revealing the gap where his number four, upper right tooth should have been.

If the police are prepared to accept that John Templeton (1945-2015) was, or at least may have been, Bible John, there is still much they could do. We know that John Templeton was cremated in 2015 and that his ashes were collected by someone rather than being scattered in the grounds of the Maryhill Crematorium. That person's name is likely included in the crematorium's records. Perhaps it was Margaret, the woman who signed John Templeton's death certificate as his partner. And what became of John Templeton's possessions? He died unexpectedly. Someone must have packed up his belongings and cleaned his flat. That person might have retained some of his possessions as keepsakes – maybe a watch or an item of clothing. There is even an outside chance that John Templeton hid his box of coins somewhere in the apartment when June insisted that he start using a joint bank account. Perhaps the coins are still there.

I asked Dr Stuart Boyer, the molecular biologist who earlier explained DNA transmission to me, whether any of these items might still yield some DNA, given the passage of time. Dr Boyer believed that it is certainly possible. But if nothing can be found, no keepsakes or coins, there is the chance that police can approach a living relative for a DNA sample. True John Templeton did not have siblings, but he had other relatives.

***

Of course, discovering the identity of Bible John was only ever part of the puzzle for me. I still want to know why John Templeton did what he did. I looked back over the books that I read about the Bible John murders and realised that most of them did not offer any explanation for the murders. Only David Wilson and Paul Harrison discussed the killer's possible motivation. In *The Lost British Serial Killer,* they conclude: "we can say with certainty that he hated women ..."[488] The murders of Patricia Docker, Jemima MacDonald and Helen Puttock were all extraordinarily vicious. John Templeton beat and kicked the women repeatedly about the head and body, then raped and strangled them at close quarters. As Joe Beattie recognised, the killer "decided on his victim, got her confidence and then murdered her. It was sadism," Beattie concluded, "of the clearest kind."[489]

But Beattie's phrase "decided on a victim" raises the issue of why Bible John chose Patricia Docker, Jemima MacDonald and Helen Puttock. He didn't know any of these women and yet he was determined to kill them. These women were not murdered at random. John Templeton targeted young mothers who had been dancing at a venue that he believed was a "den of iniquity"; a venue filled with women whom he considered to be adulterous mothers. And we know that this was almost certainly what preoccupied his mind in the moments just before the murders. Afterall, we were privy to his conversation in the taxi as he worked himself up for the kill that night. So, what did he talk about above

243

all else as he prepared to express his hatred, to vent his rage? On the night he murdered Helen Puttock, there were two recurring themes - his belief that adulterous women deserved to die and his preoccupation with the fostering of children.

John Templeton had murdered Patricia Docker some six months before he saw Emma Dresser Johnston's name on his marriage certificate. Until then, he believed his mother was a single woman named Margaret. But both women were unmarried when they gave birth to their son and, although John Templeton did not know his mother's name when he selected his first victim, he was aware that she had chosen not to keep him. She had given him up for foster care. We cannot know what the Fransmans told John Templeton about his birth parents and, in particular, his mother. They clearly had not given him his birth certificate nor told him his mother's name but they might none the less have spoken of her as an immoral or even "adulterous" woman (a term which they might have used if they believed William Templeton was married at the time Emma Johnston conceived). Still, we have no evidence of this. Any assumption that his mother was immoral or adulterous might have been John Templeton's and his alone.

We know little regarding how John Templeton felt about being a foster child. June provided our only clue when she said that, for John, "it was a case of well [my mother] didn't want me so I don't want to know her." And, although June didn't believe that John was the type of man who held a grudge, there can be no doubt that he believed he had been rejected as an infant, abandoned by his mother. It might be that June was mistaken and that John Templeton had been nursing a very deep grudge. Of course, he did not kill Patricia Docker, Jemima MacDonald and Helen Puttock because he believed he was abandoned by his presumably adulterous young mother. While this belief might have directed his rage, helped him to select his victims, he decided to rape, brutalise and murder three women because he wanted to. Joe Beattie was right, "It was sadism ... of the clearest kind." [490]

***

But there may have been even more at play in the Bible John murders – and I do mean *at play*. When I asked June about John Templeton's use of language, she said that he liked to play word games. As an example, she cited his nickname for her - "Tricky." According to June, John had derived this nickname by playing with the letters that were on her car's license plate. And I remembered June saying that John "was very careful with his speech." I wondered then, how far his word games went. Clearly, John Templeton was very literate. His occupation ensured this. So, if he had been asked what he did on Hogmanay and his response was that he didn't drink, he prayed – would this have been "prayed" or "preyed"? David Wilson and Paul Harrison raise the possibility that Bible John might have been "making a joke for himself, a play on words" with his response [491]

As mentioned earlier, David Wilson and Paul Harrison also suggested that Bible John used his time in the taxi to deliberately mislead Jeannie because he realised that she was going to be a key witness in the forthcoming police investigation. To this end, they argue, Bible John salted his conversation with lies. Although I don't believe for one moment that the killer lied in order to mislead Jeannie, I do accept that he might have been deliberately salting his conversation during the taxi ride. His biblical references and religious terminology, suggest that he might have been constructing his own narrative. It is almost as though John Templeton was deliberately creating a character, something akin to a Scottish Jack the Ripper - a killer who was engaged in a moral quest to rid the world of adulterous women. And, with the help of the moniker "Bible John," he was successful in creating this character. The spectre of Bible John has endured for decades, haunting Glasgow even after John Templeton's death.

Indeed, if John Templeton was intent on leaving an enduring legacy, he knew it was imperative that he not get caught. Afterall, the legend of Jack the Ripper has lived on in the public consciousness largely because he was never identified. Given that two plain-clothes detectives arrived on the doorstep of his Melrose Gardens apartment, John Templeton likely recognised how close he had come to being discovered and there was simply too much at stake for him to murder any more of Glasgow's young mothers. He knew that, if he was identified as Bible John, he would lose not only the social respectability he had acquired through his profession but, even more importantly perhaps, he would leave no legacy. There would be no Glaswegian bogeyman to survive the ages. Unmasked, his character would die a mortal death.

References

Primary Sources:

<u>Cemeteries and Associated Websites</u>:

Headstones from many of the cemeteries of Western Scotland.
Find a Grave UK
Deceased Online

<u>Children's Home and Scotstoun House Children's Home Site Records</u>:

"Children's Homes and Institutions in Ayrshire, Scotland", www.childrenshomes.org.uk.

"Children's Homes and Institutions in Lanarkshire, Scotland", www.childrenshomes.org.uk.

"Children's Homes: Glasgow Burgh Council Homes", www.children'shomes.org.uk.

"Glasgow, Castlemilk House: Archaeology Notes", CANMORE: National Record of the Historic Environment, www.canmore.org.uk, accessed 25th March 2021.

'Glasgow, Scotstoun House', Site Number NS56NW 105, NGR NS 5264 6805, Ordnance Survey license number 100057073, http://canmore.org.uk/site/160389, copyright and database right 2020, accessed 9th July 2020.

"30 Kingsway Court", Emporis, www.emporis.com, accessed 7th September 2021.

"Peter Atkinson: Kingsway Court, Glasgow, Scotland", www.flikr.com, accessed 7th September 2021.
'Scotstoun House', www.kilmeny.vispa.com, accessed 9th July 2020.

"Scotstoun House", Emporis, www.emporis.com, accessed 7th September 2021.

Court Records:

Divorce Court Records, Scotland, 1976-1977, 'Court of Sessions, Scotland: Divorce Case Papers', National Records of Scotland.

The State of Western Australia -v- Edwards [No 7] [2020] WASC 339.

Education Department Records:

"Bankhead Primary, Boys and Girls, 1941-1944", School Admission Registers, SR10/3/548/2/1, Glasgow City Archives, Mitchell Library.

"Bankhead Primary, Boys and Girls, 1944-1951", School Admission Registers, SR10/3/548/2/2, Glasgow City Archives, Mitchell Library.

"Bankhead School: Mitchell Library, Glasgow Collection, Postcards Collection", www.theglasgowstory.com.

"Scotstoun Primary, Boys and Girls, 1938-1942", School Admission Registers, D-ED7/276/2/4, Glasgow City Archives, Mitchell Library.

"Scotstoun Primary, Boys and Girls, 1942-1945", School Admission Registers, D-ED7/276/2/5, Glasgow City Archives, Mitchell Library.

"Scotstoun Primary, Boys, 1934-1938", School Admission Registers, D-ED7/276/3/1, Glasgow City Archives, Mitchell Library.

"Scotstoun Primary, Boys, 1945-1954", School Admission Registers, D-ED7/276/3/2, Glasgow City Archives, Mitchell Library.

"Victoria Drive Secondary School Register", SR10/3/940/4/8, Glasgow City Archives, Mitchell Library.

Electoral Registers:

Register of Electors, Glasgow Wards 13-20, 1970-1973, Mitchell Library.

Electoral Registers held by Ancestry.com –

Glasgow, Lanarkshire, Scotland, Electoral Registers, 1857-1962.

London, England, Electoral Registers, 1832-1965.

North Lanarkshire, Scotland, Electoral Registers, 1847-1969.

UK, Electoral Registers, 2003-2010.

Genealogy Websites and Databases:

Ancestry
Family Search
Genes Reunited
Geni
Glasgow Family History
Lewis, Penny L.A. and Smith. Fergus, "Old Scottish Genealogy & Family History", www.OldScottish.com
My Heritage
Rootschat

Government Websites and Forums:

"Glasgow Guide Discussion Boards", 13th February 2011-11th December 2015, www.discuss.glasgowguide.co.uk, accessed 28th September 2020.

Office for National Statistics, "New Earnings Survey (NES) timeseries of Gross Weekly earnings from 1938 to 2017", www.ons.gov.uk, accessed 17th October 2021.

"Scottish Mining Website: Index to deaths in Scotland 1950 to 1954", www.scottishmining.co.uk

Military Records:

"Australian Imperial Force – Nominal Roll", www.S3-ap-southeast-2.amazonaws.com, accessed 28th July 2021.

"Fransman William: SERN 2362: POB Amsterdam Holland: POE Liverpool NSW: NOK W Fransman Mrs W", series no. B2455,

Records authority class no. 3891, National Archives of Australia, www.recordsearch.naa.gov.au.

The National Archives, catalogue description "Records of the Military Recruitment Department, 1939-1960", www.discovery.nationalarchives.gov.uk, accessed 16th May 2021.

National Army Museum, www.nam.ac.uk, accessed 4th October 2021.

Home Guard Officer Lists 1939-45", www.forces-war-records.co.uk,accessed 5th November 2021.

Home Guard List 1941: Scottish Command, Savannah Paperback Classics publication of original material held in the Imperial War Museum.

Newspapers and Magazines:

Ardrossan and Saltcoats Herald
Ayrshire Journal
Daily Record
Evening Times
Glasgow Herald
Guardian
Herald Scotland
Independent
Observer
Scotsman
Scottish Daily Express
Sunday Herald
Telegraph

Nursing Records:

"General Nursing Council for Scotland", UK and Ireland, Nursing Registers, 1898-1968", entries for 1960, 1962, 1963, 1965, 1966 and 1968, accessed through Ancestry.com.

"Central Midwives Board of Scotland", UK and Ireland, Nursing Registers, 1898-1968", entries for 1960, 1963, 1966 and 1968, accessed through Ancestry.com.

Printing Archival Records:

The Scottish Printing Archival Trust, "Records, preserves & shares Scotland's printing heritage: Society of Master Printers of Scotland, 1973", www.scottishprintarchive.org, accessed 20th October 2021.

"Linotron 505", from *Linotype: The Film*, 1969, Mergenthaler Linotype Company, accessed on www.vimeo.com, 13th December 2021.

Recollections:

Murphy, Seamus, "My Castlemilk Home Experiences", Parts 1 and 2, available on Castlemilk History site, Facebook.com.

"WW2 People's War: An archive of World War Two memories – written by the public, gathered by the BBC: Blitz in Glasgow", www.bbc.co.uk, accessed 22nd May 2021.

Transportation Records:

City of Glasgow Corporation Transport, Official Time-Table: Motor-bus Underground Time-Table, Night Services, Fare Stages, Scale of Fares, New addition – July, 1969.

"Higher Fares for Glasgow?", Commercial Motor Archive, 22nd August 1969, www.archive.commercialmotor.com, accessed 22nd July 2021.

"British Public and National Rail Timetable List", www.railwaymuseum.org.uk, accessed 22nd July 2021.

"Glasgow Corporation Transport Bus Service Routes 1963", Glasgow Transport 1871-1973, www.semple.biz, accessed 23rd July 2021.

"Ferry Crossing (19th Century-20th Century), Canmore ID 178179, Site Number NS56NE2520, http://canmore.org.uk/site/178179, accessed 23rd July 2021.

Travel Records:

"UK and Ireland, Incoming Passenger Lists, 1878-1960", accessed through Ancestry.com.

"UK and Ireland, Outward Passenger Lists, 1890-1960", accessed through Ancestry.com.

UK BMD and other UK Govt. Records:

Scotland's People – birth, marriage, divorce and death records and censuses and at www.scotlandspeople.gov.uk

"100 Most Common Surnames, National Records of Scotland", www.nrscotland.gov.uk

Valuation Rolls, Scottish Post Office Directories and Phone Records:

Valuation Rolls 1855-1940 (available on Scotland's People).

Scottish Post Office Directories, Towns, Paisley, 1838-1854.

Scottish Post Office Directories, Towns, Glasgow, 1828-1912.

British Phone Books, 1952-1982.

www.192.com

Secondary Sources:

Reports:

Kendrick, Andrew and Hawthorn, Moyra, "National Confidential Forum for Adult Survivors of Childhood Abuse in Care: Scoping Project on Children in Care in Scotland, 1930-2005", CELCIS, University of Strathclyde, June 2012, www.fbga.redguitars.co.uk, accessed 9th July 2020.

Shaw, Tom, "Historical Abuse Systemic Review: Residential Schools and Children's Homes in Scotland 1950-1995", The Scottish Government, Edinburgh, 2007.

Books and Articles:

Abrams, Lynn, "'Blood is Thicker than Water': Family, Fantasy and Identity in the Lives of Scottish Foster Children", in Lawrence, Jon and Starkey, Pat (eds), *Child Welfare and Social Action in the Nineteenth and Twentieth Centuries: International Perspectives*, Liverpool, Liverpool University Press, 2001, pp.192-214.

Addley, Esther, "Timeline: Peter Tobin", *Guardian*, 16th December 2009, www.theguardian.com, accessed 11th June 2021.

BBC News, "1977 Anna Kenny murder: DNA tests over Angus Sinclair link", 27th October 2015, www.bbc.com.

BBC News, "The last man to do National Service", 1st June 2015, www.bbc.com accessed 16th May 2021.

Birchall, Guy, "Murder Mystery: Who were Anna Kenny, Agnes Cooney and Hilda McAuley, when were they murdered in Glasgow and were they linked to Angus Sinclair?", *Sun*, 12th April 2018.

Borunda, Alejandra, "How tampons and pads became unsustainable", *National Geographic*, National Geographic Society, 2019.

British Letterpress, "The Printing Industry in 1965: A summary of what the UK's printing industry looked like in 1965", www.Britishletterpress.co.uk, accessed 14th October 1921.

Brown, Callum, "Review of *History of Drinking: The Scottish Pub Since 1700*, review no. 1867, Reviews in History, December 2015, www.reviews.history.ac.uk, accessed 8th November 2021.

Brown, Les and Jeffrey, Robert, *Glasgow Crimefighter: The Les Brown Story*, Black and White Publishing, Edinburgh, 2005.

Cannon, Isidore Cyril, "The Compositor in London: The Rise and Fall of a Labour Aristocracy", *History Workshop*, June 30, 2012.

"Carnell Ayrshires: The Templeton Family Welcomes You", *The Ayrshire Journal*, vol.13, Spring 2017.

Cassidy, Marie, *Beyond the Tape: The Life and Many Deaths of a State Pathologist*, Hachette Books, Dublin, 2020.

Cron, Robert and Whelan, Michael, "Bible John - Unresolved", www.unresolved.me, 23rd September 2017, retrieved August 2018.

Crow, Alan and Samson, Peter, *Bible John: Hunt for a Killer*, Glasgow, First Press Publishing, 1998.

Drysdale, Neil, "Bible John: Pathologist's new book continues hunt for truth about serial killer", The Press and Journal, 16th October 2020, www.pressandjournal.co.uk, accessed 29th October 2020.

Esson, Graeme, "Angus Sinclair: A lifetime of abuse, rape and murder", BBC News, 11th March 2019.

Evans, Kathy, "Secret WW1 history of Australian soldiers with venereal disease", *Canberra Times*, 24th October 2014, www.canberratimes.com.au, accessed 2nd July 2021.

"A Dog's Life on a Sheep Farm", *Farming Independent*, 6th March 2007, www.independent.ie, accessed 28 January 2021.

Findlay, C, Cambuslang Social History 15, "A History of Cambuslang", www.docs.wixstatic.com, accessed 15th September 2020.

Finkelstein, David (ed.), *Edinburgh History of the Book in Scotland*, vol.4, Edinburgh University Press, 2007.

Goodwin, William, Linacre, Adrian and Hadi, Sibte, *An Introduction to Forensic Genetics*, 2nd ed., Oxford, Wiley-Blackwell, 2011.

Harrison, Paul, *Dancing with the Devil: The Bible John Murders*, Skipton, Vertical Editions, 2013.

Hoffman, Jan, "Do Serial Killers Just Stop? Yes, Sometimes", *New York Times*, 26th April 2018, www.nytimes.com accessed 7th November 2020.

Howie-Willis, Ian, "The Australian Army's Two 'Traditional' Diseases: Gonorrhoea and Syphilis – A Medical-Military History During the Twentieth Century", *History*, vol. 27, no. 1.

Jackson, Joe, *Chasing Killers: Three Decades of Cracking Crime in the UK's Murder Capital*, Mainstream Publishing, Edinburgh, 2008.

Knox, W. W., "The Scottish Educational System 1840-1940" in A History of the Scottish People, www.scran.ac.uk.

Leadbetter, Russell, "On the trail of decades of Glasgow's printing history", *Herald, www.heraldscotland.com,* accessed 14th October 2021.

Linklater, Magnus, "Dancing with a stranger: the Bible John case", *Scottish Review*, 1994, reprinted June 2017 in www.scottishreview.net, accessed 29th October 2020.

Lloyd, Georgina, *One Was Not Enough: True Stories of Multiple Murderers*, London, Robert Hale, 1986.

Maule, Henry, "Bible John, the Dancing Strangler, *Reading Eagle*, 27th February 1972.

McLaughlin, Bryan and Smyth, Bob, *Crimestopper: Fighting Crime on Scotland's Streets*, Black and White Publishing, Edinburgh, 2012.

McLaughlin, Mark, "Serial Killer is linked to Glasgow murders", *The Times*, 21st April 2018.

Mair, George, "Bible John: Documentary on the hunt for the notorious Glasgow serial killer Bible John features new artists impression", in *The Scotsman*, 20th November 2021.

Mayes, Andrea, "Claremont killer Bradley Edwards found guilty of Jane Rimmer and Ciara Glennon murders but not Sarah Spiers", 24th September 2020, www.abc.net.au, accessed 24th September 2020.

Mega, Marcello, "Bible John is either dead or at large … but he is NOT Peter Tobin", *Scottish Sun*, 30th September 2011, www.thesun.co.uk accessed 5th November 2020.

Meston, Prof. Michael, "Grounds for Divorce and Maintenance Between Former Spouses: Scotland" in General, A. (ed.) *Grounds for Divorce and Maintenance Between Former Spouses*, October 2002, pp.1-25, http://ceflonline.net, accessed 9th April 2022.

Mitchell, I. R., "Pat's Guide: Unlocking Maryhill – A History of its places and people", www.glasgowwestend.co.uk, accessed 20th October 2021.

"Night the school was bombed. Witness recalls carnage at Knightswood primary in the Clydebank Blitz", Herald Scotland, 19th February 2001, www.heraldscotland.com, accessed 19th February 2021.

Paton, Maureen, "Sin and the single mother: The history of lone parenthood", *Independent*, 25th May 2012.

"Primary School in the Forties – Scottish Nostalgia, 26th February 2016", History Scotland: Explore Scotland's Incredible Past, www.historyscotland.com, accessed 11th July 2020.

"Remembering the first lives lost in WW2 attacks on Clydeside", www.glasgowwestend.todaynews.co.uk, accessed 22nd May 2021.

Ritchie, Maggie, "From Titanic to the Whitehouse: New Glasgow exhibition pulls together Scotland's history in carpeting the world", Sunday Post, www.sundaypost.com, 2019, accessed 10 September 2021.

"St Andrew's Scots Kirk", www.internationalpresbytery.net, accessed 19th August 2021.

The Scottish Printing Archival Trust, "A Reputation for Excellence, Volume 2: Glasgow", 1994, www.scottishprintarchive.org, accessed 20th October 2021.

Senior Pupils of Yoker Secondary School, *Both Sides of the Burn: The Story of Yoker,* Yoker Resource Centre, 1966, 2000.

Simpson, Donald, *Power in the Blood: Whatever happened to 'Bible John'?* Glasgow, Bandwagon Publishing, 2001.

Stoddart, Charles, *Bible John: Search for a Sadist*, Paul Harris Publishing, Edinburgh, 1980.

Thane, Pat, "Unmarried Motherhood in Twentieth-Century England", *Women's History Review*, vol. 20, no. 1, February 2011, pp.11-29.

"The Manchester Typographical Society is Founded", www.historyofinformation.com, accessed 17th October 2021.

U.S. Department of Justice, F.B.I., Behavioral Analysis Unit, National Centre for the Analysis of Violent Crime, "Serial Murder: Multi-Disciplinary Perspectives for Investigators", 2008.

Whittington-Egan, Molly, *Scottish Murder Stories*, Neil Wilson Publishing, Glasgow, 1999.

Wilkinson, Roderick, *Memories of Maryhill*, Canongate Academic, Edinburgh, 1993.

Wilson, David and Harrison, Paul, *The Lost British Serial Killer: Closing the Case on Peter Tobin and Bible John*, London, Sphere, 2010.

Podcasts/Programmes:

Gillan, Audrey, "Introducing Bible John: Creation of a Serial Killer," BBC Scotland Podcast, 2022.
"The Hunt for Bible John", Series 1: Episode 1, screened BBC One Scotland, 22nd November 2021.
"The Hunt for Bible John", Series 1: Episode 2, screened BBC One Scotland, 29th November 2021.
"Serial Killer – Peter Tobin: Kill and Chill", 16th October 2019, accessed 23rd August 2020.
"Scottish Mysteries: Bible John", YouTube 2nd July 2018, podcast viewed 6th November 2020.
"Who is Bible John?" Trace Evidence podcast, Episode 008, The Bible John Murders", 25th July 2017, podcast viewed June 2019.
"Serial Killer - Bible John", for worldofkillers28, 2010, accessed on YouTube 26th July 2019.
"Serial Killer – Bible John", 14th October 2010, accessed 11th October 2018.
BBC News 16th December 2009, accessed 11 September 2019.
"Unsolved: Getting Away with Murder", Series 2, Episode 13, 'Helen Puttock/Bible John', broadcast on Grampian and Scottish Television on the 15th December 2005.
"Calling Bible John", Top Left Production for Channel 4 YouTube C4 April 1996, accessed 27th October 2020.

Public Facebook Groups:

"Being West Kilbride"
"Blasts from the Glasgow Past"
"Bygone Galashiels"
"Castlemilk History"

"Glasgow Memories"
"I went to Victoria Drive Secondary School"
"Kilmaurs and Stewarton Memories"
"Lost Glasgow"
"Muirkirk, East Ayrshire"
"Remembering Auld Ayr"
"Scotstoun memories"
"Stevenston Ayrshire, Now and Then. Memories of School, Youth clubs"

Private Facebook Groups:

"I Went to Bankhead Primary school"

NOTES

[1] Some of this description was given by Joe Jackson when he was interviewed for "Calling Bible John", Top Left Production for Channel 4, YouTube C4 April 1996, accessed 27th October 2020 and in extracts from the police notes read verbatim on Audrey Gillan's, "Introducing Bible John: Creation of a Serial Killer," BBC Scotland Podcast, 2022; *Daily Record*, 24th February 1968, p.1; *Glasgow Herald*, 10th February 1989, pp.6-7; *Glasgow Herald*, 24th February 1968, p.1; Wilson, David and Harrison, Paul, *The Lost British Serial Killer: Closing the Case on Peter Tobin and Bible John*, London, Sphere, 2010, p.32; Crow, Alan and Samson, Peter, *Bible John: Hunt for a Killer*, Glasgow, First Press Publishing, 1998, pp.22-3; Harrison, Paul, *Dancing with the Devil: The Bible John Murders*, Skipton, Vertical Editions, 2013, p.43; *Herald Scotland*, 18th February 2018; *Glasgow Herald*, 10th February 1989, pp.6-7.

[2] Wilson, David and Harrison, Paul, *The Lost British Serial Killer: Closing the Case on Peter Tobin and Bible John*, London, Sphere, 2010, p.30; Stoddart, Charles, *Bible John: Search for a Sadist*, Paul Harris Publishing, Edinburgh, 1980, p.28; Crow, Alan and Samson Peter, *Bible John: Hunt for a Killer*, Glasgow, First Press Publishing, 1998, p.23; Harrison, Paul, *Dancing with the Devil: The Bible John Murders*, Skipton, Vertical Editions, 2013, pp.43-4 and 46; Lloyd, Georgina, *One Was Not Enough: True Stories of Multiple Murderers*, London, Robert Hale, 1986, p.174; *Herald Scotland*, 18th February 2018.

[3] These police notes were read verbatim in Audrey Gillan's, "Introducing Bible John: Creation of a Serial Killer," BBC Scotland Podcast, 2022; Harrison, Paul, *Dancing with the Devil: The Bible John Murders*, Skipton, Vertical Editions, 2013, p.46; Jackson, Joe, *Chasing Killers: Three Decades of Cracking Crime in the UK's Murder Capital*, Mainstream Publishing, Edinburgh, 2008, p.65; Joe Jackson interviewed in "The Hunt for Bible John", Series 1: Episode 2, screened on BBC One Scotland, 29th November 2021. The podcast "Scottish Mysteries: Bible John", claims that the coroner confirmed that Patricia Docker had been

raped ("Scottish Mysteries: Bible John", YouTube 2nd July 2018, podcast viewed 6th November 2020).

[4] Joe Jackson interviewed for "The Hunt for Bible John", Series 1: Episode 1, screened on BBC One Scotland, 22nd November 2021; Wilson, David and Harrison, Paul, *The Lost British Serial Killer: Closing the Case on Peter Tobin and Bible John*, London, Sphere, 2010, p.33; Stoddart, Charles, *Bible John: Search for a Sadist*, Paul Harris Publishing, Edinburgh, 1980, p.29; Crow, Alan and Samson, Peter, *Bible John: Hunt for a Killer*, Glasgow, First Press Publishing, 1998, p.23; Harrison, Paul, *Dancing with the Devil: The Bible John Murders*, Skipton, Vertical Editions, 2013, p.47.

[5] Harrison, Paul, *Dancing with the Devil: The Bible John Murders*, Skipton, Vertical Editions, 2013, p.47.

[6] The article was likely that published in the *Evening Times* titled "Murder in City Lane: girl believed nude and strangled", *Evening Times*, 23rd February 1968, p.1; *Daily Record*, 24th February 1968, p.1; *Scottish Daily Express*, 24th February 1968, p.1.

[7] Stoddart, Charles, *Bible John: Search for a Sadist*, Edinburgh, Paul Harris Publishing, 1980, p.27; Alex Docker mentions his maternal grandparents John and Pauline in an interview in Audrey Gillan's, "Introducing Bible John: Creation of a Serial Killer," BBC Scotland Podcast, 2022.

[8] *Glasgow Herald*, 10th February 1968, p.1; *Daily Record*, 24th February 1968, p.1; Lloyd, Georgina, *One Was Not Enough: True Stories of Multiple Murderers*, London, Robert Hale, 1986, p.173; *Daily Record*, 24th February 1968, p.1; *Herald Scotland*, 18th February 2018; Crow, Alan and Samson, Peter, *Bible John: Hunt for a Killer*, Glasgow, First Press Publishing, 1998, pp.15-6; Harrison, Paul, *Dancing with the Devil: The Bible John Murders*, Skipton, Vertical Editions, 2013, pp.48-9; Gillan, Audrey, "Introducing Bible John: Creation of a Serial Killer," BBC Scotland Podcast, 2022; Stoddart, Charles, *Bible John: Search for a Sadist*, Edinburgh, Paul Harris Publishing, 1980, pp.32-3.

[9] Gillan, Audrey, "Introducing Bible John: Creation of a Serial Killer," BBC Scotland Podcast, 2022. The grammar used in this quote is, of course, my own.

[10] *Glasgow Herald*, 24th February 1968, p.1; *Glasgow Herald*, 27th February 1968, p.1.

[11] *Glasgow Herald*, 24th February 1968, p.1; *Daily Record*, 24th February 1968, p.1; *Scottish Daily Express*, 24th February 1968, p.1; *Glasgow Herald*, 27th February 1968, p.1.

[12] *Glasgow Herald*, 26th February 1968, p.1; *Scottish Daily Express*, 26th February 1968, p.1; *Evening Times*, 26th February 1968, p.3; *Herald Scotland*, 18th February 2018; Wilson, David and Harrison, Paul, *The Lost British Serial Killer: Closing the Case on Peter Tobin and Bible John*, London, Sphere, 2010; Cron, Robert and Whelan, Michael, "Bible John - Unresolved", www.unresolved.me, 23rd September 2017, retrieved August 2018.

[13] *Daily Record*, 26th February 1968, p.2; *Scottish Daily Express*, 19th August 1969, p.1; *Evening Times*, 26th February 1968, p.3.

[14] *Glasgow Herald*, 27th February 1968, p.1; Maule, Henry, "Bible John, the Dancing Strangler, *Reading Eagle*, 27th February 1972, p.90.

[15] *Glasgow Herald*, 28th February 1968, p.1.

[16] *Daily Record*, 1st October, 2008; "Who is Bible John? Trace Evidence podcast, Episode 008, viewed June 2019. One member of "Blasts from the Glasgow Past" explains that locals referred to Barrowland "without the definite article", Response to Patricia Blake, 14th November 2017, on "Blasts from the Glasgow Past", accessed 25th November 2020.

[17] *Daily Record*, 4th March 1968, p.11; *Scottish Daily Express*, 4th March 1968, p.8.

[18] Jackson, Joe, *Chasing Killers: Three Decades of Cracking Crime in the UK's Murder Capital*, Edinburgh, Mainstream Publishing Company, 2008, p.62.

[19] Maule, Henry, "Bible John, the Dancing Strangler, *Reading Eagle*, 27th February 1972, p.90; Cron, Robert and Whelan, Michael, "Bible John - Unresolved", www.unresolved.me, 23rd September 2017, retrieved August 2018; Harrison, Paul,

Dancing with the Devil: The Bible John Murders, Skipton, Vertical Editions, 2013, p.58.

[20] Jackson, Joe, *Chasing Killers: Three Decades of Cracking Crime in the UK's Murder Capital*, Edinburgh, Mainstream Publishing Company, 2008, pp.62-3.

[21] Retired Detective Superintendent Robert Johnstone interviewed in "The Hunt for Bible John", Series 1: Episode 1, screened on BBC One Scotland, 22nd November 2021.

[22] Jackson, Joe, *Chasing Killers: Three Decades of Cracking Crime in the UK's Murder Capital*, Edinburgh, Mainstream Publishing Company, 2008, pp.62-3; Harrison, Paul, *Dancing with the Devil: The Bible John Murders*, Skipton, Vertical Editions, 2013, pp.58-9.

[23] Wilson, David and Harrison, Paul, *The Lost British Serial Killer: Closing the Case on Peter Tobin and Bible John*, London, Sphere, 2010, p.38; *Herald Scotland*, 18th February 2018.

[24] Wilson, David and Harrison, Paul, *The Lost British Serial Killer: Closing the Case on Peter Tobin and Bible John*, London, Sphere, 2010, p.38; *Herald Scotland*, 18th February 2018.

[25] The press reported that this wedding ring had belonged to Patricia's grandmother but it might have also been hers.

[26] *Glasgow Herald*, 24th February 1868, p.1; *Scottish Daily Express*, 27th February 1968, p.7; *Scottish Daily Express*, 4th March 1968, p.8.

[27] Stoddart, Charles, *Bible John: Search for a Sadist*, Paul Harris Publishing, Edinburgh, 1980, p.31.

[28] *Guardian*, 16th March 1996, p.260.

[29] Harrison, Paul, *Dancing with the Devil: The Bible John Murders*, Skipton, Vertical Editions, 2013, pp.51 and 57.

[30] Harrison, Paul, *Dancing with the Devil: The Bible John Murders*, Skipton, Vertical Editions, 2013, p.55.

[31] *Daily Record*, 28th January 2018; This photograph, showing Millbrae Bridge was reproduced both in the photographic centre of Stoddart, Charles, *Bible John: Search for a Sadist*, Paul Harris Publishing, Edinburgh, 1980 and that of Harrison, Paul, *Dancing with the Devil: The Bible John Murders*, Skipton, Vertical Editions, 2013; Wilson, David and Harrison, Paul, *The Lost*

British Serial Killer: Closing the Case on Peter Tobin and Bible John, London, Sphere, 2010, p.34.

[32] *Herald Scotland*, 18th February 2018.

[33] Maule, Henry, "Bible John, the Dancing Strangler, *Reading Eagle*, 27th February 1972, p.90; Cron, Robert and Whelan, Michael, "Bible John - Unresolved", www.unresolved.me, 23rd September 2017, retrieved August 2018; Harrison, Paul, *Dancing with the Devil: The Bible John Murders*, Skipton, Vertical Editions, 2013, p.58.

[34] Stoddart, Charles, *Bible John: Search for a Sadist*, Paul Harris Publishing, Edinburgh, 1980, p.35.

[35] *Evening Times*, 18th August 1969, p.1; *Daily Record*, 19th August 1969, p.11; Wilson, David and Harrison, Paul, *The Lost British Serial Killer: Closing the Case on Peter Tobin and Bible John*, London, Sphere, 2010, p.47; Harrison, Paul, *Dancing with the Devil: The Bible John Murders*, Skipton, Vertical Editions, 2013, p.66; Lloyd, Georgina, *One Was Not Enough: True Stories of Multiple Murderers*, London, Robert Hale, 1986, p.177.

[36] *Scottish Daily Express*, 19th August 1969, p.1; *Daily Record*, 19th August 1969, p.11; *Evening Times*, 18th August 1969, p.1; *Evening Times*, 19th August 1969, p.7; unknown newspaper article photographed for "Calling Bible John", Top Left Production for Channel 4, YouTube C4 April 1996, accessed 27th October 2020.

[37] *Evening Times*, 18th August 1969, p.11; *Scottish Daily Express*, 19th August 1969, p.1; *Daily Record*, 21st August 1969, p.11; *Daily Record*, 23rd August 1969, p.2.

[38] Cron, Robert and Whelan, Michael, "Bible John - Unresolved", www.unresolved.me, 23rd September 2017, retrieved August 2018.

[39] Wilson, David and Harrison, Paul, *The Lost British Serial Killer: Closing the Case on Peter Tobin and Bible John*, London, Sphere, 2010, pp.47 and 52-3; Harrison, Paul, *Dancing with the Devil: The Bible John Murders*, Skipton, Vertical Editions, 2013, p.72; Stoddart, Charles, *Bible John: Search for a Sadist*, Paul Harris Publishing, Edinburgh, 1980,

pp.38-9; Jackson, Joe, *Chasing Killers: Three Decades of Cracking Crime in the UK's Murder Capital*, Mainstream Publishing, Edinburgh, 2008, p.65; "Trace Evidence podcast, Episode 008, The Bible John Murders", 25th July 2017, podcast viewed June 2019.

[40] *Evening Times*, 18th August 1969, p.1; *Daily Record*, 19th August 1969, p.11; *Scottish Daily Express*, 19th August 1969, p.1.

[41] *Evening Times*, 18th August 1969, p.11; *Evening Times*, 19th August 1969, p.7; *Scottish Daily Express*, 19th August 1969, p.1.

[42] *Scottish Daily Express*, 19th August 1969, p.1; *Scottish Daily Express*, 20th August 1969, p.7; Wilson, David and Harrison, Paul, *The Lost British Serial Killer: Closing the Case on Peter Tobin and Bible John*, London, Sphere, 2010, pp.51-2.

[43] *Evening Times*, 19th August 1969, p.7 and 21st August 1969, p.16; *Scottish Daily Express*, 19th August 1969, p.1; *Daily Record*, 21st August 1969, p.11 and 23rd August 1969, p.2.

[44] *Evening Times*, 21st August 1969, p.16; *Daily Record*, 21st August 1969, p.11; *Scottish Daily Express*, 21st August 1969, p.11; *Daily Record*, 26th August 1969, p.2; *Scottish Daily Express*, 26th August 1969, p.1; Gillan, Audrey, "Introducing Bible John: Creation of a Serial Killer," BBC Scotland Podcast, 2022.

[45] *Evening Times*, 25th August 1969, p.1; *Evening News*, 26th August 1969, p.13; *Daily Record* 26th August 1969, p.1; *Scottish Daily Express*, 26th August 1969, p.1.

[46] These were the phrases that D.I. Ricky Mason used when he was interviewed for 'Unsolved: Getting Away with Murder', Series 2, Episode 13, 'Helen Puttock/Bible John', broadcast on Grampian and Scottish Television on the 15th December 2005; Stoddart, Charles, *Bible John: Search for a Sadist*, Paul Harris Publishing, Edinburgh, 1980, p.41; Wilson, David and Harrison, Paul, *The Lost British Serial Killer: Closing the Case on Peter Tobin and Bible John*, London, Sphere, 2010, p.75.

[47] Stoddart, Charles, *Bible John: Search for a Sadist*, Paul Harris Publishing, Edinburgh, 1980, pp.41-2; Wilson, David and Harrison, Paul, *The Lost British Serial Killer: Closing the Case on Peter Tobin and Bible John*, London, Sphere, 2010, p.49.

[48] Stoddart, Charles, *Bible John: Search for a Sadist*, Paul Harris Publishing, Edinburgh, 1980, p.42.

[49] Harrison, Paul, *Dancing with the Devil: The Bible John Murders*, Skipton, Vertical Editions, 2013, p.76; Stoddart, Charles, *Bible John: Search for a Sadist*, Paul Harris Publishing, Edinburgh, 1980, pp.45 and 79-80.

[50] Harrison, Paul, *Dancing with the Devil: The Bible John Murders*, Skipton, Vertical Editions, 2013, pp.76-77, quoting from the *Scottish Daily Express*.

[51] *Evening Times*, 18th August 1969, p.11.

[52] *Evening Times*, 18th August 1969, p.11; *Daily Record*, 25th August 1969, p.6.

[53] Brown, Les and Jeffrey, Robert, *Glasgow Crimefighter: The Les Brown Story*, Black and White Publishing, Edinburgh, 2005, p.128.

[54] This was revealed by D. I. Ricky Mason in "Unsolved: Getting Away with Murder", Series 2, Episode 13, 'Helen Puttock/Bible John', broadcast on Grampian and Scottish Television on the 15th December 2005.

[55] *Evening Times*, 18th February 1989, p.4.

[56] Stoddart, Charles, *Bible John: Search for a Sadist*, Paul Harris Publishing, Edinburgh, 1980, p.37.

[57] Harrison, Paul, *Dancing with the Devil: The Bible John Murders*, Skipton, Vertical Editions, 2013, p.35.

[58] Lloyd, Georgina, *One Was Not Enough: True Stories of Multiple Murderers*, London, Robert Hale, 1986, p.178.

[59] *Evening Times*, 31st October 1969, pp.1 and 20; *Scottish Daily Express*, 1st November 1969, p.1; *Daily Record*, 1st November 1969, p.1.

[60] *Evening Times*, 31st October 1969, p.20.; Stoddart, Charles, *Bible John: Search for a Sadist*, Paul Harris Publishing, Edinburgh, 1980, p.66.

[61] *Evening Times*, 31st October 1969, p.20; *Scottish Daily Express*, 1st November 1969, p.1; Harrison, Paul, *Dancing with the Devil: The Bible John Murders*, Skipton, Vertical Editions, 2013, p.93.

[62] Gillan Audrey, "Introducing Bible John: Creation of a Serial Killer," BBC Scotland Podcast, 2022.

[63] Gillan, Audrey, "Introducing Bible John: Creation of a Serial Killer," BBC Scotland Podcast, 2022; Harrison, Paul, Dancing with the Devil: The Bible John Murders, Skipton, Vertical Editions, 2013, p.94; Cron, Robert and Whelan, Michael, "Bible John - Unresolved", www.unresolved.me, 23rd September 2017, retrieved August 2018; Guardian, 2nd September 1995, p.203; Herald Scotland, 17th August 1996; Wilson, David and Harrison, Paul, *The Lost British Serial Killer: Closing the Case on Peter Tobin and Bible John*, Great Britain, Sphere Publishing, 2010, p.61.

[64] *Herald Scotland*, 17th August 1996; Lloyd, Georgina, *One Was Not Enough: True Stories of Multiple Murderers*, London, Robert Hale, 1986, p.185; Stoddart, Charles, *Bible John: Search for a Sadist*, Paul Harris Publishing, Edinburgh, 1980, p.69; Wilson, David and Harrison, Paul, *The Lost British Serial Killer: Closing the Case on Peter Tobin and Bible John*, Great Britain, Sphere Publishing, 2010, p.87.

[65] Joe Beattie's notes read on Audrey Gillan's, "Introducing Bible John: Creation of a Serial Killer," BBC Scotland Podcast, 2022; Simpson, Donald, *Power in the Blood: Whatever happened to 'Bible John'?*, Glasgow, Bandwagon Publishing, 2001, p.16; Cron, Robert and Whelan, Michael, "Bible John - Unresolved", www.unresolved.me, 23rd September 2017, retrieved August 2018; Harrison, Paul, *Dancing with the Devil: The Bible John Murders*, Skipton, Vertical Editions, 2013, p.97.

[66] *Evening Times*, 31st October 1969, pp.1 and 20; Stoddart, Charles, *Bible John: Search for a Sadist*, Paul Harris Publishing, Edinburgh, 1980, p.47; Harrison, Paul, *Dancing with the Devil: The Bible John Murders*, Skipton, Vertical Editions, 2013, p.79; *Evening Times*, 10th November 1969, p.14; *Herald Scotland*, 13th December 1994.

[67] George Puttock interviewed for the program "Unsolved: Getting Away with Murder", Series 2, Episode 13, 'Helen Puttock/Bible John', broadcast on Grampian and Scottish Television on the 15th December 2005; *Herald Scotland*, 13th

December 1994; Harrison, Paul, *Dancing with the Devil: The Bible John Murders*, Skipton, Vertical Editions, 2013, p.81.

[68] *Sunday Herald*, 17th August 1996.

[69] Wilson, David and Harrison, Paul, *The Lost British Serial Killer: Closing the Case on Peter Tobin and Bible John*, Great Britain, Sphere Publishing, 2010, p.54; *Herald Scotland*, 17th August 1996.

[70] Magnus Linklater interviewed in "The Hunt for Bible John", Series 1: Episode 2, screened BBC One Scotland, 29th November 2021; Transcript of Jeannie's 1996 interview read in Audrey Gillan's, "Introducing Bible John: Creation of a Serial Killer," BBC Scotland Podcast, 2022.

[71] Lloyd, Georgina, *One Was Not Enough: True Stories of Multiple Murderers*, London, Robert Hale, 1986, p.182.

[72] Harrison, Paul, *Dancing with the Devil: The Bible John Murders*, Skipton, Vertical Editions, 2013, p.83-4.

[73] Stoddart, Charles, Bible John: Search for a Sadist, Paul Harris Publishing, Edinburgh, 1980, pp.ix and 57; Cron, Robert and Whelan, Michael, "Bible John - Unresolved", www.unresolved.me, 23rd September 2017, retrieved August 2018; Harrison, Paul, Dancing with the Devil: The Bible John Murders, Skipton, Vertical Editions, 2013, p.84; Guardian, 2nd September 1995, p.203; Daily Record, 3rd August 2020 (accessed online 4th August 2020).

[74] Transcript of Jeannie's 1996 interview read in Audrey Gillan's, "Introducing Bible John: Creation of a Serial Killer," BBC Scotland Podcast, 2022.

[75] *Herald Scotland*, 17th August 1996; Harrison, Paul, *Dancing with the Devil: The Bible John Murders*, Skipton, Vertical Editions, 2013, p.85.

[76] Harrison, Paul, *Dancing with the Devil: The Bible John Murders*, Skipton, Vertical Editions, 2013, pp.85-6; Wilson, David and Harrison, Paul, *The Lost British Serial Killer: Closing the Case on Peter Tobin and Bible John*, Great Britain, Sphere Publishing, 2010, p.55.

[77] Stoddart, Charles, *Bible John: Search for a Sadist*, Paul Harris Publishing, Edinburgh, 1980, p.59.

[78] Crow, Alan and Samson, Peter, *Bible John: Hunt for a Killer*, Glasgow, First Press Publishing, 1998, p.44; *Herald Scotland*, 17th August 1996; Stoddart, Charles, *Bible John: Search for a Sadist*, Paul Harris Publishing, Edinburgh, 1980, p.59; Wilson, David and Harrison, Paul, *The Lost British Serial Killer: Closing the Case on Peter Tobin and Bible John*, Great Britain, Sphere Publishing, 2010, p.56; Harrison, Paul, *Dancing with the Devil: The Bible John Murders*, Skipton, Vertical Editions, 2013, p.86.

[79] Harrison, Paul, *Dancing with the Devil: The Bible John Murders*, Skipton, Vertical Editions, 2013, pp.86-7.

[80] Stoddart, Charles, *Bible John: Search for a Sadist*, Paul Harris Publishing, Edinburgh, 1980, p.59.

[81] Harrison, Paul, *Dancing with the Devil: The Bible John Murders*, Skipton, Vertical Editions, 2013, pp.86-87 and 140; Stoddart, Charles, *Bible John: Search for a Sadist*, Paul Harris Publishing, Edinburgh, 1980, p.59 *Herald Scotland*, 17th August 1996.

[82] Harrison, Paul, *Dancing with the Devil: The Bible John Murders*, Skipton, Vertical Editions, 2013, p.87.

[83] *Herald Scotland*, 17th August 1996; *Glasgow Herald*, 1st November 1969, p.1 *Glasgow Herald*, 3rd November 1969, p.16; Charles, *Bible John: Search for a Sadist*, Paul Harris Publishing, Edinburgh, 1980, p.62.

[84] Stoddart, Charles, *Bible John: Search for a Sadist*, Paul Harris Publishing, Edinburgh, 1980, p.63; Harrison, Paul, *Dancing with the Devil: The Bible John Murders*, Skipton, Vertical Editions, 2013, p.88.

[85] *Herald Scotland*, 17th August 1996; *Scottish Daily Express*, 4th November 1969, p.1 and 5th November 1969, p.1; Crow, Alan and Samson, Peter, *Bible John: Hunt for a Killer*, Glasgow, First Press Publishing, 1998, p.46; Stoddart, Charles, *Bible John: Search for a Sadist*, Paul Harris Publishing, Edinburgh, 1980, p.64; Harrison, Paul, *Dancing with the Devil: The Bible John Murders*, Skipton, Vertical Editions, 2010, pp.88-90; Wilson, David and Harrison, Paul, *The Lost British Serial Killer: Closing the Case on Peter Tobin and Bible John*, Great Britain, Sphere Publishing, 2010, p.57.

[86] Simpson, Donald, *Power in the Blood: Whatever happened to 'Bible John'?*, Glasgow, Bandwagon Publishing, 2001, p.19; Stoddart, Charles, *Bible John: Search for a Sadist*, Paul Harris Publishing, Edinburgh, 1980, p.64; Maule, Henry, "Bible John, the Dancing Strangler, *Reading Eagle*, 27th February 1972; Harrison, Paul, *Dancing with the Devil: The Bible John Murders*, Skipton, Vertical Editions, 2013, p.90; Wilson, David and Harrison, Paul, *The Lost British Serial Killer: Closing the Case on Peter Tobin and Bible John*, Great Britain, Sphere Publishing, 2010, p.57.

[87] Joe Beattie's notes read on Audrey Gillan's, "Introducing Bible John: Creation of a Serial Killer," BBC Scotland Podcast, 2022; Stoddart, Charles, *Bible John: Search for a Sadist*, Paul Harris Publishing, Edinburgh, 1980, p.64.

[88] Former Detective Superintendent Robert Johnstone interviewed in "The Hunt for Bible John", Series 1: Episode 2, screened BBC One Scotland, 29th November 2021.

[89] Joe Beattie's notes read on Audrey Gillan's, "Introducing Bible John: Creation of a Serial Killer," BBC Scotland Podcast, 2022.

[90] Harrison, Paul, *Dancing with the Devil: The Bible John Murders*, Skipton, Vertical Editions, 2013, pp.88-89; Stoddart, Charles, *Bible John: Search for a Sadist*, Paul Harris Publishing, Edinburgh, 1980, p.63.

[91] *Glasgow Herald*, 4th November 1969, p.8; *Evening Times*, 3rd November 1969, p.1; *Evening Times*, 4th November 1969, p.15; *Scottish Daily Express*, 4th November 1969, p.1

[92] Lloyd, Georgina, *One Was Not Enough: True Stories of Multiple Murderers*, London, Robert Hale, 1986, p.183; Harrison, Paul, *Dancing with the Devil: The Bible John Murders*, Skipton, Vertical Editions, 2013, p.89; Stoddart, Charles, *Bible John: Search for a Sadist*, Paul Harris Publishing, Edinburgh, 1980, p.63.

[93] Crow, Alan and Samson, Peter, *Bible John: Hunt for a Killer*, Glasgow, First Press Publishing, 1998, p.46; Stoddart, Charles, *Bible John: Search for a Sadist*, Paul Harris Publishing, Edinburgh, 1980, p.63; *Herald Scotland*, 17th August 1996.

[94] The man did not specify whether this relative had worked at the flats or at the foster home which preceded them. Wilson, David

and Harrison, Paul, *The Lost British Serial Killer: Closing the Case on Peter Tobin and Bible John*, Great Britain, Sphere Publishing, 2010, p.57; Stoddart, Charles, *Bible John: Search for a Sadist*, Paul Harris Publishing, Edinburgh, 1980, p.64; Harrison, Paul, *Dancing with the Devil: The Bible John Murders*, Skipton, Vertical Editions, 2013, pp.89-90.

[95] Simpson, Donald, *Power in the Blood: Whatever happened to 'Bible John'?*, Glasgow, Bandwagon Publishing, 2001, p.19; Wilson, David and Harrison, Paul, *The Lost British Serial Killer: Closing the Case on Peter Tobin and Bible John*, Great Britain, Sphere Publishing, 2010, p.57.

[96] Stoddart, Charles, *Bible John: Search for a Sadist*, Paul Harris Publishing, Edinburgh, 1980, p.64; Crow, Alan and Samson, Peter, *Bible John: Hunt for a Killer*, Glasgow, First Press Publishing, 1998, p.47.

[97] Simpson, Donald, *Power in the Blood: Whatever happened to 'Bible John'?*, Glasgow, Bandwagon Publishing, 2001, p.16; Harrison, Paul, *Dancing with the Devil: The Bible John Murders*, Skipton, Vertical Editions, 2013, p.90.

[98] *Glasgow Herald*, 3rd November 1969, p.16; *Herald Scotland*, 17th August 1996; Harrison, Paul, *Dancing with the Devil: The Bible John Murders*, Skipton, Vertical Editions, 2013, p.90.

[99] Stoddart, Charles, *Bible John: Search for a Sadist*, Paul Harris Publishing, Edinburgh, 1980, p.62.

[100] Harrison, Paul, *Dancing with the Devil: The Bible John Murders*, Skipton, Vertical Editions, 2013, p.95.

[101] Harrison, Paul, *Dancing with the Devil: The Bible John Murders*, Skipton, Vertical Editions, 2013, p.91; Wilson, David and Harrison, Paul, *The Lost British Serial Killer: Closing the Case on Peter Tobin and Bible John*, Great Britain, Sphere Publishing, 2010, p.x; ("Scottish Mysteries: Bible John", YouTube 2nd July 2018, podcast viewed 6th November 2020.

[102] *Guardian*, 2nd September, 1995, p.203.

[103] Crow, Alan and Samson, Peter, *Bible John: Hunt for a Killer*, Glasgow, First Press Publishing, 1998, p.48; Harrison, Paul, *Dancing with the Devil: The Bible John Murders*, Skipton, Vertical Editions, 2013, p.91; *Guardian*, 2nd September, 1995, p.203.

[104] Charles Stoddart says "At the junction of Dumbarton Road and Gray Street" but Dumbarton Road had changed name to Argyle Street before it intersected with Gray Street (Stoddart, Charles, *Bible John: Search for a Sadist*, Paul Harris Publishing, Edinburgh, 1980, p.65); Alan Crow and Peter Sampson say the man got off the bus "at the Gray Street stop" (Crow, Alan and Samson, Peter, *Bible John: Hunt for a Killer*, Glasgow, First Press Publishing, 1998, p.48); *Guardian*, 2nd September, 1995, p.203; *Herald Scotland*, 17th August 1996.

[105] *Scottish Daily Express*, 4th November 1969, p.1.

[106] Stoddart, Charles, *Bible John: Search for a Sadist*, Paul Harris Publishing, Edinburgh, 1980, pp.56-7.

[107] Transcript of Audrey Gillan's interview with Jeannie read in her podcast, "Introducing Bible John: Creation of a Serial Killer," BBC Scotland Podcast, 2022.

[108] *Glasgow Herald*, 4th November 1969, p.8; *Evening News*, 4th November 1969, p.15; *Scottish Daily Express*, 4th November 1969, p.1.

[109] Stoddart, Charles, *Bible John: Search for a Sadist*, Paul Harris Publishing, Edinburgh, 1980, p.56.

[110] *Evening Times*, 3rd November 1969, backpage; *Glasgow Herald*, 4th November 1969, p.8; *Evening Times*, 4th November 1969, p.15; *Evening Times*, 5th November 1969, p.13; *Evening Times*, 6th November 1969, p.15; *Evening Times*, 7th November 1969, p.1; "City of Glasgow Police: Special Notice – Murder of Helen Gowans or Puttock (29)" (reproduced in the photographic section of Harrison).

[111] Stoddart, Charles, *Bible John: Search for a Sadist*, Paul Harris Publishing, Edinburgh, 1980, p.73; *Herald Scotland*, 17th August 1996.

[112] Wilson, David and Harrison, Paul, *The Lost British Serial Killer: Closing the Case on Peter Tobin and Bible John*, Great Britain, Sphere Publishing, 2010, p.62; Stoddart, Charles, *Bible John: Search for a Sadist*, Paul Harris Publishing, Edinburgh, 1980, p.74; *Herald Scotland*, 17th August 1996.

[113] Wilson, David and Harrison, Paul, *The Lost British Serial Killer: Closing the Case on Peter Tobin and Bible John*, Great

Britain, Sphere Publishing, 2010, p.62; Stoddart, Charles, *Bible John: Search for a Sadist*, Paul Harris Publishing, Edinburgh, 1980, p.74.

[114] McLaughlin, Bryan and Smyth, Bob, *Crimestopper: Fighting Crime on Scotland's Streets*, Black and White Publishing, Edinburgh, 2012, p.59.

[115] *Glasgow Herald*, 22nd November, 1969, p.1.

[116] *Evening Times*, 5th November 1969, p.13; *Evening Times*, 18th February 1989, p.4.

[117] Original news footage of D.C.S. Elphinstone Dalglish being interviewed, included in "The Hunt for Bible John", Series 1: Episode 1, screened on BBC One Scotland, 22nd November 2021.

[118] *Evening Times*, 3rd November 1969; *Daily Record*, 4th November 1969, p.1; *Evening News*, 4th November 1969, p.15; *Scottish Daily Express*, 4th November 1969, p.1; *Glasgow Herald*, 4th November 1969, p.8; "City of Glasgow Police: Special Notice – Murder of Helen Gowans or Puttock (29)" (reproduced in the photographic section of Harrison).

[119] Wilson, David and Harrison, Paul, *The Lost British Serial Killer: Closing the Case on Peter Tobin and Bible John*, Great Britain, Sphere Publishing, 2010, p.62.

[120] Stoddart, Charles, *Bible John: Search for a Sadist*, Paul Harris Publishing, Edinburgh, 1980, p.90; Wilson, David and Harrison, Paul, *The Lost British Serial Killer: Closing the Case on Peter Tobin and Bible John*, Great Britain, Sphere Publishing, 2010, p.66.

[121] *Scottish Daily Express*, 3rd November 1969, p.11; Jackson, Joe, *Chasing Killers: Three Decades of Cracking Crime in the UK's Murder Capital*, Mainstream Publishing, Edinburgh, 2008, pp.67-8.

[122] *Daily Record*, 11th November 1969, p.7; *Scottish Daily Express*, 11th November 1969, p.7; *Evening Times*, 10th October 1987, p.6; Cron, Robert and Whelan, Michael, "Bible John - Unresolved", www.unresolved.me, 23rd September 2017, retrieved August 2018; Wilson, David and Harrison, Paul, *The Lost British Serial Killer: Closing the Case on Peter Tobin and Bible John*, Great Britain, Sphere Publishing, 2010, p.65.

[123] Stoddart, Charles, *Bible John: Search for a Sadist*, Paul Harris Publishing, Edinburgh, 1980, pp.82-3.

[124] Stoddart, Charles, Bible John: Search for a Sadist, Paul Harris Publishing, Edinburgh, 1980, pp.83-5; Cron, Robert and Whelan, Michael, "Bible John - Unresolved", www.unresolved.me, 23rd September 2017, retrieved August 2018; Wilson, David and Harrison, Paul, *The Lost British Serial Killer: Closing the Case on Peter Tobin and Bible John*, Great Britain, Sphere Publishing, 2010, p.65.

[125] *Scottish Daily Express*, 11th November 1969, p.7; Wilson, David and Harrison, Paul, *The Lost British Serial Killer: Closing the Case on Peter Tobin and Bible John*, Great Britain, Sphere Publishing, 2010, p.65.

[126] *Evening Times*, 10th October 1987, p.6; Cron, Robert and Whelan, Michael, "Bible John - Unresolved", www.unresolved.me, 23rd September 2017,retrieved August 2018; Wilson, David and Harrison, Paul, *The Lost British Serial Killer: Closing the Case on Peter Tobin and Bible John*, Great Britain, Sphere Publishing, 2010, p.65.

[127] Cassidy, Marie, Beyond the Tape: The Life and Many Deaths of a State Pathologist, Hachette Books, Dublin, 2020, p. 89; Cron, Robert and Whelan, Michael, "Bible John - Unresolved", www.unresolved.me, 23rd September 2017, retrieved August 2018; Wilson, David and Harrison, Paul, The Lost British Serial Killer: Closing the Case on Peter Tobin and Bible John, Great Britain, Sphere Publishing, 2010, p.65; Evening Times, 10th October 1987, p.6.

[128] *Herald Scotland*, 17th August 1996; Wilson, David and Harrison, Paul, *The Lost British Serial Killer: Closing the Case on Peter Tobin and Bible John*, Great Britain, Sphere Publishing, 2010, p.65; Stoddart, Charles, *Bible John: Search for a Sadist*, Paul Harris Publishing, Edinburgh, 1980, p.87.

[129] Wilson, David and Harrison, Paul, *The Lost British Serial Killer: Closing the Case on Peter Tobin and Bible John*, Great Britain, Sphere Publishing, 2010, p.63.

[130] Stoddart, Charles, *Bible John: Search for a Sadist*, Paul Harris Publishing, Edinburgh, 1980, pp.11 and 18.

[131] Magnus Linklater interviewed in "The Hunt for Bible John", Series 1: Episode 2, screened BBC One Scotland, 29th November 2021.

[132] *Sunday Herald*, 17th August 1996.

[133] Harrison, Paul, *Dancing with the Devil: The Bible John Murders*, Skipton, Vertical Editions, 2013, pp.67 and 130; *Herald Scotland*, 17th August 1996.

[134] Simpson, Donald, *Power in the Blood: Whatever happened to 'Bible John'?*, Glasgow, Bandwagon Publishing, 2001, p.149.

[135] Wilson, David and Harrison, Paul, *The Lost British Serial Killer: Closing the Case on Peter Tobin and Bible John*, Great Britain, Sphere Publishing, 2010, p.58.

[136] McLaughlin, Bryan and Smyth, Bob, *Crimestopper: Fighting Crime on Scotland's Streets*, Black and White Publishing, Edinburgh, 2012, p.59.

[137] McLaughlin, Bryan and Smyth, Bob, *Crimestopper: Fighting Crime on Scotland's Streets*, Black and White Publishing, Edinburgh, 2012, pp.57-60; Brown, Les and Jeffrey, Robert, *Glasgow Crimefighter: The Les Brown Story*, Black and White Publishing, Edinburgh, 2005, pp.131-4; Jackson, Joe, *Chasing Killers: Three Decades of Cracking Crime in the UK's Murder Capital*, Mainstream Publishing, Edinburgh, 2008, pp.66-70.

[138] Brown, Les and Jeffrey, Robert, *Glasgow Crimefighter: The Les Brown Story*, Black and White Publishing, Edinburgh, 2005, p.127.

[139] Wilson, David and Harrison, Paul, *The Lost British Serial Killer: Closing the Case on Peter Tobin and Bible John*, Great Britain, Sphere Publishing, 2010, pp.63-75; Brown, Les and Jeffrey, Robert, *Glasgow Crimefighter: The Les Brown Story*, Black and White Publishing, Edinburgh, 2005, pp.131-4; McLaughlin, Bryan and Smyth, Bob, *Crimestopper: Fighting Crime on Scotland's Streets*, Black and White Publishing, Edinburgh, 2012, pp.57-60.

[140] Cron, Robert and Whelan, Michael, "Bible John - Unresolved", www.unresolved.me, 23rd September 2017, retrieved August 2018.

[141] Brown, Les and Jeffrey, Robert, *Glasgow Crimefighter: The Les Brown Story*, Black and White Publishing, Edinburgh, 2005, p.131; "Scottish Mysteries: Bible John", YouTube 2nd July 2018, podcast viewed 6th November 2020.

[142] Harrison, Paul, *Dancing with the Devil: The Bible John Murders*, Skipton, Vertical Editions, 2013, pp.94 and 154.

[143] Stoddart, Charles, *Bible John: Search for a Sadist*, Paul Harris Publishing, Edinburgh, 1980, p.72.

[144] Harrison, Paul, *Dancing with the Devil: The Bible John Murders*, Skipton, Vertical Editions, 2013, p.100.

[145] *Herald Scotland*, 17th August 1996.

[146] Harrison, Paul, *Dancing with the Devil: The Bible John Murders*, Skipton, Vertical Editions, 2013, pp.143-4.

[147] Wilson, David and Harrison, Paul, *The Lost British Serial Killer: Closing the Case on Peter Tobin and Bible John*, Great Britain, Sphere Publishing, 2010, p.58.

[148] Stoddart, Charles, *Bible John: Search for a Sadist*, Paul Harris Publishing, Edinburgh, 1980, p.104.

[149] Wilson, David and Harrison, Paul, *The Lost British Serial Killer: Closing the Case on Peter Tobin and Bible John*, Great Britain, Sphere Publishing, 2010, p.70.

[150] Wilson, David and Harrison, Paul, *The Lost British Serial Killer: Closing the Case on Peter Tobin and Bible John*, Great Britain, Sphere Publishing, 2010, p.70.

[151] Stoddart, Charles, *Bible John: Search for a Sadist*, Paul Harris Publishing, Edinburgh, 1980, p. 105.

[152] Harrison, Paul, *Dancing with the Devil: The Bible John Murders*, Skipton, Vertical Editions, 2013, p.91; "Scottish Mysteries: Bible John", YouTube 2nd July 2018, podcast viewed 6th November 2020.

[153] Stoddart, Charles, *Bible John: Search for a Sadist*, Paul Harris Publishing, Edinburgh, 1980, p.104.

[154] Stoddart, Charles, *Bible John: Search for a Sadist*, Paul Harris Publishing, Edinburgh, 1980, p.105.

[155] *Scottish Daily Express*, 11th November 1969, p.7.

[156] Wilson, David and Harrison, Paul, *The Lost British Serial Killer: Closing the Case on Peter Tobin and Bible John*, Great Britain, Sphere Publishing, 2010, p.83.

[157] Stoddart, Charles, *Bible John: Search for a Sadist*, Paul Harris Publishing, Edinburgh, 1980, pp.56-7.

[158] Wilson, David and Harrison, Paul, *The Lost British Serial Killer: Closing the Case on Peter Tobin and Bible John*, Great Britain, Sphere Publishing, 2010, p.84.

[159] "Glasgow Memories", posted 1st October 2021, accessed 2nd October 2021.

[160] Stoddart, Charles, *Bible John: Search for a Sadist*, Paul Harris Publishing, Edinburgh, 1980, pp.87-8.

[161] Stoddart, Charles, *Bible John: Search for a Sadist*, Paul Harris Publishing, Edinburgh, 1980, p.56.

[162] Stoddart, Charles, *Bible John: Search for a Sadist*, Paul Harris Publishing, Edinburgh, 1980, p.64.

[163] Stoddart, Charles, *Bible John: Search for a Sadist*, Paul Harris Publishing, Edinburgh, 1980, p.57.

[164] Harrison, Paul, *Dancing with the Devil: The Bible John Murders*, Skipton, Vertical Editions, 2013, p.89; Stoddart, Charles, *Bible John: Search for a Sadist*, Paul Harris Publishing, Edinburgh, 1980, p.63.

[165] Wilson, David and Harrison, Paul, *The Lost British Serial Killer: Closing the Case on Peter Tobin and Bible John*, Great Britain, Sphere Publishing, 2010, p.83.

[166] *Glasgow Herald*, 4th November 1969, p.8; *Evening Times*, 3rd November 1969, p.1; *Scottish Daily Express*, 4th November 1969, p.1.

[167] Harrison, Paul, *Dancing with the Devil: The Bible John Murders*, Skipton, Vertical Editions, 2013, p.132.

[168] Harrison, Paul, *Dancing with the Devil: The Bible John Murders*, Skipton, Vertical Editions, 2013, pp.151-2.

[169] Harrison, Paul, *Dancing with the Devil: The Bible John Murders*, Skipton, Vertical Editions, 2013, p.87.

[170] Harrison, Paul, *Dancing with the Devil: The Bible John Murders*, Skipton, Vertical Editions, 2013, p.87.

[171] Whittington-Egan, Molly, *Scottish Murder Stories*, Neil Wilson Publishing, Glasgow, 1999, p.171.

[172] Stoddart, Charles, *Bible John: Search for a Sadist*, Paul Harris Publishing, Edinburgh, 1980, pp.136-7.

[173] Harrison, Paul, *Dancing with the Devil: The Bible John Murders*, Skipton, Vertical Editions, 2013, p.154.

[174] Crow, Alan and Samson, Peter, *Bible John: Hunt for a Killer*, Glasgow, First Press Publishing, 1977, pp.64-5, citing Norman Adams, *Goodbye, Beloved Brethren* pub. 1972; Stoddart, Charles, *Bible John: Search for a Sadist*, Paul Harris Publishing, Edinburgh, 1980, pp.135-6; *Herald Scotland*, 30th January 1996.

[175] Harrison, Paul, *Dancing with the Devil: The Bible John Murders*, Skipton, Vertical Editions, 2013, p.177.

[176] Wilson, David and Harrison, Paul, *The Lost British Serial Killer: Closing the Case on Peter Tobin and Bible John*, Great Britain, Sphere Publishing, 2010, p.59.

[177] Stoddart, Charles, *Bible John: Search for a Sadist*, Paul Harris Publishing, Edinburgh, 1980, p.22.

[178] Brown, Les and Jeffrey, Robert, *Glasgow Crimefighter: The Les Brown Story*, Black and White Publishing, Edinburgh, 2005, p.128.

[179] Wilson, David and Harrison, Paul, *The Lost British Serial Killer: Closing the Case on Peter Tobin and Bible John*, Great Britain, Sphere Publishing, 2010, p.86.

[180] Stoddart, Charles, *Bible John: Search for a Sadist*, Paul Harris Publishing, Edinburgh, 1980, p.31; Harrison, Paul, *Dancing with the Devil: The Bible John Murders*, Skipton, Vertical Editions, 2013, pp.46 and 96; Wilson, David and Harrison, Paul, *The Lost British Serial Killer: Closing the Case on Peter Tobin and Bible John*, Great Britain, Sphere Publishing, 2010, p.61; Whittington-Egan, Molly, *Scottish Murder Stories*, Neil Wilson Publishing, Glasgow, 1999, p.168; Brown, Les and Jeffrey, Robert, *Glasgow Crimefighter: The Les Brown Story*, Black and White Publishing, Edinburgh, 2005, p.129.

[181] *Herald Scotland*, 18th February 2018.

[182] Wilson, David and Harrison, Paul, *The Lost British Serial Killer: Closing the Case on Peter Tobin and Bible John*, Great Britain, Sphere Publishing, 2010, p.89.

[183] Harrison, Paul, *Dancing with the Devil: The Bible John Murders*, Skipton, Vertical Editions, 2013, p.95.

[184] Whittington-Egan, Molly, *Scottish Murder Stories*, Neil Wilson Publishing, Glasgow, 1999, p.169.

[185] Whittington-Egan, Molly, *Scottish Murder Stories*, Neil Wilson Publishing, Glasgow, 1999, pp.168-9.

[186] Wilson, David and Harrison, Paul, *The Lost British Serial Killer: Closing the Case on Peter Tobin and Bible John*, Great Britain, Sphere Publishing, 2010, p.89.

[187] Crow, Alan and Samson, Peter, *Bible John: Hunt for a Killer*, Glasgow, First Press Publishing, 1998, p.99.

[188] Borunda, Alejandra, "How tampons and pads became unsustainable", *National Geographic*, National Geographic Society, 2019.

[189] Gillan, Audrey, "Introducing Bible John: Creation of a Serial Killer," BBC Scotland Podcast, 2022.

[190] "The History of Menstrual Health", *SimpleHealth*, 12th March 2019, www.simplehealth.com

[191] Whittington-Egan, Molly, *Scottish Murder Stories*, Neil Wilson Publishing, Glasgow, 1999, p.168; Crow, Alan and Samson, Peter, *Bible John: Hunt for a Killer*, Glasgow, First Press Publishing, 1998, p.99; *Herald Scotland* 29th January 1996; *Guardian*, 16th March 1996.

[192] Whittington-Egan, Molly, *Scottish Murder Stories*, Glasgow, Neil Wilson Publishing, 1999, pp.173-4.

[193] Stoddart, Charles, *Bible John: Search for a Sadist*, Paul Harris Publishing, Edinburgh, 1980, p.81.

[194] Harrison, Paul, *Dancing with the Devil: The Bible John Murders*, Skipton, Vertical Editions, 2013, p.158.

[195] Cassidy, Marie, *Beyond the Tape: The Life and Many Deaths of a State Pathologist*, Hachette Books, Dublin, 2020, pp. 231-2; Drysdale, Neil, "Bible John: Pathologist's new book continues hunt for truth about serial killer", *The Press and Journal*, 16th October 2020, www.pressandjournal.co.uk, accessed 29th

October 2020; Crow, Alan and Samson, Peter, Bible John: *Hunt for a Killer*, Glasgow, First Press Publishing, 1998, p.88.

[196] *Herald Scotland*, 4th July 1996; *Sunday Herald*, 17th August 1996; Gillan, Audrey, "Introducing Bible John: Creation of a Serial Killer," BBC Scotland Podcast, 2022.

[197] *Sunday Herald*, 17th August 1996.

[198] Cassidy, Marie, Beyond the Tape: The Life and Many Deaths of a State Pathologist, Hachette Books, Dublin, 2020, p.232. While there have been suggestions that Helen's stockings were stored in a plastic bag and even that they had been dried over a heater, Magnus Linklater claims that the semen stain "was preserved, frozen and held by Joe Beattie's team" (Linklater, Magnus, "Dancing with a stranger: the Bible John case", Scottish Review, 1994, reprinted June 2017 in www.scottishreview.net, accessed 29th October 2020).

[199] "Cops came to my door looking for a murderer; Husband was given DNA test", the freelibrary.com, *Daily Record*, 1996.

[200] Goodwin, William, Linacre, Adrian and Hadi, Sibte, *An Introduction to Forensic Genetics*, 2nd ed., Oxford, Wiley-Blackwell, 2011, pp.117-9; Wilson, David and Harrison, Paul, *The Lost British Serial Killer: Closing the Case on Peter Tobin and Bible John*, London, Sphere, 2010, p.167.

[201] *Herald Scotland*, 23rd October 2005; Brown, Les and Jeffrey, Robert, *Glasgow Crimefighter: The Les Brown Story*, Edinburgh, Black & White Publishing, 2005, pp.132-3.

[202] Brown, Les and Jeffrey, Robert, *Glasgow Crimefighter: The Les Brown Story*, Edinburgh, Black & White Publishing, 2005, p.133.

[203] *Herald Scotland*, 23rd October 2005.

[204] McLaughlin, Bryan and Smyth, Bob, *Crimestopper: Fighting Crime on Scotland's Streets*, Edinburgh, Black & White Publishing, 2012, pp.57-8.

[205] *Daily Express*, 4th November, 2012; Cron, Robert and Whelan, Michael, "Bible John - Unresolved", www.unresolved.me, 23rd September 2017, retrieved August 2018.

[206] *Daily Express, 4th November, 2012; Cron, Robert and Whelan, Michael, "Bible John - Unresolved",*

www.unresolved.me, 23rd September 2017, retrieved August 2018; Wilson, David and Harrison, Paul, *The Lost British Serial Killer: Closing the Case on Peter Tobin and Bible John*, London, Sphere, 2010, p.64.

[207] "Trace Evidence podcast, Episode 008, The Bible John Murders", 25th July 2017, podcast viewed June 2019.

[208] *Evening Times*, 7th February 1983, p.2; Crow, Alan and Samson, Peter, *Bible John: Hunt for a Killer*, Glasgow, First Press Publishing, 1977, pp.87-8.

[209] *Evening Times*, 7th February 1983, p.2.

[210] *Evening Times*, 7th February 1983, p.2.

[211] Crow, Alan and Samson, Peter, *Bible John: Hunt for a Killer*, Glasgow, First Press Publishing, 1998, pp.87-8; Harrison, Paul, *Dancing with the Devil: The Bible John Murders*, Skipton, Vertical Editions, 2013, p.178.

[212] *Telegraph*, 15th October 2000; Harrison, Paul, *Dancing with the Devil: The Bible John Murders*, Skipton, Vertical Editions, 2013, p.119.

[213] *Telegraph*, 15th October 2000; Harrison, Paul, *Dancing with the Devil: The Bible John Murders*, Skipton, Vertical Editions, 2013, p.118.

[214] *Sunday Herald*, 16th October 2000.

[215] Harrison, Paul, *Dancing with the Devil: The Bible John Murders*, Skipton, Vertical Editions, 2013, p.119.

[216] Simpson, Donald, *Power in the Blood: Whatever happened to 'Bible John'?*, Glasgow, Bandwagon Publishing, 2001, pp.27-8.

[217] Simpson, Donald, *Power in the Blood: Whatever happened to 'Bible John'?*, Glasgow, Bandwagon Publishing, 2001, pp.xi and 47.

[218] Simpson, Donald, *Power in the Blood: Whatever happened to 'Bible John'?*, Glasgow, Bandwagon Publishing, 2001, pp.63 and 130.

[219] Simpson, Donald, *Power in the Blood: Whatever happened to 'Bible John'?*, Glasgow, Bandwagon Publishing, 2001, pp.85 and 94.

[220] Harrison, Paul, *Dancing with the Devil: The Bible John Murders*, Skipton, Vertical Editions, 2013, pp. 151 and 180.

[221] *Daily Record*, 25th August 2013; Harrison, Paul, *Dancing with the Devil: The Bible John Murders*, Skipton, Vertical Editions, 2013, pp.120 and 155.

[222] *Daily Record*, 25th August 2013.

[223] Harrison, Paul, *Dancing with the Devil: The Bible John Murders*, Skipton, Vertical Editions, 2013, p.142; *Daily Record*, 25th August 2013.

[224] Harrison, Paul, *Dancing with the Devil: The Bible John Murders*, Skipton, Vertical Editions, 2013, p.145.

[225] Stoddart, Charles, *Bible John: Search for a Sadist*, Edinburgh, Paul Harris Publishing, 1980, pp.18-9.

[226] *Evening Times*, 18th February 1989, p.4.

[227] *Daily Record*, 13 June 2010.

[228] Wilson, David and Harrison, Paul, *The Lost British Serial Killer: Closing the Case on Peter Tobin and Bible John*, London, Sphere, 2010, p.3.

[229] Wilson, David and Harrison, Paul, *The Lost British Serial Killer: Closing the Case on Peter Tobin and Bible John*, London, Sphere, 2010, p.ix.

[230] *Daily Record*, 13th June 2010.

[231] Mega, Marcello, "Bible John is either dead or at large … but he is NOT Peter Tobin", Scottish Sun, 30th September 2011, www.thesun.co.uk accessed 5th November 2020; *Daily Record*, 25th August 2013; Harrison, Paul, *Dancing with the Devil: The Bible John Murders*, Skipton, Vertical Editions, 2013, p.172.

[232] Wilson, David and Harrison, Paul, *The Lost British Serial Killer: Closing the Case on Peter Tobin and Bible John*, London, Sphere, 2010, p.182.

[233] Mega, Marcello, "Bible John is either dead or at large … but he is NOT Peter Tobin", Scottish Sun, 30th September 2011, www.thesun.co.uk accessed 5th November 2020; Daily Express, 4th November, 2012; Cron, Robert and Whelan, Michael, "Bible John - Unresolved", www.unresolved.me, 23rd September 2017, retrieved August 2018.

[234] Cron, Robert and Whelan, Michael, "Bible John - Unresolved", www.unresolved.me, 23rd September 2017, retrieved August 2018.

[235] Harrison, Paul, *Dancing with the Devil: The Bible John Murders*, Skipton, Vertical Editions, 2013, p.144.

[236] *Daily Record*, 5th March 2010; McLaughlin, Bryan and Smyth, Bob, *Crimestopper: Fighting Crime on Scotland's Streets*, Edinburgh, Black & White Publishing, 2012, pp.60-1.

[237] *Guardian*, 29th January 1996, p.6.

[238] *Guardian*, 16th March 1996, p.260; *Herald Scotland*, 17th August 1996.

[239] Crow, Alan and Samson, Peter, *Bible John: Hunt for a Killer*, Glasgow, First Press Publishing, 1998, p.55; McLaughlin, Bryan and Smyth, Bob, *Crimestopper: Fighting Crime on Scotland's Streets*, Edinburgh, Black & White Publishing, 2012, p.60.

[240] Simpson, Donald, *Power in the Blood: Whatever happened to 'Bible John'?*, Glasgow, Bandwagon Publishing, 2001, p.161.

[241] *Herald Scotland*, 17th August 1996.

[242] Whittington-Egan, Molly, *Scottish Murder Stories*, Glasgow, Neil Wilson Publishing, 1999, p.174.

[243] *Guardian*, 16th March 1996, p.260.

[244] "Extract of an entry in a Register of Deaths", DE 1216882, District no. 579, Year 1980, Entry No. 44, reproduced in Crow, Alan and Samson, Peter, *Bible John: Hunt for a Killer*, Glasgow, First Press Publishing, 1998, centre illustrations.

[245] *Herald Scotland*, 30th January 1996.

[246] *Guardian*, 16 March 1996, p.260; *Herald Scotland*, 17th August 1996; Crow, Alan and Samson, Peter, *Bible John: Hunt for a Killer*, Glasgow, First Press Publishing, 1998, pp.59 and 61.

[247] *Herald Scotland*, 30th January 1996; Crow, Alan and Samson, Peter, *Bible John: Hunt for a Killer*, Glasgow, First Press Publishing, 1998, pp.62-3.

[248] Crow, Alan and Samson, Peter, *Bible John: Hunt for a Killer*, Glasgow, First Press Publishing, 1998, p.70.

[249] *The Observer*, 4th February 1996, p.14; *Guardian*, 16th March 1996.

[250] Crow, Alan and Samson, Peter, *Bible John: Hunt for a Killer*, Glasgow, First Press Publishing, 1998, p.104; *Herald Scotland*, 30th January 1996.

[251] Cassidy, Marie, *Beyond the Tape: The Life and Many Deaths of a State Pathologist*, Hachette Books, Dublin, 2020, p.232; *Herald Scotland*, 30th January 1996; *Glasgow Herald*, 5th July 1996.

[252] Gillan, Audrey, "Introducing Bible John: Creation of a Serial Killer," BBC Scotland Podcast, 2022; Glasgow Herald, 5th July 1996; Cassidy, Marie, Beyond the Tape: The Life and Many Deaths of a State Pathologist, Hachette Books, Dublin, 2020, 232; Whittington-Egan, Molly, Scottish Murder Stories, Glasgow, Neil Wilson Publishing, 1999, p.174; Guardian, 16th March, 1996, p.260; Drysdale, Neil, "Bible John: Pathologist's new book continues hunt for truth about serial killer", The Press and Journal, 16th October 2020 www.pressandjournal.co.uk, accessed 29th October 2020.

[253] *Herald Scotland*, 30th January 1996; *Guardian*, 16th March, 1996, p.260; Drysdale, Neil, "Bible John: Pathologist's new book continues hunt for truth about serial killer", *The Press and Journal*, 16th October 2020, www.pressandjournal.co.uk, accessed 29th October 2020.

[254] Whittington-Egan, Molly, *Scottish Murder Stories*, Glasgow, Neil Wilson Publishing, 1999, p.174; *Guardian*, 29th January, 1996, p.6; *Independent*, 2nd February 1996; Drysdale, Neil, "Bible John: Pathologist's new book continues hunt for truth about serial killer", *The Press and Journal*, 16th October 2020, www.pressandjournal.co.uk, accessed 29th October 2020.

[255] *Herald Scotland*, 26th June 1996.

[256] *Glasgow Herald*, 5th July 1996 and 17th August 1996; *Independent*, 2nd February 1996.

[257] *Herald Scotland*, 26th June 1996 and 17th August 1996.

[258] Cassidy, Marie, *Beyond the Tape: The Life and Many Deaths of a State Pathologist*, Hachette Books, Dublin, 2020, p.232; Linklater, Magnus, "Dancing with a stranger: the Bible

John case", *Scottish Review*, 1994, reprinted June 2017 in www.scottishreview.net, accessed 29th October 2020.

[259] *Guardian*, 2nd February, 1996, p.5.

[260] Cassidy, Marie, *Beyond the Tape: The Life and Many Deaths of a State Pathologist*, Hachette Books, Dublin, 2020, p.233; Drysdale, Neil, "Bible John: Pathologist's new book continues hunt for truth about serial killer", *The Press and Journal*, 16th October 2020, www.pressandjournal.co.uk, accessed 29th October 2020.

[261] *Glasgow Herald*, 5th July 1996.

[262] *Glasgow Herald*, 5th July 1996.

[263] Gillan, Audrey, "Introducing Bible John: Creation of a Serial Killer," BBC Scotland Podcast, 2022.

[264] *Glasgow Herald*, 5th July 1996.

[265] "Serial Killer – Bible John", YouTube, accessed 11th October 2018.

[266] *Glasgow Herald*, 5th July 1996; *Guardian*, 16th May 1996.

[267] *Herald Scotland*, 24th June 1996.

[268] *Herald Scotland*, 22nd July 1996.

[269] *Herald Scotland*, 27th July 1996.

[270] Harrison, Paul, *Dancing with the Devil: The Bible John Murders*, Skipton, Vertical Editions, 2013, p.144.

[271] Gillan, Audrey, "Introducing Bible John: Creation of a Serial Killer," BBC Scotland Podcast, 2022.

[272] Dr Stewart Boyer, interviewed 4th September 2020. As Dr Cassidy suggests, "your nuclear DNA identifies you and you alone", (Cassidy, Marie, *Beyond the Tape: The Life and Many Deaths of a State Pathologist*, Hachette Books, Dublin, 2020, p.101).

[273] Cassidy, Marie, *Beyond the Tape: The Life and Many Deaths of a State Pathologist*, Hachette Books, Dublin, 2020, p.101.

[274] Dr Stewart Boyer, interviewed 4th September 2020.

[275] *Observer*, 4th February 1996, p.14.

[276] Dr Stewart Boyer, interviewed 4th September 2020.

[277] The National Records of Scotland provide such a list and it includes all of these surnames. "100 Most Common Surnames, National Records of Scotland, www.nrscotland.gov.uk.

[278] Lewis, Penny L.A. and Smith. Fergus, "Old Scottish Genealogy & Family History", www.OldScottish.com.

[279] A number of family genealogists on Ancestry.com suggest that John (b.1871) married Margaret McKay (b.1776) in Glasgow in 1796. This would mean that John married Mary at the unlikely age of 15. The 1851 survey indicates that, at the time, he was 73 and Mary MacKay 74. This means that Mary's husband John was born in 1777-78. Birth records suggest that there was indeed a John Templeton born in Glasgow in 1777 (the son of James Templeton and Mary Muir). At the end of the day, John (b.1781) more likely married Jean Brown in Kilmarnock in 1808. He was registered as 60 years old in the 1841 census and 70 years old in the 1851 census.

[280] Harrison, Paul, *Dancing with the Devil: The Bible John Murders*, Skipton, Vertical Editions, 2013, p.84.

[281] Lloyd, Georgina, *One Was Not Enough: True Stories of Multiple Murderers*, London, Robert Hale, 1986, p.182.

[282] Wilson, David and Harrison, Paul, *The Lost British Serial Killer: Closing the Case on Peter Tobin and Bible John*, London, Sphere, 2010, p.54.

[283] Harrison, Paul, *Dancing with the Devil: The Bible John Murders*, Skipton, Vertical Editions, 2013, p.84.

[284] Simpson, Donald, *Power in the Blood: Whatever happened to 'Bible John'?*, Glasgow, Bandwagon Publishing, 2001, pp.xiv-xv.

[285] Dr Stewart Boyer, interviewed 4th September 2020.

[286] There was one John Templeton one who was born in Canada but moved to England at both born in England, who moved to Scotland in adulthood but they have not been included in this cohort because they would have had English accents.

[287] Harrison, Paul, *Dancing with the Devil: The Bible John Murders*, Skipton, Vertical Editions, 2013, p.132.

[288] *Herald Scotland*, 17th August 1996.

[289] *Scottish Daily Express*, 26th August 1969, p.1; *Evening Times*, 25th August 1969, p.1 and 26th August 1969, p.13; *Daily Record*, 26th August 1969, p.1.

[290] *Evening Times*, 3rd November 1969, p.1 and 4th November, 1969 p.15 and 5th November 1969, p.13; *Glasgow Herald*, 4th November 1969, p.8; *Scottish Daily Express*, 4th November 1969, p.1 and 5th November 1969, p.1; *Daily Record*, 4th November 1969, p.1.

[291] *Evening Times*, 3rd November 1969, p.1 and 4th November, 1969 p.15; *Glasgow Herald*, 4th November 1969, p.8; *Scottish Daily Express*, 4th November 1969, p.1; *Daily Record*, 4th November 1969, p.1.

[292] "A Dog's Life on a Sheep Farm", *Farming Independent*, 6th March 2007, www.independent.ie, accessed 28 January 2021.

[293] Jym Francey to "Old Pictures of Kilmarnock", posted 10th December 2021.

[294] Both photographs were posted by Alex Johnson to "Bygone Galashiels", 24th February 2017, accessed 24th November 2020.

[295] *Glasgow Herald*, 4th November 1969, p.8; *Evening Times*, 3rd November 1969, p.1; *Scottish Daily Express*, 4th November 1969, p.1.

[296] Harrison, Paul, *Dancing with the Devil: The Bible John Murders*, Skipton, Vertical Editions, 2013, p.132.

[297] Harrison, Paul, *Dancing with the Devil: The Bible John Murders*, Skipton, Vertical Editions, 2013, p.132.

[298] Valuation Roll of the County of Ayr for the Year 1940-1940. – Parish of Mauchline, VR009000229-/351, Ayr County, p.351.

[299] Valuation Roll of the County of Dumfries for the Year 1940-1940. – Parish of Applegarth, VR009700068-/73, Dumfries County, p.73.

[300] *British Phone Books*, 1968.

[301] *British Phone Books*, 1974, 1975 and 1982.

[302] "Carnell Ayrshires: The Templeton Family Welcomes You", *The Ayrshire Journal*, vol.13, Spring 2017, p.36. There is a colour photograph of John Drennan Templeton in this magazine but, as his features are fine and his ears close to his head, there is no facial features with which I can eliminate him from the John Templeton cohort.

[303] Obituary for Dr John Stewart Templeton published in the *Herald Scotland* on the 7th May 2021.

[304] Harrison, Paul, *Dancing with the Devil: The Bible John Murders*, Skipton, Vertical Editions, 2013, pp.151-2.

[305] Wilson, David and Harrison, Paul, *The Lost British Serial Killer: Closing the Case on Peter Tobin and Bible John*, Great Britain, Sphere Publishing, 2010, p.57; Stoddart, Charles, *Bible John: Search for a Sadist*, Paul Harris Publishing, Edinburgh, 1980, p.64.

[306] Stoddart, Charles, *Bible John: Search for a Sadist*, Paul Harris Publishing, Edinburgh, 1980, p.63.

[307] Stoddart, Charles, *Bible John: Search for a Sadist*, Paul Harris Publishing, Edinburgh, 1980, p.63; Harrison, Paul, *Dancing with the Devil: The Bible John Murders*, Skipton, Vertical Editions, 2013, p.89; *The Glasgow Herald*, 17th August 1996.

[308] 'Location of Scotstoun House – The Hidden Glasgow Forums' http://www.hiddenglasgow.com, accessed 9th July 2020; Senior Pupils of Yoker Secondary School, *Both Sides of the Burn: The Story of Yoker,* Yoker Resource Centre, 1966, 2000, pp.39-40 and 131; 'Glasgow, Scotstoun House', Site Number NS56NW 105, NGR NS 5264 6805, Ordnance Survey license number 100057073, http://canmore.org.uk/site/160389, copyright and database right 2020, accessed 9th July 2020; 'Children's Homes and Institutions in Lanarkshire, Scotland', www.childrenshomes.org.uk; 'Scotstoun House', www.kilmeny.vispa.com, accessed 9th July 2020; Responses to Bill McAdam's post on "Scotstoun memories", 19th December 2017, accessed 1st September 2020; Response to Diane Parker's post in "I went to Victoria Drive Secondary School", 1st July 2019, accessed 6th June 2021; "Lost Glasgow", 28th April 2015, accessed 1st October 2020; Elizabeth Fullerton to "Scotstoun Memories", 26th October 2016, accessed 5th October 2020; Response to Ann Scott's post to "Scotstoun memories", 20th March 2021, accessed 20th March 2021.

[309] Response to Irene Yule's post to "Scotstoun memories", 25th May 2019, accessed 1st September 2020; Response to Ann

Scott's post to "Scotstoun memories", 20th March 2021, accessed 20th March 2021.

[310] My own photograph of the Templeton gravesite in Mauchline Cemetery.

[311] John Templeton's obituary, published in the *Herald Scotland* on the 18th June 2019.

[312] All three of them have Facebook and their cousins number among their Facebook friends.

[313] Annie Burns' headstone in Strathhaven Cemetery.

[314] Christine Bell Ondersma to "Being West Kilbride", 5th November 2015, accessed 9th September 2020.

[315] Obituary for Eliza Templeton nee Anderson published in the *Ardrossan and Saltcoats Herald* on the 22nd February 2012.

[316] Shirley Templeton to "Stevenston Ayrshire, Now and Then. Memories of School, Youth clubs.", 14th April 2018, accessed 30th August 2020 and Shirley Templeton to "Stevenston Ayrshire, Now and Then. Memories of School, Youth clubs.", 25th April 2017, accessed 8th September 2020.

[317] Shirley Templeton to "Stevenston Ayrshire, Now and Then. Memories of School, Youth clubs.", 14th April 2018, accessed 30th August 2020.

[318] 1940, Valuation Rolls, VR1010201667-/174, Burgh of Glasgow, Parish of Govan.

[319] 1940, Valuation Rolls, County of Moray.

[320] Thane, Pat, "Unmarried Motherhood in Twentieth-Century England", *Women's History Review*, vol. 20, no. 1, February 2011, pp.16-21; Paton, Maureen, "Sin and the single mother: The history of lone parenthood", *Independent*, 25th May 2012.

[321] Ancestry.com, private message received 18th March 2022.

[322] England & Wales, Civil Registration Marriage Index, 1916-2005; "England and Wales Marriage Registration Index, 1837-2005", www.familysearch.org.

[323] Ancestry.com, private message received 18th March 2022.

[324] Note, Margaret was born on the 4th January 1918, Margaret Barr Martin Ness Smith Templeton's Birth Certificate, 1918, Ayrshire, available on Scotland's People; Keith Coventry

from Pegasus Investigations Ltd was able to find John McAdam's birthday for me.

[325] 1901 Census, Kirkland Rows, 35, Dreghorn, Ayrshire; 1911 Census for Dreghorn, Census 589/3/37, p. 37; Alexander Templeton's death certificate.

[326] Andrew Frew's parentage is written on his marriage and death certificates.

[327] Mary McSephney Robertson Keegans Frew's death certificate, 1943, Muirkirk, available on Scotland's People; Joan McAdam Frew's death certificate, 1943, Muirkirk, available on Scotland's People.

[328] Andrew Frew's headstone in Muirkirk Cemetery; "Scottish Mining Website: Index to deaths in Scotland 1950 to 1954", www.scottishmining.co.uk.

[329] Daniel McIsaac's death certificate.

[330] Annie Craig and William Stewart Burns's headstone in Muirkirk Cemetery.

[331] Martha Frew – Francis Caven to "Muirkirk, East Ayrshire", 5th April 2016, accessed 3rd September 2020; William Frew – Francis Caven to "Muirkirk, East Ayrshire", 6th April 2016, accessed 3rd September 2020; John Frew - Eleanor Dodds to "Muirkirk, East Ayrshire", 9th May 2020, accessed 2nd September 2020; Nicholas Blair to "Muirkirk, East Ayrshire", 24th August 2020, accessed 2nd September 2020; Nicholas Blair to "Muirkirk, East Ayrshire", 25th August 2020, accessed 2nd September 2020; Elizabeth and James – Ian Wilson to "Muirkirk, East Ayrshire", 16th January 2011, accessed 3rd September 2020; James Frew – Agnes Scotland to "Muirkirk, East Ayrshire", 14th January 2019, accessed 2nd September 2020; Margaret Frew - Margaret Jordan to "Muirkirk, East Ayrshire", 23rd February 2019, accessed 2nd September 2020; Andrew Frew – Ann Walker to "Muirkirk, East Ayrshire", 7th April 2014, accessed 4th September 2020; Catherine McIsaac – Bill Loneskie, via Morag Taylor Gibson on behalf of Catherine McIsaac, to "Muirkirk, East Ayrshire", 7th February 2019, accessed 2nd September 2020; Isabella McIsaac – Myra

Scott to "Muirkirk, East Ayrshire", 3rd February 2019, accessed 3rd September 2020.

[332] John Smith to "Muirkirk, East Ayrshire", 14th May 2012, accessed 4th September 2020.

[333] Andrew Frew's Death Certificate, 1953 Muirkirk, available on Scotland's People; "Scottish Mining Website: Index to deaths in Scotland 1950 to 1954", www.scottishmining.co.uk.

[334] This could have been number 65. The family moved into number 129 when it was built, a few years later.

[335] Patricia Morgan to "Muirkirk, East Ayrshire", 23rd September 2020, accessed 29th September 2020.

[336] "Registering illegitimate births – Guides, Scotland's People", www.scotlandspeople.gov.uk.

[337] Adrian Duffield to "Muirkirk, East Ayrshire", 19th July 2009, accessed 4th September 2020.

[338] James Park to "Muirkirk, East Ayrshire", 29th August 2014, accessed 4th September 2020.

[339] 1901 Census, "Kirkland Rows, 35, Dreghorn, Ayrshire".

[340] 1851 Census, "Toll, Kilmaurs, Cunningham, Ayrshire".

[341] 1851 Census, "Toll, Kilmaurs, Cunningham, Ayrshire".

[342] 1841 Census, "Crosshouse, Kilmaurs, Ayrshire"; 1851 Census, "Anderson's Land, Kilmaurs, Cunningham, Ayrshire".

[343] The National Archives, catalogue description "Records of the Military Recruitment Department, 1939-1960", www.discovery.nationalarchives.gov.uk, accessed 16th May 2021.

[344] "The last man to do National Service", BBC News, 1st June 2015, www.bbc.com, accessed 16th May 2021; The National Archives, catalogue description "Records of the Military Recruitment Department, 1939-1960", www.discovery.nationalarchives.gov.uk, accessed 16th May 2021.

[345] Email from Forces War Records, 23rd May 2021.

[346] 1901 Census, "Murcons Close, Mauchline, Ayrshire".

[347] *British Phone Books*, 1952-1982. A check of www.192.com names Agnes as a co-habitant, indicating that this is John McAdam Templeton.

[348] Wilson, David and Harrison, Paul, *The Lost British Serial Killer: Closing the Case on Peter Tobin and Bible John*, Great Britain, Sphere Publishing, 2010, p.91.

[349] Findlay, C, Cambuslang Social History 15, "A History of Cambuslang", www.docs.wixstatic.com, accessed 15th September 2020; "Primary School in the Forties – Scottish Nostalgia, 26th February 2016", History Scotland: Explore Scotland's Incredible Past, www.historyscotland.com , accessed 11th July 2020.

[350] Many schools in the area were administered by the Glasgow Corporation Education Department, ("Schools, Pupils and Teachers", www.glasgowfamilyhistory.org.uk; Les More to "Memories of Springburn, Balornock & Barmulloch", 31st August 2020, accessed 26th October 2020).

[351] The Glasgow City Archives have a note on their catalogue which suggests that the records prior to 1941 did not survive the bombing.

[352] "Scotstoun Primary, Boys and Girls, 1942-1945", School Admission Registers, D-ED7/276/2/5, Glasgow City Archives, Mitchell Library; "Scotstoun Primary, Boys, 1934-1938, D-ED7/276/3/1; "Scotstoun Primary, Boys and Girls, 1938-1942", D-ED7/276/2/4; "Scotstoun Primary, Boys, 1945-1954, D-ED7/276/3/2; "Bankhead Primary, Boys and Girls, 1941-1944", School Admission Registers, SR10/3/548/2/1, Glasgow City Archives, Mitchell Library; "Bankhead Primary, Boys and Girls, 1944-1951", School Admission Registers, SR10/3/548/2/2, Glasgow City Archives, Mitchell Library.

[353] Valuation Roll of the Burgh of Dumfries, 1930-1931, VR002400027; Valuation Roll of the Burgh of Dumfries, 1935-1936, VR002400031.

[354] Alice Jane Kerr's death certificate, 1940, 685/5 1489; 1940 Valuation Roll, VR011400118-515.

[355] Secret Scotland: Recognition sought for Dumfries and Galloway munitions workers", www.secretscotland.worldpress.com, accessed 1st December 2021; Liptrott, Sharon, "Bid to compile list of region's

munitions workers", *Daily Record*, 4th January 2012, www.dailyrecord.co.uk, accessed 20th October 2012.

[356] William Templeton said that his parents were both Scottish born in Divorce Court Records, Scotland, 1976-1977, 'Court of Sessions, Scotland: Divorce Case Papers', National Records of Scotland.

[357] National Army Museum, www.nam.ac.uk, accessed 4th October 2021.

[358] Home Guard List 1941: Scottish Command, Savannah Paperback Classics publication of original material held in the Imperial War Museum; Home Guard Officer Lists 1939-45", www.forces-war-records.co.uk, accessed 5th November 2021.

[359] "Glasgow's Munitions Industry", www.wightonfamily.ca, accessed 20th October 2021.

[360] "Bankhead Primary, Boys and Girls, 1941-1944", School Admission Registers, SR10/3/548/2/1, Glasgow City Archives, Mitchell Library; "Bankhead Primary, Boys and Girls, 1944-1951", School Admission Registers, SR10/3/548/2/2, Glasgow City Archives, Mitchell Library.

[361] "Bankhead Primary, Boys and Girls, 1944-1951", SR10/3/548/2/2.

[362] "Bankhead Primary, Boys and Girls, 1944-1951", SR10/3/548/2/2.

[363] "Bankhead Primary, Boys and Girls, 1944-1951", SR10/3/548/2/2.

[364] Valuation Rolls for 1940, VR010201658-/323, Glasgow Burgh.

[365] Stoddart, Charles, *Bible John: Search for a Sadist*, Paul Harris Publishing, Edinburgh, 1980, pp.62-3.

[366] William's date of birth was recorded on the Item list for "Fransman William" at, National Archives of Australia, www.recordsearch.naa.gov.au; "Fransman William: SERN 2362: POB Amsterdam Holland: POE Liverpool NSW: NOK W Fransman Mrs W", series no. B2455, Records authority class no. 3891, National Archives of Australia, www.recordsearch.naa.gov.au.

[367] 1921 Census, 685/819 page 4 of 23.

[368] *Glasgow Herald*, 4th November 1969, p.8; *Evening Times*, 3rd November 1969, p.1; *Evening Times*, 4th November 1969, p.15; *Scottish Daily Express*, 4th November 1969, p.1.

[369] "General Nursing Council for Scotland", UK and Ireland, Nursing Registers, 1898-1968", entries for 1960, 1962, 1963, 1965, 1966 and 1968, accessed through Ancestry.com.

[370] "UK and Ireland, Outward Passenger Lists, 1890-1960".

[371] "UK and Ireland, Incoming Passenger Lists, 1878-1960".

[372] "Central Midwives Board of Scotland", UK and Ireland, Nursing Registers, 1898-1968", entries for 1960, 1963, 1966 and 1968, accessed through Ancestry.com.

[373] "30 Kingsway Court", Emporis, www.emporis.com, accessed 7th September 2021; "Scotstoun House", Emporis, www.emporis.com, accessed 7th September 2021; "Peter Atkinson: Kingsway Court, Glasgow, Scotland", www.flikr.com, accessed 7th September 2021.

[374] "Australian Imperial Force – Nominal Roll", www.S3-ap-southeast-2.amazonaws.com, accessed 28th July 2021.

[375] 1940 Valuation Rolls, VR010201671-/297, Glasgow Burgh, p.297; William Fransman's death certificate, Statutory Registers, Deaths, 644/7 454.

[376] Response to Irene Yule's post in "Scotstoun memories", 25th May 2019, accessed 27th August 2021.

[377] Edinburgh Valuation Rolls, 1915.

[378] Response to Ann Scott's post to "Scotstoun memories", 20th March 2021, accessed 13th August 2021.

[379] Response to Irene Yule's post in "Scotstoun memories", 15th February 2021, accessed 27th August 2021; Response to Irene Yule's post to "Scotstoun memories", 25th May 2019, accessed 27th August 2021.

[380] Stoddart, Charles, *Bible John: Search for a Sadist*, Paul Harris Publishing, Edinburgh, 1980, pp.135-6.

[381] Joan Downie interviewed in "The Hunt for Bible John", Series 1: Episode 2, screened BBC One Scotland, 29th November 2021.

[382] Detective Inspector Ricky Mason interviewed for 'Unsolved: Getting Away with Murder', Series 2, Episode 13,

'Helen Puttock/Bible John', broadcast on Grampian and Scottish Television on the 15th December 2005.

[383] Stoddart, Charles, *Bible John: Search for a Sadist*, Paul Harris Publishing, Edinburgh, 1980, p.63.

[384] Former Detective Superintendent Robert Johnstone interviewed in "The Hunt for Bible John", Series 1: Episode 2, screened BBC One Scotland, 29th November 2021.

[385] WordSense Dictionary, "den of iniquity (English) Origin and history", https://www.wordsense.eu, accessed online 17th June 2022; "den of iniquity – Prases.com", https://www.phrases.com, accessed online 17th June 2022.

[386] Lloyd, Georgina, *One Was Not Enough: True Stories of Multiple Murderers*, London, Robert Hale, 1986, p.182.

[387] Stoddart, Charles, *Bible John: Search for a Sadist*, Paul Harris Publishing, Edinburgh, 1980, p.59.

[388] Harrison, Paul, *Dancing with the Devil: The Bible John Murders*, Skipton, Vertical Editions, 2013, p.154.

[389] Crow, Alan and Samson, Peter, *Bible John: Hunt for a Killer*, Glasgow, First Press Publishing, 1977, pp.64-5, citing Norman Adams, *Goodbye, Beloved Brethren* pub. 1972; Stoddart, Charles, *Bible John: Search for a Sadist*, Paul Harris Publishing, Edinburgh, 1980, pp.135-6; *Herald Scotland*, 30th January 1996.

[390] "Central Midwives Board of Scotland", UK and Ireland, Nursing Registers, 1898-1968", entries for 1960, 1963, 1966 and 1968, accessed through Ancestry.com.

[391] UK and Ireland, Outward Passenger Lists, 1890-1960.

[392] UK and Ireland, Outward Passenger Lists, 1890-1960.

[393] "St Andrew's Scots Kirk", www.internationalpresbytery.net, accessed 19th August 2021.

[394] Howie-Willis, Ian, "The Australian Army's Two 'Traditional' Diseases: Gonorrhoea and Syphilis – A Medical-Military History During the Twentieth Century", *History*, vol. 27, no. 1; Evans, Kathy, "Secret WW1 history of Australian soldiers with venereal disease", *Canberra Times*, 24th October 2014, www.canberratimes.com.au, accessed 2nd July 2021.

[395] "Fransman William: SERN 2362: POB Amsterdam Holland: POE Liverpool NSW: NOK W Fransman Mrs W", series no. B2455, Records authority class no. 3891, National Archives of Australia, www.recordsearch.naa.gov.au.

[396] "Fransman William: SERN 2362: POB Amsterdam Holland: POE Liverpool NSW: NOK W Fransman Mrs W", series no. B2455, Records authority class no. 3891, National Archives of Australia, www.recordsearch.naa.gov.au.

[397] This phrase was not necessarily William Fransman's. It may have reflected John Templeton's interpretation of his words.

[398] "Bankhead Primary, Boys and Girls, 1944-1951", SR10/3/548/2/2; Victoria Drive Secondary School Register", SR10/3/940/4/8.

[399] "Victoria Drive Secondary School Register", SR10/3/940/4/8.

[400] British Letterpress, "The Printing Industry in 1965: A summary of what the UK's printing industry looked like in 1965", www.Britishletterpress.co.uk, accessed 14th October 2020; "The Manchester Typographical Society is Founded", www.historyofinformation.com, accessed 17th October 2021; Cannon, Isidore Cyril, "The Compositor in London: The Rise and Fall of a Labour Aristocracy", *History Workshop*, June 30, 2012; Responses to Cannon, Isidore Cyril, "The Compositor in London: The Rise and Fall of a Labour Aristocracy", *History Workshop*, June 30, 2012, www.historyworkshop.org.uk, accessed 17th October 2021.

[401] Finkelstein, David (ed.), *Edinburgh History of the Book in Scotland*, vol.4, Edinburgh University Press, 2007; www.cartridgesave.co.uk, accessed 12th Oct ober 2021.

[402] "Linotron 505", from Linotype: The Film, 1969, Mergenthaler Linotype Company, accessed on www.vimeo.com, 13th December 2021.

[403] Stoddart, Charles, *Bible John: Search for a Sadist*, Paul Harris Publishing, Edinburgh, 1980, pp.56-7.

[404] Stoddart, Charles, *Bible John: Search for a Sadist*, Paul Harris Publishing, Edinburgh, 1980, p.64.

[405] "The Manchester Typographical Society is Founded", www.historyofinformation.com, accessed 17th October 2021.

[406] Responses to Cannon, Isidore Cyril, "The Compositor in London: The Rise and Fall of a Labour Aristocracy", *History Workshop*, June 30, 2012, www.historyworkshop.org.uk, accessed 17th October 2021.

[407] Cannon, Isidore Cyril, "The Compositor in London: The Rise and Fall of a Labour Aristocracy", *History Workshop*, June 30, 2012.

[408] Cannon, Isidore Cyril, "The Compositor in London: The Rise and Fall of a Labour Aristocracy", *History Workshop*, June 30, 2012.

[409] Responses to Cannon, Isidore Cyril, "The Compositor in London: The Rise and Fall of a Labour Aristocracy", *History Workshop*, June 30, 2012, www.historyworkshop.org.uk, accessed 17th October 2021.

[410] Responses to Cannon, Isidore Cyril, "The Compositor in London: The Rise and Fall of a Labour Aristocracy", *History Workshop*, June 30, 2012, www.historyworkshop.org.uk, accessed 17th October 2021.

[411] Interview with June.

[412] Harrison, Paul, *Dancing with the Devil: The Bible John Murders*, Skipton, Vertical Editions, 2013, pp.151-2.

[413] Stoddart, Charles, *Bible John: Search for a Sadist*, Paul Harris Publishing, Edinburgh, 1980, p.59.

[414] Fransman, William, Statutory Registers Deaths 644/7 454.

[415] Stoddart, Charles, *Bible John: Search for a Sadist*, Paul Harris Publishing, Edinburgh, 1980, p.64; Wilson, David and Harrison, Paul, *The Lost British Serial Killer: Closing the Case on Peter Tobin and Bible John*, Great Britain, Sphere Publishing, 2010, p.57.

[416] Harrison, Paul, *Dancing with the Devil: The Bible John Murders*, Skipton, Vertical Editions, 2013, p.90.

[417] Simpson, Donald, *Power in the Blood: Whatever happened to 'Bible John'?*, Glasgow, Bandwagon Publishing, 2001, p.19.

[418] City of Glasgow Corporation Transport, Official Time-Table: Motor-bus Underground Time-Table, Night Services, Fare Stages, Scale of Fares, New addition – July, 1969.

[419] "British Public and National Rail Timetable List", www.railwaymuseum.org.uk, accessed 22nd July 2021; City of Glasgow Corporation Transport, Official Time-Table, New addition – July, 1969.

[420] "Higher Fares for Glasgow?", Commercial Motor Archive, 22nd August 1969, www.archive.commercialmotor.com, accessed 22nd July 2021.

[421] Wilson, David and Harrison, Paul, *The Lost British Serial Killer: Closing the Case on Peter Tobin and Bible John*, Great Britain, Sphere Publishing, 2010, p.70.

[422] Stoddart, Charles, *Bible John: Search for a Sadist*, Paul Harris Publishing, Edinburgh, 1980, p.104.

[423] "Glasgow Corporation Transport Bus Service Routes 1963", Glasgow Transport 1871-1973, www.semple.biz, accessed 23rd July 2021; "Ferry Crossing (19th Century-20th Century), Canmore ID 178179, Site Number NS56NE2520, http://canmore.org.uk/site/178179, accessed 23rd July 2021.

[424] Harrison, Paul, *Dancing with the Devil: The Bible John Murders*, Skipton, Vertical Editions, 2013, p.91; "Scottish Mysteries: Bible John", YouTube 2nd July 2018, podcast viewed 6th November 2020.

[425] Stoddart, Charles, *Bible John: Search for a Sadist*, Paul Harris Publishing, Edinburgh, 1980, p.104.

[426] City of Glasgow Corporation Transport, Official Time-Table, New addition – July, 1969.

[427] City of Glasgow Corporation Transport, Official Time-Table, New addition – July, 1969.

[428] Stoddart, Charles, *Bible John: Search for a Sadist*, Paul Harris Publishing, Edinburgh, 1980, pp.105-6.

[429] Wilson, David and Harrison, Paul, *The Lost British Serial Killer: Closing the Case on Peter Tobin and Bible John*, Great Britain, Sphere Publishing, 2010, p.71.

[430] Stoddart, Charles, *Bible John: Search for a Sadist*, Paul Harris Publishing, Edinburgh, 1980, pp.104-6.

[431] Register of Electors, Glasgow, 1969, vol. 1970 Wards 9-21.

[432] Wilson, David and Harrison, Paul, *The Lost British Serial Killer: Closing the Case on Peter Tobin and Bible John*, Great Britain, Sphere Publishing, 2010, p.85.

[433] RCE 292/1977/Glasgow, included on the couple's Marriage C, District 644-3,1969, Entry No. 415 in the District of Glasgow.

[434] Divorce Court Records, Scotland, 1976-1977, 'Court of Sessions, Scotland: Divorce Case Papers', 4710/77, National Records of Scotland.

[435] Divorce Court Records, Scotland, 1976-1977, 'Court of Sessions, Scotland: Divorce Case Papers', 4710/77, National Records of Scotland.

[436] This date was entered as a correction on the original marriage certificate.

[437] Wilson, David and Harrison, Paul, *The Lost British Serial Killer: Closing the Case on Peter Tobin and Bible John*, Great Britain, Sphere Publishing, 2010, pp.74-5.

[438] Wilson, David and Harrison, Paul, *The Lost British Serial Killer: Closing the Case on Peter Tobin and Bible John*, Great Britain, Sphere Publishing, 2010, pp.74-5.

[439] Crow, Alan and Samson, Peter, *Bible John: Hunt for a Killer*, Glasgow, First Press Publishing, 1998, p.108.

[440] Stoddart, Charles, *Bible John: Search for a Sadist*, Paul Harris Publishing, Edinburgh, 1980, p.128; Lloyd, Georgina, *One Was Not Enough: True Stories of Multiple Murderers*, London, Robert Hale, 1986, pp.189-90.

[441] Esson, Graeme, "Angus Sinclair: A lifetime of abuse, rape and murder", BBC News, 11th March 2019; McLaughlin, Mark, "Serial Killer is linked to Glasgow murders", The Times, 21st April 2018; BBC News, "1977 Anna Kenny murder: DNA tests over Angus Sinclair link", 27th October 2015, www.bbc.com.

[442] BBC News, "1977 Anna Kenny murder: DNA tests over Angus Sinclair link", 27th October 2015, www.bbc.com.

[443] Stoddart, Charles, *Bible John: Search for a Sadist*, Paul Harris Publishing, Edinburgh, 1980, p.126; Lloyd, Georgina, *One Was Not Enough: True Stories of Multiple Murderers*, London, Robert Hale, 1986, p.188; Crow, Alan and Samson,

Peter, *Bible John: Hunt for a Killer*, Glasgow, First Press Publishing, 1998, pp.108-9.

[444] Stoddart, Charles, *Bible John: Search for a Sadist*, Paul Harris Publishing, Edinburgh, 1980, pp.128-9; Lloyd, Georgina, *One Was Not Enough: True Stories of Multiple Murderers*, London, Robert Hale, 1986, p.190; Crow, Alan and Samson, Peter, *Bible John: Hunt for a Killer*, Glasgow, First Press Publishing, 1998, p.110.

[445] Stoddart, Charles, *Bible John: Search for a Sadist*, Paul Harris Publishing, Edinburgh, 1980, pp.127-8; Lloyd, Georgina, *One Was Not Enough: True Stories of Multiple Murderers*, London, Robert Hale, 1986, pp.188-9.

[446] Birchall, Guy, "Murder Mystery: Who were Anna Kenny, Agnes Cooney and Hilda McAuley, when were they murdered in Glasgow and were they linked to Angus Sinclair?", *Sun*, 12th April 2018.

[447] Birchall, Guy, "Murder Mystery: Who were Anna Kenny, Agnes Cooney and Hilda McAuley, when were they murdered in Glasgow and were they linked to Angus Sinclair?", *Sun*, 12th April 2018.

[448] Esson, Graeme, "Angus Sinclair: A lifetime of abuse, rape and murder", BBC News, 11th March 2019.

[449] Esson, Graeme, "Angus Sinclair: A lifetime of abuse, rape and murder", BBC News, 11th March 2019.

[450] 'Unsolved: Getting Away with Murder', Series 2, Episode 13, 'Helen Puttock/Bible John', broadcast on Grampian and Scottish Television on the 15th December 2005.

[451] Hoffman, Jan, "Do Serial Killers Just Stop? Yes, Sometimes", *New York Times*, 26th April 2018, www.nytimes.com accessed 7th November 2020.

[452] Hoffman, Jan, "Do Serial Killers Just Stop? Yes, Sometimes", *New York Times*, 26th April 2018, www.nytimes.com accessed 7th November 2020.

[453] U.S. Department of Justice, F.B.I., Behavioral Analysis Unit, National Centre for the Analysis of Violent Crime, "Serial Murder: Multi-Disciplinary Perspectives for Investigators", 2008, p.5.

[454] The State of Western Australia -v- Edwards [No 7] [2020] WASC 339; Mayes, Andrea, "Claremont killer Bradley Edwards found guilty of Jane Rimmer and Ciara Glennon murders but not Sarah Spiers", 24th September 2020, www.abc.net.au, accessed 24th September 2020.

[455] Hoffman, Jan, "Do Serial Killers Just Stop? Yes, Sometimes", *New York Times*, 26th April 2018, www.nytimes.com accessed 7th November 2020.

[456] Hoffman, Jan, "Do Serial Killers Just Stop? Yes, Sometimes", *New York Times*, 26th April 2018, www.nytimes.com accessed 7th November 2020.

[457] *Scottish Daily Express*, 10th November 1969, p.16.

[458] *Evening Times*, 19th August 1969, p.7.

[459] Wilson, David and Harrison, Paul, *The Lost British Serial Killer: Closing the Case on Peter Tobin and Bible John*, Great Britain, Sphere Publishing, 2010, p.75.

[460] Stoddart, Charles, *Bible John: Search for a Sadist*, Paul Harris Publishing, Edinburgh, 1980, p.112.

[461] Stoddart, Charles, *Bible John: Search for a Sadist*, Paul Harris Publishing, Edinburgh, 1980, pp.112-3; Lloyd, Georgina, *One Was Not Enough: True Stories of Multiple Murderers*, London, Robert Hale, 1986, p.187.

[462] Stoddart, Charles, *Bible John: Search for a Sadist*, Paul Harris Publishing, Edinburgh, 1980, pp. 113-5; Lloyd, Georgina, *One Was Not Enough: True Stories of Multiple Murderers*, London, Robert Hale, 1986, p.187.

[463] Response to Margo Sharp's post to "I went to Victoria Drive Secondary School", 17th July 2021, accessed 19th July 2021.

[464] Jill Bavin-Mizzi's post to "I Went to Bankhead Primary school", 23rd August 2021.

[465] Stoddart, Charles, *Bible John: Search for a Sadist*, Paul Harris Publishing, Edinburgh, 1980, p.22.

[466] Stoddart, Charles, *Bible John: Search for a Sadist*, Paul Harris Publishing, Edinburgh, 1980, p.56.

[467] "Dancing With Death", *Daily Record*, 1st October 2008.

[468] Wilson, David and Harrison, Paul, *The Lost British Serial Killer: Closing the Case on Peter Tobin and Bible John*, Great Britain, Sphere Publishing, 2010, p.83.

[469] *Evening Times*, 7th November 1969, p.1; *Scottish Daily Express*, 8th November 1969, p.6.

[470] *Evening Times*, 7th November 1969, p.1.

[471] Linklater, Magnus, "Dancing with a stranger: the Bible John case", *Scottish Review*, 1994, reprinted June 2017 in www.scottishreview.net, accessed 29th October 2020.

[472] Old footage of an interview with Joe Beattie in "The Hunt for Bible John", Series 1: Episode 2, screened BBC One Scotland, 29th November 2021.

[473] Old footage of an interview with Joe Beattie in "The Hunt for Bible John", Series 1: Episode 2, screened BBC One Scotland, 29th November 2021.

[474] Transcript of Audrey Gillan's interview with Jeannie read in her podcast, "Introducing Bible John: Creation of a Serial Killer," BBC Scotland Podcast, 2022.

[475] Transcript of Audrey Gillan's interview with Jeannie read in her podcast, "Introducing Bible John: Creation of a Serial Killer," BBC Scotland Podcast, 2022.

[476] Wilson, David and Harrison, Paul, *The Lost British Serial Killer: Closing the Case on Peter Tobin and Bible John*, Great Britain, Sphere Publishing, 2010, p.75.

[477] Harrison, Paul, *Dancing with the Devil: The Bible John Murders*, Skipton, Vertical Editions, 2013, pp.85-6.

[478] Stoddart, Charles, *Bible John: Search for a Sadist*, Paul Harris Publishing, Edinburgh, 1980, p.41.

[479] Harrison, Paul, *Dancing with the Devil: The Bible John Murders*, Skipton, Vertical Editions, 2013, p.132.

[480] Murray, Paula, "New sketch of serial killer Bible John's crooked teeth revealed in BBC documentary", *Scottish Daily Express*, 20th November 2021.

[481] *Glasgow Herald*, 4th November 1969, p.8; *Evening News*, 4th November 1969, p.15; *Scottish Daily Express*, 4th November 1969, p.1.

[482] *Evening Times*, 3rd November 1969, p.1.

[483] *Daily Record*, 4th November 1969, p.1.

[484] *Scottish Daily Express*, 4th November 1969, p.1; *Glasgow Herald*, 4th November 1969, p.8.

[485] Stoddart, Charles, *Bible John: Search for a Sadist*, Paul Harris Publishing, Edinburgh, 1980, p.56.

[486] Stoddart, Charles, *Bible John: Search for a Sadist*, Paul Harris Publishing, Edinburgh, 1980, p.87.

[487] Stoddart, Charles, *Bible John: Search for a Sadist*, Paul Harris Publishing, Edinburgh, 1980, p.85.

[488] Wilson, David and Harrison, Paul, *The Lost British Serial Killer: Closing the Case on Peter Tobin and Bible John*, Great Britain, Sphere Publishing, 2010, p.90.

[489] Stoddart, Charles, *Bible John: Search for a Sadist*, Paul Harris Publishing, Edinburgh, 1980, p.22.

[490] Stoddart, Charles, *Bible John: Search for a Sadist*, Paul Harris Publishing, Edinburgh, 1980, p.22.

[491] Wilson, David and Harrison, Paul, *The Lost British Serial Killer: Closing the Case on Peter Tobin and Bible John*, Great Britain, Sphere Publishing, 2010, p.87.

TABLE OF CONTENTS

Finito di stampare
nel mese di giugno 2024
presso Rotomail Italia S.p.A. – Vignate (MI)